DUST BOWL TO DISNEY

Dust Bowl to Disney

The Lost Memoir of Danny Alguire

By Danny Alguire

Edited by Lucas O. Seastrom, Hal Smith, and Didier Ghez

BearManor Media
2023

Dust Bowl to Disney
The Lost Memoir of Danny Alguire

© Copyright by Reuben Daniel Alguire, 1990
Modern copyright by Charlotte Bryant McCormack, 2023

All rights reserved.

No portion of this publication may be reproduced, stored, and/or copied electronically (except for academic use as a source), nor transmitted in any form or by any means without the prior written permission of the publisher and/or author.

Published in the United States of America by:

BearManor Media

4700 Millenia Blvd.
Suite 175 PMB 90497
Orlando, FL 32839

bearmanormedia.com

Printed in the United States.

Typesetting and layout by PKJ Passion Global

ISBN—978-1-62933-967-2

Table of Contents

Foreword by Charlotte Bryant McCormack	vii
Editors' Introduction	xi
Dust Bowl to Disney	1
Afterword: Remembrances	174

Appendix

Tribute to Benny Strickler by Danny Alguire	182
Danny Alguire Remembered by Chris Tyle	189
Danny Alguire and the Southwestern Trumpet Style by Hal Smith	193
For Whom the Brass Bell Tolls by Hal Smith	198
A Cinderella Story: The Firehouse Five Plus Two in 1950 by Lucas O. Seastrom	207
Notes on the U.S.S. *Alchiba* by Lucas O. Seastrom	227
Notes on Wolfgang Reitherman and Disney Feature Animation by Lucas O. Seastrom	229
Interview with Danny Alguire by Hal Smith and Chris Tyle	233
"Lost Love" Lyrics Written by Danny Alguire	243
Alguire's Chili Recipe	244
Recommended Listening compiled by Hal Smith	247
Bibliography	252
About the Editors & Contributors	260

Alguire's "Epilogue #2"	264
Index	265

Foreword

By Charlotte Bryant McCormack

Danny Alguire was my stepfather. I met him as a junior high school student in Burbank, California when he courted and eventually married my mother, Irene Bryant. The family connection aside, Dan was also my friend.

Danny Alguire at home in Beaverton, Oregon in the 1970s.
Courtesy of Charlotte Bryant McCormack.

The very fact that you're holding this book in your hands is a miracle. A few years before his passing in 1992 (just short of his eightieth birthday), Dan had sent the typed manuscript to an old Navy friend from World War II, William McDonald, in hopes that he might enjoy reading it. The book had already received comments and critiques from the various Alguire family relatives, as well as old Disney Studios colleagues. Though he didn't know it then, Dan would never see his book again after sending it to McDonald. Our family had considered it lost for years—that is until the son of Dan's old friend rediscovered it in his family archives. Scrolled across the manuscript box was "If Found Please Return to R.D. Alguire" and the old, outdated address. It took him four months, but he found me, via my brother, and the rest is for you to read now.

From the moment I met him, Dan was a class act, a real gentleman. By that time in the late 1960s, he had already lived quite a life, enduring a great depression, a world war, years of traveling on the road as a musician, many odd-jobs, and a first marriage that tragically ended with his wife Betty's death from cancer.

But he also had been having a whole lot of fun. Dan was one of the best cornet and trumpet players anyone in the western United States could hear. Before the war, he played with Bob Wills and His Texas Playboys, the best in western swing music. Dan didn't just play his horn, he sang too, and one of his vocals, "Home in San Antone," was a hit record across the United States. Bob Wills' line "Come on in, Danny" is still preserved on that recording. As you'll read, that experience was a big break for Dan, and he enjoyed every minute of it.

His time with Bob Wills turned my stepfather into the kind of musician perfect for a new jazz band being formed around 1949. A number of artists and animators at the Walt Disney Studios had been jamming together at lunchtime for years. They started playing gigs in their spare time outside of work, and they weren't half-bad. The trombone player, Ward Kimball, was an original guy with a sense of humor. He had an old antique fire engine that he was taking on a caravan from Los Angeles to San Diego. The band would fit perfectly in the back. So they dressed up in old fireman's costumes, piled in, and played jazz all the way down the coast. They called themselves the Firehouse Five, and being a seven-piece band, added a "Plus Two" at the end.

The Firehouse Five Plus Two became a household name around the world. They even played the opening day of Disneyland and headlined at the park for years afterward. All those Disneyland guests didn't realize that the band was made up of directors, composers, and animators from the Disney Studios. Their music was happy, sincere, and lots of fun. I had never heard anything like it when I first saw them, and by that time they'd been playing together for twenty years!

You'll read all these stories, and a lot more, from Dan himself. He writes like he used to talk: simple, down to earth, funny, and self-deprecating. I can almost hear that sweet Oklahoma drawl of his as I read, and it brings back many fond conversations about life and philosophy that he had with me. Dan spent a good part of his later career as an assistant director at the Disney Studios helping Walt Disney and his artists bring animated movies to the big screen. So he picked up a few pieces of wisdom about storytelling too. It all shows here in these pages.

Editors' Introduction

There is a history of American traditional jazz that seems almost underground. From its origins in New Orleans as a composite of diverse musical forms to a rapid diffusion across the United States, it is music both cosmopolitan and parochial. It's an oral tradition, passed from musician to musician and best evangelized from the live bandstand, but has often relied on seminal recordings to sow inspiration for new generations of players and new innovations in style. At times, traditional jazz emerged on the stage of American popular music, courtesy of great promoters such as King Oliver, Louis Armstrong, Jelly Roll Morton, and Bix Beiderbecke. But there were others, legends in their own realms, arbiters of a form that underpinned American musical growth in the twentieth century. Players such as Kid Ory, Lu Watters, Benny Strickler, and Bob Scobey.

Alguire taking a solo in the late 1960s.
Courtesy of Charlotte Bryant McCormack.

Reuben Dan Alguire—Dan or Danny to those who knew him—was a horn player who straddled the popular and provincial stages of traditional jazz music. The proponent of an unusual, southwestern style of trumpet playing spent over two decades as first cornet in the Firehouse Five Plus Two, a popularly-styled band that appeared many times on television, sold countless records, and introduced unnumbered listeners young and old to the magic of traditional jazz (including a number of the people who've now compiled this volume).

The Firehouse Five Plus Two—a part-time band comprised mostly of full-time artists and personnel at the Walt Disney Studios—did their own take on the classic jazz form, swirling a gumbo pot of sounds: New Orleans, Dixieland, West Coast, Two-Beat, Southern California Hot Jazz. Taxonomy aside, it had clear and uninhibited appeal. They spoke a universal language, and were, as Alguire himself writes, "the most unique band in the history of jazz. This bunch of firemen—characters on stage—who looked like they just tumbled out of the screen, yet played great music, were a total entertainment package."

The Firehouse Five Plus Two joins other jazz bands at the Orange County Airport in September, 1967. L to R: In the Firehouse Five are K. O. Eckland, tambourine and piano; Danny Alguire, cornet; Eddie Forrest, drums; Ward Kimball, trombone. Members of the Young Men from New Orleans, Harvey Brooks, bass drum and piano; Alton Redd, snare drum; Bernard Carrere, string bass; Joe Darensbourg, clarinet; Mike Delay, trumpet. In the background on the wagon are musicians from Doc Souchon's band. Courtesy of the New Orleans Jazz Museum.

Members of the Firehouse Five Plus Two perform at the
Orange County Airport in September, 1967. L to R:
Danny Alguire, cornet; Eddie Forrest, drums; K. O. Eckland,
tambourine and piano. Courtesy of the New Orleans Jazz Museun.

A key ingredient to the Firehouse Five's commercial success were the swinging brass melodies of Alguire's cornet. It was unlike most horn sounds any other jazz band at the time had achieved. The difference came from Alguire's own background playing in western swing bands during the 1940s, including the world-renowned Bob Wills and His Texas Playboys. As will be explored, this distinctive, head-turning sound had a lineage that wonderfully blended regional character with popular charm. Firehouse Five Plus Two chief and first trombonist Ward Kimball best summarized Alguire's role in their unique group, "In looking back it becomes obvious to me that Danny Alguire playing his steady cornet was the glue that held the band together."

The uncovering of Alguire's memoir is a moment of luck and discovery. At this intersection of American history, a diverse array of topics and interests synthesize, from the Great Depression to the Pacific Theater of World War II to the Walt Disney Studios in some of its most prosperous years to the exhilarating albeit uncertain realms of professional Country & Western and jazz music.

Long considered lost, the re-discovered manuscript is presented here as Alguire wrote it. He is a practiced storyteller, blending a Southwestern sense of folkloric charm with a healthy dose of self-deprecating humor. His voice is lean, efficient, and does not fail at holding the reader's interest. The story is unmistakably American with its tales of perseverance, hope, and renewal. This modest yet fascinating memoir is a testament to Danny Alguire's enduring spirit and character, as well as a virtuous encouragement to discover your own voice in whatever form it might make itself known.

With few exceptions for grammatical corrections, Alguire's writing remains pure in its original form. Accompanying endnotes are provided at the end of each chapter for extended commentary and useful information on the various locations, persons, and historical events through which Alguire travels. At the text's conclusion, an appendix of supplementary material presents a cornucopia of insight and further reading. This includes original supplements prepared by Alguire himself, new historical essays, and more.

At certain points in the writing, Alguire inserted quotes from colleagues into the text, including those from newly conducted interviews. Rather than re-incorporate into an endnote or appendix, these have been left alone in their original placement so as to retain Alguire's vision and not disrupt his intended narrative flow. Additional pieces of commentary left separate from the main text have been included as endnotes.

Having worked nearly two decades at the Walt Disney Studios as an assistant director in animation production, Alguire occupied an unusual and privileged vantage point from which to appreciate the work of his Disney colleagues. The self-effacing narrative of his own life is matched by eloquent description and analysis of Disney animation production, a form of appreciation that was still rare for its day.

At the time of Alguire's writing in the 1980s, Disney animation was enduring a loss in relevance and audience demand. To many, the beloved animated features of Walt Disney's era were distant memories, if remembered at all. To Alguire, someone intimately involved in the creation of many such classics, these films deserved attention. He might very well have felt spurred on by the 1981 publication of *The Illusion of Life: Disney Animation*, an opus on the art form's golden age authored by Alguire's colleagues Ollie Johnston and Frank Thomas, the latter of whom was also a bandmate in the Firehouse Five Plus Two. This helps contextualize the amount of chapters Alguire commits to remembering his Disney tenure, from which we as readers now benefit. Luckily at the time, the drought of popular interest was soon to be remedied with a new slate of blockbuster animated features beginning with *The Little Mermaid* in 1989. It was still going strong when Alguire passed away in 1992, the year of *Aladdin's* release.

Of course, this narrative begs the reader to listen to music, even to learn to play it oneself. "I wish it was possible to bring the sound of our brand of Dixieland to these pages," Alguire writes of the Firehouse Five Plus Two. A discography of recommended listening is provided in the appendix in chronological order. Treat it as a virtual soundtrack to Alguire's story.

A supporting character in Alguire's musical biography is trumpeter Benny Strickler, who had the lead chair with Bob Wills and His Texas Playboys when Alguire joined the group in the early 1940s. Strickler's significance, both personally for Alguire and generally in the style of trumpet playing they mutually developed, is not to be underestimated. Strangely, Alguire does not commit much space in the memoir itself to covering this topic. Perhaps he had felt that he had made his point clear in other writings and testimonies. Thus the appendix provides expanded information and insight into Strickler's music career, much of it from Alguire himself. His characteristic deference to Strickler is on full display, as *Jazz Report* editor Paul E. Affeldt noted at the time, "a story about a warm, friendly musician, by a warm and friendly musician." Alguire was committed to ensuring that his late friend and mentor's career did not go unnoticed. The influence and inspiration that he received from Strickler, first playing together with Bob Wills and then upon soulful reflection for years to come, is essential to appreciating Alguire's own approach to music.

In a way, Alguire's devoted appreciation of Strickler reads as a testament to the values and significance that he himself provided for younger listeners and musicians in his own moment throughout the 1950s, 1960s, and 1970s. Some of those recipients of Alguire's influence and inspiration share their impressions here, including drummer Hal Smith, and trumpeters Theodore Thomas (son of Frank Thomas) and Chris Tyle.

Acknowledgements

We, the editors, are indebted to many for the publication of this memoir and accompanying supplements. Historians Joe Campana and Paul Hagglund were supportive in their respective fields, most especially in the preservation of rare materials. In addition, Dave Radlauer helped to preserve audio of one of the few surviving interviews with Alguire. Derek Coller was helpful with additional research, as was the late Barbara Martin of *Western Swing Monthly*. The Hyperion Historical Alliance graciously allowed us to republish an essay originally included in their annual journal. Jenna Benton lent her adept skills to the design of the book's cover, and she also provided touch-ups to many of the illustrations seen throughout. Jim Hollifield, Steven Reeser, Joseph Spencer, Dr. David Stricklin, Dr. Charles Townsend, Marc Caparone, Todd James Pierce, Robert Reitherman, Bruce Reitherman, and Pete Vilmur each provided their own measure of support. Diane Breazeale and the family of Benny Strickler graciously allowed the publication of photographs from their private collection, as did Christopher Lord and the family of Ward Kimball, along with Leon D. Oakley, Carolyn Wills, the Estate of Bob Wills, the OKPOP Museum, and the New Orleans Jazz Museum. Theodore Thomas and Chris Tyle made contributions adding to the volume's richness and insight. We'd also like to thank Ben Ohmart, Sarah Joseph, and the team at BearManor Media for helping bring this work to the reading public. Most of all, Charlotte Bryant McCormack generously responded to our inquiries about the memoir's existence, and met our idea to publish it with enthusiasm. Her allowance, support, and participation made this effort possible. Her heartfelt affection for her stepfather remains an inspiration.

Lucas O. Seastrom, Hal Smith, Didier Ghez

Chapter 1:

"Yes Sir! That's My Baby" [1]

During the fifty-plus years I played and sang professionally, I was asked many questions about music. I was most often asked why I enjoyed it so much. People would drop by the bandstand at Disneyland or at one of the Firehouse Five Plus Two dances. "Dan," they would say, "you look like you're having such a good time. Where does it come from?"

I knew very early in life that I had a good ear for melody and a great feel for tempo, but I wasn't so sure about my motivation. Although I realized that music came easy and that I was always drawn to it, I didn't always listen to the voice within me that whispered, "Danny boy, stay with your music." And whenever I strayed from music, I got into a heap of trouble.

It was a steamy August evening in Chickasha, Oklahoma in 1912, when my father Burt, a professional drummer, began to pace back and forth in the kitchen. He had a playing job that night and was worried, wondering whether to go play or get a sub and stay home. My grandfather Rueben Tye, M.D. was preparing for the delivery. He had been a doctor in Chickasha, Indian Territory way before statehood in 1907 and had delivered hundreds of babies. One more tonight was no big thing (even if it was his grandson).

The bespectacled Dr. Tye looked up at my sweating Dad pacing the floor, and the more he paced, the more it upset Grandpa. "Well, Burt," he said, "you're not doing any good here. I can't deliver the baby until it comes. Why don't you go play the job. God knows you need the money."

So Dad threw up his hands and rushed out the door in frustration to play drums while I was born. When he hurried home after midnight, there I was, sleeping away.

Told he had a son, Dad looked down at me next to Mom and smiled. "Well, there is our little striped kitten."

Just before I was born, a cat with kittens lived in the barn out back of Grandpa's house. The mama cat had this curious habit of bringing one little striped kitten to the house. It was either the mama cat's favorite or she was trying to get rid of it. (I always worried about that.) She would drag it in and leave all the others back in the barn. So, Dad would take the striped kitten back with the others. First thing you know, the cat would have the kitten back in the house. "Tell you what, Bessie," Dad said to Mom one day, "we'll call Dan our little striped kitten."

That nickname held for a long time, but later it kind of bothered me. Would they, too, carry me out and drop me someday? Years after my birth, when my brain began to function a little, I learned that during Mom's pregnancy, Dad would be banging away on those drums, practicing. So I figured maybe all that racket somehow penetrated Mom's abdomen while I was developing and somehow....

Well, Dad was a good drummer and he kept up the practice during my early years of life. Can you imagine a baby trying to sleep with all those drums popping? I don't know. Maybe it did some damage.

A few years after my birth we moved into what I thought at the time was a big two-story house. It was right next door to Grandma and Grandpa on Colorado Street. By then Dad was a bookkeeper with Linton Grain Company, but he still played drums on occasional dances.[2]

My first memories would be of that huge two story house and Dad practicing with his drums. And even today, if I close my eyes and listen, I can hear the best of my father's drums and see him smile, keeping that beat all the while.

I used to sit on the front porch steps, waiting for him to return from work. Someone might come along and ask, "What are you doing, Dan?"

"I'm waiting for my Daddy to come home."

And every day he did come home, gave me a hug and a kiss. He loved me. I could depend on Dad. I knew that early on and I never doubted his love. And my how that marvelous love in our family would influence my life.

Older brother, George, sister Bernice, and I had some good times, but after Robert, the youngest of the children, was born in 1917, our mother was really tied down with our new little "Bud." I was five when "Bud" came along and I felt ignored. Mom was busy with the two older children, and the baby, and keeping house. She didn't have time to watch me. "Oh, no. Time for the striped kitten to go," I thought.

So this was the beginning of my "running away" episodes. They'd find me and bring me back. "Why do you run away, Dan?" Mom would ask.

"I don't run away. I just *walk* down the street." In my mind running away was, well, running. Never understood what she was talking about. All I did was just walk away—happily, too, I might add.

More than once, she caught me knocking the high hook off the screen door with a broomstick, but I usually slipped out the door before she grabbed me.

Looking back, I was just lonesome. Even that early, I loved people, so I took off to find them. Mother had her hands full, caring for the children, trying to keep house and cook and wash and iron; not an easy task in those days. How did women do it all?

Not only did I "run" away; one time I "rode" away. Mom looked out the front window to see me clinging to the back step of the ice wagon waving to her. It sped down the street, pulled by two high-stepping mules. The iceman brought me home, giving Mom a few gray hairs.

I often ended up at the Frisco Depot. I would perch myself up on a baggage cart and watch the trains whistle by, picking up soot and dirt all the while. I liked the sounds of those old steam engines and the rhythm of the clattering tracks; good sounds; sounds you don't forget. [3]

One day this policeman saw me. "What are you doing here, son?"

I wasn't frightened. In my mind I had done no wrong.

"Just watching the trains go by," I said.

"Where do you live?"

"Down that way," I pointed.

"Well, get up here on my motorcycle." He sat me in front of him on the motorcycle and we puttered down the street. I enjoyed the ride, wind blowing in my face. "Now which way?" he asked, and I kept pointing. Finally, we got to the turn and I pointed again. "Here?" he asked. I nodded, and pointed to my house.

We sputtered to a stop under the rustling branches of our big elm tree and he shut off the engine.

He led me up to the front door and knocked and Mom came to the door. "Lady," he asked, "do you know where I found this boy?"

"I wouldn't be at all surprised," Mother answered, glancing down at me.

"Frisco Depot."

"What was he doing?"

"Well, he was sitting on a baggage truck, watching the trains, but I knew he was a runaway, so I got him and I brought him here. He showed me all the way home."

"Well," Mother sighed. She opened the screen door. "You get in here, Dan. You're going to get a good spanking."

"Now, don't whip him. He was a good little boy, and he didn't cause any harm. He didn't get hurt, and he showed me where he lived and all, so don't whip him."

Mother looked at him and then at me, and thought a minute. "All right. I won't whip him."

I rarely got a whipping, but I probably needed one then. I kept on running away.

My poor grandfather, Dr. Tye. He had so many grandchildren—around fourteen in all. Grandpa wasn't sure how many grandchildren he had, or what they all looked like.

One day, he was walking home from his downtown office, and my brother George was walking down the street in the opposite direction. He passed my grandfather without saying a word. Grandpa walked on a few steps and paused. "Is that one of my grandchildren?" he wondered. "No, I guess not." He walked on a few steps and stopped again, puzzled. "Yeah, I believe it is." And he turned around to look. "I think that's George, Bessie's boy." He shouted. "George?"

George didn't answer.

Grandpa walked a few steps further, stopped, turned and looked again. "Well I know that's George." He spoke more firmly this time. "George!" George walked up to him. "Where you going?"

"Just down the street."

"You are George, aren't you?"

"Yes."

"Well, you come along."

They say it's a wise father that knows his own child, but, in this case, it was a befuddled grandfather that didn't know his own grandchild. Fourteen grandchildren aren't easy to remember. Anyway, he got George home.

George was a good kid. But I was the better runaway, by far.

During my breeze through kindergarten I began to enjoy the school songs and I got hooked on eating wheat paste (water, flour, and a little perfume). It smelled good and tasted good. Nothing wrong in eating some. Apparently never hurt me.

By 1918, when I turned six and Dad got a job with the U.S. Department of Agriculture, I had kicked the paste habit and we moved to Fort Worth, Texas. I had already become a star first grade singer in Chickasha with songs like, "In the Blue Ridge Mountains of Virginia." I loved my friends in Chickasha. I cried when we left. (But I would return later for high school and my first paying job in music.)

When we arrived in Fort Worth, Dad rented a baggage truck (an old Model-T Ford) and piled some of our belongings in the back. Our furniture came by train. And Dad drove us to a house he had previously rented.

I noticed a drugstore across the street, which I figured would be my candy store. And it was. I can still smell the special aroma of all those goodies and taste the licorice and cinnamon sticks.

World War I was still on; soldiers everywhere. I asked Mother about it and she tried to explain we were fighting a war in Europe, but I couldn't grasp the meaning of all that.

One of the first things I remember about music, besides Dad's drums and singing in kindergarten, was a woman singer next door. I used to lie in bed and listen to her practice in her living room early in the evening, right after supper. She sang a very popular tune at that time, written by the well-known composer Victor Herbert, "Kiss Me Again." [4] The lyrics went: "Kiss me again. Kiss me again. Kiss me again and again… and I thought, "Gosh, there's a lot of kissing going on in this song." She would sing it in operatic style. Pretty lusty, too.

Victor Herbert wrote some beautiful things: "Thine Alone," "Italian Street Song," "Indian Summer," and others. When he wrote "Kiss Me Again," he meant it as a parody. "I got so sick and tired of all those kissing songs popular at the time," he later wrote, "that I was really making fun of them. I'll put so many kisses in this song, that they'll get tired of hearing about kissing." But the darn song turned out to be a big hit. Some woman made a recording of the song and it became famous.

I got acquainted with a kid on the corner, by the name of Bud Trout. His folks ran a grocery store. Older brother Jim had some records that he played for me; the first jazz record I ever heard, such as it was then. It was a Ted Lewis record.

Ted Lewis was quite famous—worked mostly stage shows. Even though Ted was a horrible clarinet player, he had a lot of showmanship, and always hired good musicians to back him up. Later on, I go to hear him in-person in Kansas City, on stage, and he was a great showman. He wore a top hat and had a cane, and he played the most "corn-ball" clarinet you ever heard in your life. He got a lot of great musicians started in his day. Among them was Benny Goodman. When I heard Lewis on stage in Kansas City at the Main Street Theatre later in 1923, I thought they were the greatest jazz band in the world, not knowing I was soon to hear all the other great black jazz bands in Kansas City. [5]

In 1918 in Fort Worth, I also heard Paul Whiteman and his orchestra on records. One of his tunes was "Dardanella." [6]

So Ted Lewis and Paul Whiteman were the first jazz and dance orchestras I ever heard. I was discovering my interest in music and remember clearly as a boy how people changed their moods when they listened to music. It was a good feeling that I learned very early.

Dad's first job in Fort Worth was "broomcorn analyst." When Dad and his father had moved from South Dakota years before, they took up farming near Chickasha and grew broomcorn, so Dad knew broomcorn. It was not easily grown. Its first growth resembles regular corn. Right out of the top grows the strands of broomcorn. These were cut and laid on racks under a covered shed until the live sap dried out. Then it was threshed and baled and sold to broom factories. It could vary in quality a lot. Greedy brokers would swoop in and buy up high-grade broomcorn from a farmer for a low price, and then sell it at a big profit.

Dad worked out a system of grading that was quite accurate and wrote the government pamphlet on broomcorn. He saved the farmers a lot of money. [7]

A few years later in 1923, just after we moved to Kansas City, he sent out questionnaires to farmers, asking what kind of broomcorn crop they expected to have. Most reported a poor crop, but the brokers thought the crop would be overproduced and the price would be low. But Dad was sure of his figures. Years later, he told George and me that he could have hooked up with a wealthy cheat, bought up most of the crop, and made a killing. But Dad wouldn't even consider doing such a thing. He was an honest man. Poor, but honest.

In Fort Worth, we moved again. My brother George and I walked to the Alexander Hogg School, named after one of the early Texas pioneers, who had a daughter named "Ima." Ima Hogg. That got to be a big joke around the surrounding country. My teacher was Miss Quigly.

In the fourth grade, they began to include music in our classes and had us sing. And, boy, I loved that. Some girl and I got up in front of the class and sang duets or I would sing a solo. I wasn't scared at all. Didn't bother me to get up in front of a group and sing.

About that time (I was about eight), Dad decided that George and I ought to start playing music so he got George a drum, and bought me a mellophone (shaped like a French horn, but has valves instead of pistons). Here I was, nurtured in the womb by drums and Dad gave me a mellophone! "I want to play drums," I told him. (I wanted to bang them when Dad was asleep like he did to me as a poor baby.)

"No, I don't want two drummers," Dad said.

I didn't see anything wrong with two drummers. Anyway, I would sneak in and play George's drum too. I managed to wake everybody up a few times.

We joined the Fort Worth Rotary Club Boys Band and our uniforms were U.S. Army uniforms (war surplus). We had wrap leggings and billed caps and the regulation khaki shirt, tie, and pants. I began to learn to read music.

One night in the practice hall they had me sitting on a stool that had no back to it, so I figured out that if I turned my stool around behind the guy next to me and faced backwards, I could lean up against the back of his chair. Of course, when I did that, I wasn't facing the director. But, I was quite comfortable playing that way—until the director spotted me.

He stopped the band. "Say, Dan, why are you facing the wrong way?"

"Well, I… I face this way so I'll have something to lean against."

"Well, you can't play correctly unless you face the director and watch my stick." That got a big laugh.

I figured I didn't need direction anyway. Once the band started and the beat was going, I knew where I was.

One time, the Rotary Club Boys Band was scheduled to play at a state-wide druggists' convention down in Galveston, Texas. They paid for the band to go down by train, but they weren't going to let me go, because I was too young (about nine by then). But Dad spoke to the band director. "If I pay for Dan's fare will you take him along?"

"Yes, we will," he said.

On the train down, they put George and me together in an upper berth. And what did I do, but wet the bunk. George was furious. He punched me with his elbow. "Get over on your own side!" It was a horrible night. I slept on my own wet side of the bed.

In Galveston the next day, after our playing stint, we had some recreation time. They took us down to the beach. We rented some things to float on, a horseshoe-shaped cork seat covered with canvas, with straps coming down that made into a seat. You sat in this contraption, floating on the water. A wave hit me and turned me over and I got my head tangled up in the webbing and started swallowing salt water. A lifeguard pulled me up by the hair, sputtering out of the water.

By the time we got back to Fort Worth, George wasn't speaking to me. He said if I wet the bed again, he would throw me off the train.

It was on that train back to Fort Worth that I first realized how much I loved music. I felt it, dreamed it, and heard it in my sleep. Every train sound I heard became a rhythm. (At the time, I was just trying hard to think of something else, afraid I would wet the bed again!)

But little did I know how far music would take me or from how many jams it would rescue me. Music was now an irreversible part of my life and, though I didn't know it at the time, would lead me by the hand through some rough spots in life. But, no—I wouldn't listen!

Chapter Endnotes

1. The chapter titles throughout the book are jazz and folk standards, most of which were recorded by the Firehouse Five Plus Two at various points in their tenure. "Yes Sir! That's My Baby" was originally released on 78 rpm (GOOD TIME JAZZ No. 14) opposite "Pagan Love Song" and was an early hit for the band. It was later included on the 33 1/3 LP, "The Firehouse Five Story Vol. 1." The song was one of the earliest recorded by the band to feature a vocal chorus section. Alguire himself was typically the lead singer of the group.
2. According to *A Standard History of Oklahoma*, the Linton Grain Company handled more than $1 million in wheat in January and February, 1915. A "$20,000 modern elevator plant" was eventually in use at the Chickasha location. Proprietor Fred R. Linton was a native of Illinois, and later worked in Kansas City around the same time that a young Walter Elias Disney was growing up in the area. The Grain Company in Chickasha was strategically well-placed "with reference to the grain belt and railroad facilities," making it a major location for grain production in the region.

3. This is the St. Louis & San Francisco Railway depot in Chickasha, located at 6th and Michigan Avenues. The "Frisco" arrived in Chickasha in 1902—10 years before Alguire's birth.
4. Victor Herbert was a major figure among the songwriters and composers of Tin Pan Alley, then at the height of its primacy and popular appeal.
5. Ted Lewis was born Theodore Leopold Friedman in Centerville, Ohio in 1890. He began playing piccolo, then clarinet as a pre-teen. He started his singing career in 1906 and worked his way into Vaudeville, including tours with Jack Lewis—billed as "Lewis and Friedman." He became "Ted Lewis" after theater manager changed the name of the act to "Lewis and Lewis," explaining that the shorter name fit better on the marquee. Lewis led his first band in 1916. At the high-class Rector's restaurant, between sets, he won a battered top hat in a card game. One night, following an intermission, he returned to the bandstand wearing the top hat, tipped it to the audience and asked "Is everybody happy?" The phrase and the top hat became his trademarks. He recorded extensively, and many sides became hits—including his theme song "When My Baby Smiles At Me," "Tiger Rag," and the iconic "Me And My Shadow." Over the years, his recording sessions often included hot jazzmen such as Muggsy Spanier, Benny Goodman, Jack Teagarden, Frank Teschemacher, Jimmy Dorsey, Don Murray, and Fats Waller. Ted Lewis performed for over 60 years, and passed away in New York City in 1971. For information from the website of the Ted Lewis Museum in Circleville, Ohio, visit: www.tedlewismuseum.org.
6. Paul Whiteman was also the subject of a memorable caricature in the 1935 Walt Disney *Silly Symphonies* cartoon, *Music Land*. "The King," as his character was known, was a

rotund saxophone who ruled over the free-spirited Isle of Jazz. Designed by studio artist Albert Hurter, the character was animated by Clyde Geronimi and Leonard Sebring.

7. G. B. Alguire was a prominent figure in the midwestern broomcorn industry in the 1920s and thirties. As a United States Department of Agriculture representative, he pushed for the standardization and increased efficiency in broomcorn production. "Standardization of broomcorn is a necessary thing," he told a group of Illinois farmers in 1926. "It is needed just as much as the grading of corn, wheat, oats, potatoes, fruits, wool, and other farm commodities, which are already being graded according to a government standard." See the Bibliography for additional sources on the elder Alguire's career.

Chapter 2:

"Down Where the Sun Goes Down"

One night in 1920, before Grandpa (Dr. Tye) and Grandma moved from Chickasha to Texas, my Aunt Verna, staying with them in Chickasha, heard a noise in the house and came downstairs. She confronted this burglar. "What do you want?" she asked.

"I want money," he growled. I guess he thought she was alone.

"Well, we haven't got any," she snapped back.

About this time, Dr. Tye, who was getting pretty old, heard the commotion and hollered from upstairs. "What's going on down there, Verna?"

"There's a man in the house."

"What does he want?"

"He says he wants money."

The burglar glared at her. "Who's that?" he asked.

And Aunt Verna, a pretty brave little woman, perhaps a hundred pounds, stood right up to him. "That's my Father, and don't you touch a hair on his head!" which was funny, because Grandpa was as bald as a billiard ball.

The burglar hollered, "You stay up there, old man. Don't you come down here!" He ran out without taking anything.

And it was that year, 1920, that Dr. Tye and Grandma retired from Chickasha and moved close to Burleson, Texas, sixteen miles south of Fort Worth. They built a house, put in a new well and all. The water tasted great, always cold.

But Dr. Tye's health was failing.

"Gee, I was kind of scared of Grandpa as a kid," I used to tell Mom.

"He had dyspepsia," Mother said. "Ulcers."

"I was afraid of him. He always looked so gruff and he ruled that family with an iron hand."

"I'm sorry you remember him like that," Mother said, "because Poppa was a very kind man, and a very good doctor."

In Clarendon, Texas in the 1890s, there was a Jewish family named Marcus, who ran a clothing store, and Grandpa was the doctor that delivered a Marcus baby in Clarendon. That baby was the "Marcus" of Neiman-Marcus Department Store in Dallas. Mr. Marcus kept in touch with Dr. Tye until Grandpa's death and was always fond of him. He even sent him presents throughout the years. Grandpa also became a surgeon for the Fort Worth and Denver Railroad while he maintained a horse and buggy practice.

It was in 1893, when they opened up Oklahoma Indian Territory to settlers, that Grandpa moved his family to Chickasha, bought some land, built a home, and erected the two-story Tye Building where he set up practice in Chickasha continuing until 1920, when he retired and moved to his farm near Burleson, Texas.

One Sunday down on the farm in Texas before Grandpa died, someone knocked at the front door. Grandma swung open the door and a poor ragged-looking man stood there, eyes puffy and red. He was dirty and smelled of smoke. "I understand that there's a doctor here," he said holding a tattered hat in his hands and looking hopeful.

"Yes, my husband's a doctor," Grandma said. "He's retired."

The poor man dropped his head and rolled his hat in his fingers, and then looked up at her. "Well ma'am we're campin', eh, livin' down by the creek. I have a child that's mighty sick. Runnin' a fever. I wondered if Doc, ah, if Doc had some medicine for him."

"Just a minute," Grandma said. She called Grandpa.

He came to the door in his black suit and string tie and the man tried to describe what was ailing the child. "Well," Grandpa said, "wait a minute. I'll get some medicine." And he fetched an amber bottle full of pills. "Try these."

"How much do I owe you?" asked the man.

"Oh, I don't know. A dollar, I guess."

So the man dropped his head, plunged a hand into his dirty overalls and pulled out a silver dollar, took the medicine, thanked Grandpa, and left.

And after he left, my grandmother jumped up. "Why did you charge him a dollar for that medicine? That poor man," she said, tears in her eyes. "It was probably the last dollar he had."

"Well, I don't know. He asked me how much, and I just said, 'A dollar.'"

"Well, I think that was terrible!"

She was mad at him for charging the man a dollar which even to me, at my age, sounded like a lot of money.

But Grandpa told her, "Sudie, a man needs to keep his pride."

Dr. Tye would soon die. Not long before, they had moved his bed in the front room and his wife walked into the room one morning. "Good morning," she said. "How do you feel?"

"Sudie," he said, looking serious, "I want you to go down to the foot of the bed and look straight at me. You see anything wrong with my face?"

Startled, she stared at him. "No. I don't think so, except…yes!" Her lips parted and she sucked in a quick breath. "One side of your face…Oh, my God. You…."

"Yeah. I had a stroke last night."

Matter-of-factly, "Had a stroke."

And sure enough, he did. It wasn't long after that, Grandpa died; a second stroke in 1922.

We were living in Fort Worth when the phone rang that day. Mother answered it. It was her mother. January, 1922. Reuben P. Tye, M.D., horse and buggy doctor from Chickasha, Indian Territory, was dead.

Mother took it bravely. I don't recall seeing her cry, but I know she did. She never liked for us to see her cry. She and her sisters always spoke so proudly of their "Poppa."

He was buried at Rose Cemetery in Chickasha, Oklahoma, 1922. I remember seeing my grandfather, the man who brought me into the world, in his casket, before they took him away.

Later that same year in Fort Worth, I heard a knock on the door and answered it. It was night, about 7:00 p.m. It was a Western Union boy.

"Is your folks at home?" he asked.

I called Mother. I stood at the door with the Western Union boy and looked at the telegram. It had a black mark around the edge or some black "X's" or something. "What do those black marks mean?" I asked him.

"Death in the family," he said in a monotone, rolling his eyes to the floor.

It struck me. "Oh," I said. "Death in the family," rang in my thoughts.

Mom came to the door, took the telegram and read it. I remember the message word-for-word. "D. E. Alguire killed in automobile accident. Come," it said.

"Come…."

Dad loved his father. He seemed to get so much strength from his father and Mom said that it hit him hard, and he cried. None of us went. He went alone; took a train to Oklahoma City for the funeral. Couldn't afford to take the rest of us.

So, in 1922, I lost both my grandfathers. And it was a shame. My grandfather Alguire was a real hardy man—slim and vigorous. And Dr. Tye was a fine pioneer doctor.

A couple of summers before Grandpa Alguire died, Dad sent us by train for two weeks to visit his folks on the farm. We loved it, because they had fruit orchards and fields to run in. And when he'd mow, we'd run behind the mower smelling that fresh cut alfalfa and scare out all the rabbits. We tried to catch the little ones.

Grandpa Alguire bred horses, he had a magnificent black stallion named "Prince." Farmers from all around would bring their mares to breed with Prince. Of course, by this time we were getting pretty "savvy." We knew that when they brought a mare, Prince was going to breed her. So George and I would sneak to the hay loft where we could look out onto the breeding area about forty feet square.

In the middle were two posts twelve feet apart, topped by a single rail to which they would hitch the mare. Grandpa would lead Prince up to the mare on the other side of the rail. They would sniff. Prince soon got the message. And then Grandpa would lead Prince around behind the mare. When he got close to the mare he would just let him go.

Of course, we watched it all. Probably our first exposure to breeding. Didn't know a thing about humans, but we sure knew about horses.

The way Grandpa Alguire got killed was a freaky thing. He and my uncle Henry were driving west into Oklahoma City in his 1919 Dodge touring car. While making a left turn over the railroad tracks, the car bumped around and, somehow or another, Grandpa lost control of the car. Right past the tracks was a fifteen or twenty-foot ditch on the right. The car flipped and rolled into the ditch. The steering wheel crushed Grandpa's chest. He died instantly. Uncle Henry, riding with him, was injured, but he survived.

After Grandpa died, Grandma stayed there awhile; a few months, maybe. Then she sold the farm.

Dad said it was a good farm. Grandpa had horses, pecan orchards, apricots, peaches, and apples, and he farmed. He grew wheat, oats, and alfalfa for his stock.

Grandpa had milk cows. He would do the milking every night and every morning. We followed him to the house in the evenings. He had two pails of milk, one in each hand, and he would swing along singing and walking in rhythm. He used to sing "Buffalo Gals":

Buffalo Gals, are you coming out tonight,
Coming out tonight, coming out tonight.
Buffalo Gals, aren't you coming out tonight and
Dance by the light of the moon.

I loved it.

Grandpa would lift his violin down off the wall, and play a few tunes. That's where Dad and I got our musical talent.

Grandpa was short and wiry. Maybe five-seven, 140 pounds, but strong for his size. He used to sing to Grandma, "When You and I were Young, Maggie." A lot of music in him.

The upshot of the whole thing was this: it all came to a disappointing end for the Alguires. The 160 acres that Grandpa owned, four miles east of Oklahoma City, was close to where oilmen brought in the "Mary Sudik" (first discovery well for the Oklahoma City oilfield in 1928). If Grandpa had lived (and he was very healthy) a few more years on that farm, he would have been sitting on top of a lot of oil. And Grandma sold it, just before they found oil!

The next year, 1923, Dad got a promotion and would be transferred to Kansas City, Missouri. But things were looking bad. Both our grandfathers dead, the farm gone. And here, we had to move to Kansas City. The move was so abrupt. Although we didn't realize it at the time, a Depression was looming and a lot of hard times were in store for us and for a lot of folks.

Chapter 3:

"Working Man Blues"

So in August, 1923, Dad loaded up our 1918 Dodge touring car and we left Fort Worth for Kansas City.

We stopped by Chickasha and stayed with some of Mother's old friends, the Mills family, just for a couple of nights. While we were there, the morning paper headlines indicated Warren G. Harding, the President of the United States, had died suddenly in San Francisco. I'm not sure they ever found out the cause of death. He either had a heart attack, some said, or stomach trouble, maybe cancer. Anyway, I don't think it was ever publicly revealed. Some thought he was poisoned.

"Well, if the President's dead, who's going to be the new President?" I asked Mother that day.

"The vice-president takes over. His name is Calvin Coolidge." Anyway, Coolidge was re-elected in 1924.

One of the sons of the Mills family had a nice collie. The next day (the day before we left), he was run over and killed. The boy cried like a baby. We all did, because he had lost his dog. And it was another new sorrow none of us kids had known.

Dad liked to get up before dawn. It was mostly dirt roads, so we took off early from Chickasha. We chugged off in the old Dodge traveling north through Oklahoma to Blackwell and finally reached a little town in southern Kansas called Cherryvale. Dad found rooms.

At the hotel, we found a puppy we called "Mopsy" and sneaked him into the room.

We didn't make too many miles in those days on dirt roads.

It was mid-summer, about 100 degrees. We would rumble along, Dad spitting tobacco juice out the window. When we saw he was going to spit, we would all duck to the right.

No pavement, just sandy road with two ruts. One time, Dad said, "Look! I don't even have to steer the car." He held his hands up, and the tires just followed the ruts. All of a sudden, he looked out and here comes the left rear tire right along his side. Eyes wide, "Oh boy! The wheel came off," he said.

Not the wheel, but the tire and the rim. So, we came to a quick stop. The car had oak spokes and it was so hot that the wooden spokes shrunk and the tire and rim just flew off the wheel.

Dad and George searched through a field and found a couple of fence posts to put under the car. The soil was so sandy that we couldn't get the jack to stand on a solid base to lift the wheel up. George was thirteen or fourteen, so he was a help to Dad. They struggled with this piece of wood underneath the car, shoved the jack up on it, and raised the wheel up off the ground.

They cut some leather straps off our suitcase and made shims, which they wedged between the oak wheel and the rim, so that the lugs would stay on to hold the tire, and we continued rumbling through the country, grasshoppers buzzing and splatting on the windshield.

I loved the trip. Big adventure.

George's interest was focused on the side of the road, where these tall sunflowers grew ten or twelve feet high. "Well, I'll just pick a sunflower," he thought.

He grabbed hold of one of these sunflower stems and, of course, that stuff is just like steel cable. You couldn't pull one out with a tractor. It jerked George up against the two rods that held up the top. Otherwise, it would have pulled him clear out of the car. Naturally, he let go real quick. Imagine, trying to pull a sunflower out of the ground! Dad gave him a pretty good lecture. Bernice and Bud and I laughed, but Dad and Mom didn't laugh. Neither did George.

When we got to Olathe, Kansas, near Kansas City, it was dark. We slept that night and drove off early the next day.

When we reached Kansas City, I wanted to run away again, back to Chickasha; anywhere, but this big dirty city. And I missed my music.

Chapter 4:

"What Is This Thing Called Love"

In Kansas City by noon, Dad drove to the home of Mr. and Mrs. Warner, a third cousin. Now here was this old lady and her husband, well into their seventies, and I thought it was pretty rude of Dad... of course, I don't know what he thought. Maybe, third cousins were kind enough for that.

We pulled up in front of their house and piled out. I think we spent a couple of nights with them, running in and out of the house, banging the screen doors. I think the old couple was just about ready for a heart attack. It was terrible, imposing like that. Perhaps Dad phoned Mrs. Warner first and was invited to spend the night. I hope so.

Within a day or two, just a half a block away, Dad rented an upstairs apartment and the people living below were Jewish or Italian, and they cooked with garlic and *wow*! We got our first aroma of garlic.

Dad bought a furnished house on the south side for $7,000 in a nice neighborhood; our first real home. In the attic was a three-quarter sized pool table. Public pool halls were considered a bad influence on young kids, so this pool table in the attic was put to plenty of use.

I sailed through the fifth and sixth grades at Bancroft Grade School and then I transferred to Westport Junior High School. The cafeteria was what I remembered best. For fifteen cents, I could get roast beef with noodles, gravy, and two pieces of bread. After Mother's cooking, this food was terrific!

Mother's only fault was that she was not a good cook. But our family was close. We loved each other, and I thought for the first years of my life, until I was nine or ten, that everybody had a family like ours: a mother, a father, and children, and everyone got along. No hassles. And no separations. I asked Mother about it later in life. "Didn't you and Dad ever fight?"

"Oh yes," she said. "Sometimes we did. But we made it a rule never to have our differences in front of you children. We would go into the bedroom or the bathroom and solve our problems."

"I can't remember that I ever saw you or Dad argue over anything important." (A few years later there might have been some differences that we heard, but nothing big.) That was a fine thing. But it was a jolt to later learn the realities of life.

God bless Mother. She was a good teacher. I don't think she was cut out to be a wife or a mother. All she liked to do was read. She loved history and had a memory that was unbelievable; dates, places. Many a time I came home from school and found her sitting in the living room, reading away.

She wasn't the greatest housekeeper, either. She kept the place clean, but she didn't like it. I didn't blame her. Nobody complained. We were happy.

She was the world's worst cook. She would overcook the meat. Dad would bring home top sirloin steak; twenty-five cents a pound (and Kansas City had the best). He liked his meat rare. So Mom cooked it rare. For the rest of us, she would cook it to death. I caught on pretty quick and asked her to cook mine rare like Dad's.

She made cakes. They fell. She made pies. The crust was so hard, you couldn't cut it. Every Sunday, same menu-roast, cooked to death, and gravy with lumpy potatoes. And her salad: shred some lettuce, slice some tomatoes in a big bowl and drown it with mayonnaise. It was so soggy, you could hardly eat it. Of course, we didn't have refrigeration, and you couldn't keep the lettuce crisp, but Mom just didn't have that knack. "Mother, God bless you, you tried." She admitted she couldn't cook. But we survived, because she was a mother who loved us all. We had our faults too. It was amazing how we all wanted to see each other happy.

In Kansas City, George and I joined the Kansas City Rotary Club Boys Band. We had nice blue uniforms with cap and big white plume. That was good band, except I got tired of playing mellophone. I was listening to the trumpet section and *boy*! that's where the melody was.

So I went to Dad. "I'm tired of playing mellophone," I said. "No melody, I want a trumpet." Dad bought me a trumpet. It was a King trumpet, gold, with fancy designs on the bell. Cost Dad about $200 and I had it for a long time. [1]

Pretty soon I got bored with the Boy's band and I started listening to jazz records. I'd play along with the record as best I could. I got better and better. And I knew I would learn more. I was hooked.

Mom tried to put some weight on my sister Bernice, but she couldn't seem to do it. She wasn't sick, just thin and timid. Just grew up skinny. She had a friendly personality, and was always good to George, Bud, and me; taught all of us how to dance. She was a natural, and had the greatest sense of tempo I ever saw.

"You know who my favorite musician is?" she asked me once.

"No, who?"

"Louis Armstrong. He has a great sense of rhythm."

"Well," I said, "you're right. No one could budge him once the beat started."

Bernice took up piano. Often Dad would get out his violin and we played songs that Dad wrote or sheet music that Bernice would bring home. I played trumpet lead and Dad played harmony on violin; George on drums. Sis could read music, but couldn't "fake" anything, nothing by ear. But, she was a born dancer.

In 1925, the fast, tricky dancing was called "Gandy Dancing." This was revived in California in the 1940s, and called, "The Balboa." New step? No way!

In 1927 and 1928 Bernice and George, and their friends in Kansas City would go over to the "Pla-Mor Ballroom" on Main Street in Kansas City and dance on Saturdays and Sundays to Chick Scoggins and his orchestra. The "Charleston" was going strong. From 1926 to 1929 Bernice and George and their whole gang and all her sorority pals were into dancing in a big way. [2]

Bernice organized a sorority, and our house was filled with kids all the time. They were rolling back the rug, putting on the records and dancing. That was the big thing, house dancing, and Bernice was the ringleader. All the guys that danced with Bernice said, "You could turn a somersault and she'd follow you."

Mom and Dad didn't mind the kids and all the activity. No problems. We all loved people. We shared all that we had: food, house, music. It was a beautiful thing.

And I started to recognize that I had some musical talent.

Some people have a sense of rhythm and no sense of melody or tone and others have a good sense of tone, but no rhythm, and some have both. They are the ones that do pretty well musically. When you have both, you have what you need to make it and should go for it. I felt fortunate that I had a sense of tone and a sense of rhythm.

George did, too. But George didn't care for his drums by then. He later took up guitar and violin. And Bernice got us to dance. Our lives, like never before, were overflowing with music.

Chapter Endnotes:

1. First producing trombones in 1894, King remains one of the preeminent makers of brass instruments in the United States. Noted musicians including Tommy Dorsey and Charlie Parker played King instruments. The company has operated in the area around Cleveland, Ohio since its inception.
2. From its debut on Thanksgiving, 1927 that attracted thousands of patrons, the Pla-Mor ballroom was one of

Kansas City's most popular jazz venues. It boasted a 14,000 square foot ballroom resting on some 7,000 metal springs which allowed the floor to flex with the dancers' movements. Racially segregated, the Pla-Mor became the subject of controversy when bandleader Cab Calloway was violently evicted in 1945. In the waning post-war years, the ballroom ultimately closed its doors and was demolished in the early 1970s, around the same time the Firehouse Five Plus Two retired from regular playing.

Chapter 5:

"The World Is Waiting For the Sunrise"

I'm not blaming my Mom or Dad—but I've often wondered why I didn't get motivated more. I don't know. It's something that parents can instill into their children, to want them to amount to something. My sister and two brothers had motivated children, all college graduates. All did well. Did the motivation come from their parents?

I was good in school. I could absorb the stuff, but I didn't seem to have that kick in the butt that it took to say: "Boy! I'm going into geology or journalism," or whatever, and go after it.

I just fell into everything. The nearest I ever came to being motivated was when I got into music, and I didn't get into that like I should have.

Never had a lesson in my life. I learned it on my own, which was wrong. I should have gone to a good teacher, and learned to play correctly. I would have gone much further and played better.

I must say that I finally did get motivated when I went to work at Disney Studios. I was contributing to the magical creations of Disney. And I had my jazz music with the Firehouse Five Plus Two.

But before I got there, I began to wonder what success really was. Money? Power? I felt guilty that I wasn't a hard driving dynamo with motivation. I was too happy, I thought.

I'm not blaming my parents at all, because I loved them both dearly. I couldn't ask for better parents. Maybe we had too much love, too much happiness in our family. We grew up not knowing or seeing much conflict. We all felt good about ourselves. Maybe we shouldn't have been so complacent. Does a lack of self-esteem stimulate motivation and drive you to do more and more because you don't feel good about yourself? Maybe we needed more pain. Why, Dad only whipped George and me once.

It was when we moved into our second house back in Fort Worth in 1918, our second move. In moving the furniture into the house, the movers knocked a chip off the door jamb. Strangely enough, just before that, Dad had given both George and me a new pocket knife. Dad looked at the hall door that day and it looked like it could have been done with a knife.

He came to George and me, knowing we had these new knives. "Did you cut that wood?"

"No," I said, "I didn't do it."

"I didn't do it, Dad," said George.

One thing Dad couldn't tolerate was lying, and he was convinced that we were lying to him. So we got a strapping. "We didn't do it, Dad," we cried all the while he whipped us.

The next day the movers returned and one of them came up to Dad. "Oh, Mr. Alguire, we accidentally knocked that piece of wood off the door. We'll get it fixed for you."

Dad was devastated. I never knew this, but Mom told me years later that Dad went into the bedroom, closed the door, lay down on the bed, and wept. He had whipped us for nothing. He never raised a hand to us from that day forward. Maybe that was wrong, maybe we needed more. (Easy for me to say now.)

When I was a kid, I got a few "switchings" from Mother—swat my legs with a little peach switch. But there was never any violence in our family. Not at all. Did we grow up thinking life would be so painless? Did all this goodness suppress motivation?

One thing, though, was kind of amusing. Mom was ambidextrous. Mom said that when she first went to school, she was naturally left-handed, but, you know, they tried to make everyone right-handed in school then. Once-in-awhile, she would box my ears a little for something. It was pretty hard to duck her, because I didn't know with which hand she was going to hit me! But, it never hurt. And anyway, I probably deserved it. Maybe I needed more, left or right!

Chapter 6:

"Doctor Jazz"

After my sophomore year in Kansas City, during March or April—I know it was still kind of chilly—I came down with pleurisy. Dr. Monahan came to our house, rammed a needle between my ribs, and drained some fluid from my pleural cavity. I was in bed a couple of weeks. It was that Kansas City cold.

I recovered, but that year, 1928, Dad and Mom sent me to Oklahoma to stay with my grandmother thinking the dry air would be more healthful. So, I left Kansas City on the train, alone, to go and live with Grandma, my Aunt Verna, and her two children for the summer back in Chickasha.

I got acquainted with some new kids. And then September came. Instead of coming back to Kansas City, we all agreed that maybe I ought to go to school in Chickasha. I wanted to stay also, because I liked my friends and the winter would be milder.

So, I showed up at Chickasha High School on opening day, September, 1928.[1] There was a little student hangout across the street from the high school called "The Black Cat." I went in and struck up a conversation with a guy named B. J. Vaughan. I told him I played trumpet.

"We got an orchestra, we're trying to get organized. I play alto sax and I'm the leader," he said. "Would you like to play with us?"

"Oh, yeah!"

"We play dance music and all that stuff."

We wore black and yellow striped blazers and called ourselves, "The Yellow Jackets." One night, a guy comes by the bandstand. "I know why they named your band the 'Yellow Jackets,'" he said with a smirk.[2]

"Why?" I asked.

"Because every time we come to your dance, we get stung!"

We were all kids, just trying to learn to play music. Later, we got to the jazz.

Before we left Kansas City, I was playing trumpet for myself, practicing, trying to learn, and was listening to all the jazz bands on stage shows and on records.

Kansas City in the 1920s was the hot bed of jazz bands, mostly black bands. They had the great Bennie Moten orchestra, "Andy Kirk and his Twelve Clouds of Joy," "The Alabamans," and "The Blue Devils," all good black jazz bands, so I was picking up on them.

One summer night in Kansas City, several of us walked down to Eighteenth and Vine, which was the black area in Kansas City. Of course, we couldn't get in, because we were white and too young. "Blacks only, brother." So, we sneaked around back. They had the dance hall all screened-in, but the wooden flaps were up for the summer heat. And back behind the place, if we crawled up a steep embankment, eight or ten feet up, we figured we could be right behind the bandstand. So we did—crawled up and enjoyed the music. I went to that "box-seat" many times.

Bennie Moten's Jazz Band. Boy! I didn't know what it was, but I knew it was for me. "That's the music I want to play," I would tell my friends.

I didn't know it at that time (about 1924), but I was listening to probably one of the world's greatest jazz bands.[3] A few years later, after Bennie Moten died, the group was taken over by Count Basie, who took the band to even greater heights.

This was my initiation into jazz, and it blew my mind. They played so great, and that's what I wanted to be: a jazz trumpet player.

So, when I arrived in Chickasha and talked to B. J. Vaughan about playing in a "real band," the visions of the jazz bands back in Kansas City danced in my mind. I saw myself up on the bandstand playing trumpet in a mist.

"You'll be our second trumpet player," he said. "We got a trombone player, three saxes, a drummer, a piano player and a banjo player. And we're adding a tuba."

Big band stuff. "Great!" I said. "When do we start?"

We'd gather in somebody's home on the weekends, practice mail order stock arrangements by Archie Bleyer and others. And we practiced hard. It was the first time I saw the words, "Swing It," on the start of the last chorus of an arrangement.

We began to get jobs. We played the American Legion Hall for our school friends and booked out-of-town jobs a few times. We played for a big crowd at Anadarko, Oklahoma for some occasion. Eleven bucks apiece. That's what ruined me. 'All you do is play this fun music,' I thought, 'and get $11 for it?'

Of course, we didn't get $11 every night. We played our share of "water hauls" (small crowds). We'd split up maybe two or three bucks apiece or less. But we were learning. We improved.

Later on, we got a piano player that took charge, an older musician. He rehearsed us better. And we improved rapidly. And so, here I was, still in high school making money with a trumpet, watching people dance and have fun. Little did I know I would be doing that for another fifty years!

Chapter Endnotes:

1. In an additional fragment left with Alguire's manuscript, Disney animator and Firehouse Five Plus Two band leader Ward Kimball would recount from the days of their famed jazz band, "There were many times that the Firehouse Five boys would be sitting around bee-essing before doing a concert or a dance and we would try to talk Danny into singing his Chickasha High School fight song. If he had enough shots under his belt, Danny might stand up and with a straight face, in a sing-song, flat voice, and oblige us with

his rendition of the funniest school song I've ever heard. This old school bit always had a relaxing effect on us and we would then go out on the stage an' knock 'em dead! There was nothing like a good story or joke to loosen up the band with a laugh or two."

2. Original note from Alguire: "They had another trumpet player in the Yellow Jackets, named Bill Van Wie. Last I heard, he was owner and editor of the *Blanchard, Oklahoma News*. On piano we had Bill Norris. Leader and First Sax: B. J. Vaughan. Tenor Sax: Bob Conrad. Trombone: Shakey Davis (Kilgore, Texas). Drummer: Gerald Bednar. Harold Hafer, banjo. Later Bill Bednar on tuba."

3. Bennie Moten and his band, including trumpeters Lammar Wright and Ed Lewis, were significant musical influences on the style of playing adopted by Alguire and others, including Benny Strickler. This approach to trumpet and cornet is sometimes described as a "southwestern" style. Moten passed away on April 2, 1935.

Chapter 7:

"Sobbin Blues"

It all started in October, 1929 when the stock market crashed.

Grandmother lost all her money in Cities Savings and Loans. It went belly-up overnight. People were distraught, pounding on closed bank doors, money gone. The only income Grandma had to live on was rent from the Tye office building that Grandpa had left them in Chickasha. They were doing better than most. But at the end of my senior year in high school, 1930, I went back to Kansas City for a summer job with the Kansas City Board of Trade before returning for college at Oklahoma University.

My cousin, Frances, was attending Oklahoma University. "Oh, you've got to go to Oklahoma University and pledge a fraternity," she said. (Like pledging was more important than learning!) She helped get me in Phi Delta Theta. I pledged, but told them I had to have a job in the kitchen for my room and board, $42.00 a month in the fraternity house. All my Dad could afford was $25.00 a month. (He was still working for the government.)

For two years, I went to school and did alright. I was in journalism, but took some geology, too. I wasn't mature enough to get motivated. I wanted to play music. Unfortunately, I wasn't good enough to play in the college dance bands; only the school marching band.

When I was a freshman, I got my tail paddled a lot by the fraternity members, but when I became a member, I never laid a hand on anyone. I didn't believe in hazing and hell week and all that baloney.

I returned to Kansas City in the summers (1931-1933) where George (with Dad's help) bought an ice route. Boy, things were tough. We were right in the middle of the Depression. George worked in the filling station, George's brother-in-law and Bud sold ice out of the small ice house, and I drove two of the routes. I quit college after my second year and we all survived somehow.

Sometimes I'd stay with George and his new wife, Cynthia. She kept house (very neat, too) and did all the cooking. Our favorite dish was floured hamburger, cooked, and then milk was added to give it a gravy taste. We were lucky to have hamburgers. Some folks didn't even have milk.

It was 1933 when Dad got fired. Franklin D. Roosevelt came into office and he started cutting out departments, including Dad's.

"There goes the poor farmers," Dad said. "they're going to get skinned alive again now."

One of Dad's jobs was to publish bulletins and market reports on broomcorn value each year. They cut all that out, and if anyone was bitter at Roosevelt, it was my father. You could just say the word "Roosevelt," and his face turned scarlet. He never got over it.

Somehow or another when he had his government job, he felt secure. Dad always wanted security, you know, money in the bank. "That's what counts." After he lost his job, Dad was never the same. When he became expendable, it took his incentive away. He ran scared. It broke him. Broke his spirit. He was fifty-five; too late to start over and no jobs anyway. There were thousands like Dad in those days.

I often wondered if that Depression was really necessary. It all seemed so shocking, so tragic—and so unnecessary.

The jazz, the blues that rippled through the night air in Kansas City's black neighborhoods eased the confusion about a world I didn't understand. America and Kansas City were reeling from unemployment and hopelessness was rampant. Music, as it would throughout my life, came to my rescue and I realized more than ever what a joy it was to make people happy with music. I began to feel a sense of worth, of doing something to ease the pain so many people lived with at this particular time in history. It was odd. I felt so sorry for these poor struggling folks. I'll never forget the vacant, hopeless faces of so many people. Young as I was, I felt just playing trumpet might cheer the aching hearts around me. So I played all I could, although the jobs were not steady. In those days, everyone needed relief of some sort. Some chose jumping from buildings or a pistol to the head. And I sought relief in music.

Dad got about $2,000 severance pay from his job. It wasn't a big pension, but it was $2,000.

George and I were still at the filling station, and we ran the ice routes. We had two trucks and were getting by on that, but Dad and Mom packed their clothes, and just walked out of the house and left it, mortgage and all. He couldn't pay it. He just walked away, as thousands were doing all over America. It hurt his pride. They couldn't make the payments, probably forty bucks a month, but he didn't have it, except for his severance pay. He was never the same again.

He decided that his best bet was to get into the broomcorn brokerage business. Oklahoma was the best spot to go. So Dad and Mom moved to Chickasha and rented a house. Bernice was married and living in Bokchito, Oklahoma with her husband's folks.

And by October, 1933, the rest of us left Kansas City and wound up in good old Chickasha, Oklahoma again. I ran into a drummer friend from the high school dance band, Jack Wantland, and he talked me into going to Texas, to sell postal telegraph clocks!

We'd go into a town—we had a pretty good sales gimmick—and sold these clocks which ran off of a plug-in. It kept accurate time. Western Union clocks were the thing. They were rigged up from a central place so that every hour, on the hour, one could press a button and an electric magnet would pull all clocks in town onto the correct time on the hour. So, that was quite a selling point for them—electric, central control.

But you rented them for $15 a month. You never got to buy the Western Union clock. So we'd say, "Well, you've had this clock for… what, ten years? At so much a month? Look at all the money you've paid out, and you still don't even own the clock. You buy our clock for $15 and you'll have the same accurate time." And they were good clocks!

Of course, we'd get a percentage on every sale and we made a little money, but that finally blew over. Jack took off and I returned to Chickasha.

But we came up with other ideas. We had to.

Chapter 8:

"Red Hot River Valley"

By early spring 1934, still in Chickasha, Dad had an idea. "Tell you what let's do," he said. "Let's go out to west Texas, out around Littlefield, and try to promote the growth of broomcorn and I'll buy the broomcorn." Poor Dad. He was getting desperate. The $2,000 was about gone.

We had a thresher and a baler which George built. He rigged up this hydraulic baler; worked real good, too. You know, he'd start a little motor which powered a hydraulic lift to press these bales. Then we'd tie them off with baling wire. The only trouble was, the "dust bowl" had started in west Texas and they couldn't grow much broomcorn. We'd thresh whatever we could; wasn't much.

George and I went out first and started selling seed, for the 1934 spring planting. With just a little more rain, it could have been good....

Just a little more rain.

Dad, Mother, and Bud, now graduated from high school, came out later to Littlefield where George was building the baler. When harvest time came along, we started threshing and baling.

Ed Chesnut, Bernice's husband, was helping us thresh and bale broomcorn, too. He called me his "ole broomcorn buddy." They stayed awhile, and then packed up and went back to Oklahoma City with their new baby.

In Oklahoma City, Ed worked for Armour Meat Packing plant and other places where he could get work. They were making it some way. I don't know how. Boy, I guess when Dan was born, that was about the bottom of the barrel. (The economy, I mean!)

But earlier, out in West Texas, I was starved for music. I got an orchestra together. Bill Norris came out from Chickasha. He got a job on the weekly newspaper as a reporter and was playing piano. We had a sax player and a bass player and we played a few jobs around. Didn't make too much money, but it helped; brother, did it help. Again, music rescued me. We had good crowds at fifty cents a couple. When times are rough, music helps.

In the meantime, I was getting a little better on trumpet. Finally, Bill Norris' brother, George, came out from Oklahoma and got in the CCC Camp for a while.[1] All of a sudden, he and Bill decided to go to California and so they took off. And the music slowed down.

In the summer of 1935, Dad, George, Ed, and I took the broomcorn machinery and rumbled into south Texas threshing and baling broomcorn through the Rio Grande Valley. We made a little money.

And then one night I got a call from a guy up in Lubbock, so I grabbed a bus for Lubbock to play in his dance band, "Jimmie Thornton and his Orchestra." I didn't go back to south Texas.

When they got through down there, George, Bud, Ed, and Dad came back to Littlefield. But, before I left south Texas, we all went across the border one dusty Sunday to Matamoros, Mexico and saw bulls that hot dusty summer day. It was horrible. You could smell the blood. The flies did, too.

I played in Lubbock awhile and then I got a letter from Bill Norris out in Los Angeles. "Dan, get on out here!" he said. "There's some playing out here. There's nothing back there. You can make it in California!"

I figured music was better than baling broomcorn, so I packed one small suitcase for California. The next problem was raising the money to get there.

Chapter Endnotes:

1. The Civilian Conservation Corps, a nationwide work relief program founded in 1933 as a major component of President Franklin Roosevelt's New Deal.

Chapter 9:

"Walk Right In"

Someone mentioned a "stock pass" to me one day. "What's a stock pass?" I asked.

Well, the Santa Fe Railroad ran through Lubbock, Texas. When a stockman took his stock (hogs, sheep, or cattle) to market they gave him a "stock pass" to ride in the caboose to market. Years later, the stockmen started doing all their business by phone or telegram and using trucks, but Santa Fe kept that stock pass available for every load of stock that was moving anywhere. So I hustled down to the stock yards. "Yeah. We'll give you a stock pass," they said.

They told me what train to catch and when. I showed the conductor my papers and boarded the train. So in January, 1936, I rode a caboose from Lubbock, Texas to Los Angeles, California smelling cow dung all the way. I had my suitcase full of clothes—not too full—and my horn, and a couple of bucks. So it took us (me and the cattle) two nights and three aromatic days to get to L.A. The train would lay over in some town for a couple of hours and I would run over to a café and get a bowl of beans or a hamburger and wash up the best I could.

When the train clanked into the yards in Los Angeles, they screeched to a halt at the main Union Station. To get to the station platform I had to walk through two passenger trains, so it looked like I was coming out of a passenger train when I hopped out onto the main platform and a "red cap" ran up to me.

"Can I carry your luggage, sir?" he asked.

Heck, I only had my horn and one bag. "No. It's all right, I'll handle it." God, I'm sure he had more money than I did. I had thirty-five cents in my pocket! But I was in L.A., sun shining, January, 1936.

Bill Norris' place was close—First and Olive. I jumped a streetcar going west on First and got off at Olive Street in the California sunshine. No smog then. It was a rooming house.

"Welcome to California!" shouted Bill and his brother, George. We shook hands all around. Two beds in a large room. $4 a week rent. He and George helped me out and fed me for a few weeks, until I got on my feet and got a job.

George was working in a bookie place, writing racehorse tickets, and Bill had a job typing in one of the department stores for $18 a week. It wasn't long after that, Bill started getting some piano calls, one in Bakersfield.[1] His brother George went with him and got a job with a cotton broker and I moved to a small apartment.

I finally started playing at $2 a night plus tips at a smoke-filled joint called "The Hot Shot" in L.A. I had a lot to learn. I had my own pet keys for all the tunes I knew, but one night, we had a new singing waitress.

She came up to the band stand. "I want to do 'Honeysuckle Rose' in A flat," she said, looking at me from the corners of her eyes with some degree of doubt.

I turned to the piano player, Bob. "Gee, Bob, I don't know this in A flat," I whispered. "I only play it in F."

Bob was an old timer. "Well, Dan," he said, "you're just about to learn to play it in A flat." Later, he told me, "You go home and you get your horn out, and you learn to play in all the keys. Take one tune that you can play in F and learn to play it in A flat and G and C and so forth, so you'll be prepared. These singers don't always sing in the same key as you play."

So I practiced like crazy. I'd go home at night and practice until my lips were raw, but I held the job and I kept learning. The other guys carried me along.

We had drums, piano, trumpet, and sax. Then, we got a better job down by San Pedro, at the L.A. harbor, a place called the "Ambassador Cellar" and, *wow!* it paid big: $4 a night plus tips. And all the seafood was great. I worked there from May until Christmas 1936, and then I got a steady job in L.A. at "The Gables," with a four-piece band until spring 1937 when my brother Bud suddenly appeared at the door.[2]

He was trying to find a job. He and his wife, Linnie Bea had been choking with dust and starving in Artesia, New Mexico. I got Bud a job at the Gables waiting tables, washing dishes, or whatever he could do. Didn't pay much. But finally, "I'm not going to make it here," Bud said. "I gotta go home."

I was getting kind of homesick myself. I had been in California about a year and a half. "I'll go with you," I said. We packed up and headed back east.

I was running again. I should have listened to the music voice within me. Here I was, making good money with music. Easy! But what did I do? Walk away from it. I don't know why we do stupid things.

Chapter Endnotes:

1. Over a hundred miles north of Los Angeles in the southern portion of the Central Valley, Bakersfield was the seat of Kern County, a region at the center of the agricultural labor struggles soon to be immortalized by John Steinbeck in his 1939 novel, *The Grapes of Wrath*.
2. That August of 1936, a young couple, Ward Kimball and Betty Lawyer, were married in a small ceremony. Both artists at the Walt Disney Studios in the Silverlake neighborhood of Los Angeles, the Kimballs soon joined Betty's parents at their home in the suburb of Alhambra. By that time, Ward, an amateur trombonist, was regularly organizing lunchtime jam sessions with fellow artists at the Disney Studios.

Chapter 10:

"Lonesome Mama Blues"

After hitch-hiking to Phoenix, we ran out of money. We dropped into the Avalon Club in downtown Phoenix and there was a woman playing piano and organ. Her husband played drums and trombone (a strange combination). I walked up and smiled. "Could you use another musician? I play trumpet."

"Do you sing?" they asked.

"Yeah."

"Then why don't you sit in? Play with us a little. We'll see how you sound."

So I sang and played the rest of the evening.

They liked what they heard. "Fine. You're hired."

We rented a little room in a hotel across the street, and Bud stayed a few days until I got a little money ahead, but then Bud came to me, feeling pretty low. "I've got to get on home, Dan. I can't stay here any longer."

I had saved a few bucks, so I gave him what money I had. "I better stay here and work a little longer," I told him. "I'll come on to Artesia as soon as I can get enough money ahead." So my brother Bud took off. He caught a freight train and hitch-hiked and made it back to Artesia, New Mexico.

In May, 1937, all of a sudden, it got hot in Phoenix. "Oh, boy. I've got to get out of here," I thought. The hotel room was unbearable during the day, like a furnace. I had to "live" at the joint where I worked. They had water air conditioning. After two more weeks, I took off.

I hitch-hiked to Safford, Arizona in that relentless sun and found myself on the street out of money and wondering what I was going to do next besides find water to drink. And by gosh, if I didn't run into B.J. Vaughan, the guy I used to play with in high school in Chickasha. He was a traveling salesman. I couldn't believe it. I thought he was a mirage.

"By God!" he said, "What are you doing in this hell hole?"

"I'm broke. Trying to get home," I moaned, mouth dry and spirits low.

He drove me to some town in New Mexico where he turned north to Albuquerque, slipped me some money and I resumed hitch-hiking. (I got to see B.J. and his wife in San Francisco about 1968 at a concert I was playing with the Firehouse Five Plus Two. Shortly after that, B.J. had a fatal heart attack.)

I checked the map to find Artesia, New Mexico and I had to go a crazy way, up north and east across the mountains, but I got a ride with this sleazy guy who reeked with sweat, bourbon, and nicotine.

"Well, I'm going to Cloudcroft," he slurred, "if that'll help you."

"Yeah. Sure will."

I got a little scared because he was boozing it up and driving like a madman, laughing, sipping on his jug and swerving all over the highway. I was afraid he would run us off the road! I was more than happy to jump out of his car at Cloudcroft and watch him squeal back on the highway.

I looked around the town. Nothing. Six p.m., alone on an empty road. It was one of the lowest points in my life. I sat down on my suitcase, trumpet at my dusty feet and just couldn't hold back the tears. Here I was (whatever I was) twenty-five years old—nothing. Going nowhere.

It was one of the few times I cried in my life. At least the tears washed the dust from my eyes and nose.

"Well, this is not going to help," I thought, but I did feel better after crying.

A guy came along in a truck and took me all the way to Artesia. I hopped off his truck at dusk and, exhausted, slumped into

Bud's house. I showered and Linnie fixed a hot meal for me. It tasted great; just beans and tortillas and hot peppers, I think.

Some of Linnie's relatives gave me a ride to Littlefield, Texas to see Mother and Dad. Dad had a crew threshing and baling broomcorn, toughing it out.

I walked around in a stupor, just lost, hanging around like a lost hound. "I better go back to California," I thought. "Nothing's happening here. God, Dan! You just got here." My brain was shot.

I had been homesick and I was glad to see Dad and Mom. After ten days, I broke it to them. "I've got to go back to California. That's the only place I can work." I told them good-bye. I was running again.

I ran into a little luck. They used to pay you for driving used cars to California and that's what this new friend planned to do. My ability to make friends saved me again. I didn't realize at the time what a great asset it was to make friends easily. So I got a ride with him. Didn't cost much. I got my old job back, too. I worked a few more months and then in 1938, things began to brighten.

In October, the old Chickasha piano pal, Bill Norris, started a new job in Bakersfield. So I moved there. I joined the musician's union. Scale was about four bucks a night; good job.

It was a roadhouse; one of those places about four or five miles out of town where cheating wives and cheating husbands met their lovers. It was a dark, dimly lit place—a good rendezvous place—and the tips were good.

Before I knew it, I was hauling in sixty-five bucks a week, counting tips. I bought a 1929 Ford. First car I ever owned. The band was very good and we played two years before the place changed hands and went to pot. I returned to L.A. in 1940 and started playing at "Frank's Place" with a friend of mine.

From then on I was never out of work too long. I wasn't making as much in Los Angeles, but I was doing just fine.

And it was in 1940 that I married Betty Bahn. We had dated awhile so we just went ahead and got married. Funny, I knew the war was coming. I had this strange notion. I wanted someone to come home to. She was of German descent, a great cook, and we got along fine.

By November, 1941, I'd saved up a little money and decided to take a bus back to Oklahoma and visit the folks, who were now living in Oklahoma City. I would be gone a couple of weeks. I left the car (by now we had a 1935 Chevy) with Betty and took off.

In Oklahoma City I heard that Benny Strickler, a friend of mine and a fine jazz trumpet player, had joined the Bob Wills band.

I was puzzled to learn that he was in a Western band. I would soon find out why. I read in the paper that they were playing in Oklahoma City at the Trianon Ballroom that night. So, I drove down to see Benny.

Chapter 11:

"Home in San Antone"

When I arrived at the Trianon Ballroom that night in November, 1941, I was absolutely amazed at the size of the crowd. The ballroom was up on the second floor and I'll bet it took me a half an hour to get upstairs. I never saw such a mass of people in my entire life—laughing, dancing, happy people. "This is a Western band? What in the world is going on?" When I finally got upstairs, I fought my way through the bodies and smoke to the bandstand. I guess there were 3,000 people, and on a Tuesday night! "What in the world does this Bob Wills have to draw so many people on a Tuesday night?" (And that was just the beginning. I would later become even more amazed at the crowds that Bob Wills drew.)

A performance by Bob Wills and His Texas Playboys in 1941-42.
L to R: unknown announcer, Louis Tierney, Benny Strickler, Don Harlan (partly hidden), Bob Wills (on "Punkin"), Eldon Shamblin. Courtesy of the Estate of Bob Wills/OKPOP Museum Collection.

When I saw Benny Strickler playing his trumpet, I thought back to when I first heard the Wills recording of "Big Beaver." It was a far cry from standard Western Music, and the sound I was hearing from the bandstand at that moment was certainly not typical Western Music. Benny was happy to see me.[1]

"Hey, Dan," he shouted, "got your horn with you? Go get it and sit in with us."

Strickler was the finest trumpeter I had ever heard. He had worked with Joe Venuti and other jazz bands and had even turned down a job with Artie Shaw just before he joined Wills. I could not imagine why this guy who loved jazz would even consider a Western band, but I later found out that when Benny Strickler heard Bob's recording of "Big Beaver," just as I had heard it in California, he had realized that Bob Wills' band was much more than Western Music. It was a special type of jazz and Benny wanted to be part of it. Strickler met Bob in Hollywood when Bob was there for a movie and recording session and staying at the Hollywood Plaza Hotel. Benny approached Bob and told him he wanted a job in the band and Bob immediately answered, "O.K." Benny told me later, with a laugh, that Bob said, "I could tell by looking at him that he was a good musician."[2]

I got my horn from the car and played the rest of the evening. Benny told me to take some of his solos so Bob could hear how I played. After the dance he took me up and introduced me to Bob Wills.

"Well," Bob drawled, "how do you do? I like your playing. Would you like to join our little band?"

We shook hands. "You bet," I said.

"Fine. You're hired. Come on up to Tulsa in the next day or so. We'll get you going."

Bob was expanding his band. He wanted to play any kind of a job. That same night he hired two more jazz musicians, Woody Wood and Alex Brashear. Woody played clarinet as good as Artie Shaw and Benny Goodman. Alex had played trumpet with Jack Teagarden.

Bob Wills.

God, I couldn't believe it. Just like that, I was a member of Bob Wills and His Texas Playboys. I was impressed with the music they played that night. The band had a beat that wouldn't quit and the crowd was having such a good time dancing to that great rhythm. They were an absolutely beautiful bunch of musicians.

Well, I hurried home and told the folks about it. They were excited that I would be in Tulsa, near Oklahoma City, and near home again. I had been gone since 1936. And they were eager to meet my new wife. So now I faced the task of telling Betty that she must come to Oklahoma. I called her the next day. "Guess what?" I said.

"What?"

"I joined the Bob Wills band."

"You did what?"

"I joined Bob Wills' band. It's a good job." I waited for her response. Nothing. "I'm tired of working in those joints out there." She was silent. "I think I can get somewhere here…in Bob's band."

There was a long pause. "What do you want me to do?" she asked.
"Call Olan Grove." He was a good friend. "I'll get an apartment."
"Okay," she said, a little bewildered.

"Now, you have money in the bank. Take it all out in travelers checks, pay up our debts and have Olan bring you to Tulsa in our car. Store whatever you don't have room for."

She wasn't upset, just shocked. She thought it would be a better opportunity for us. Betty and I got along all right. I was a peaceful man. She was a peaceful woman. She didn't have many faults. Very neat. Good housekeeper, good cook, and very loyal.

"Okay. Will do," she said.

"Keep me posted," I said. "Call me on the way a couple of times."

She did. Let me knew where she was. I got the apartment and had a phone put in.

The band rehearsed every day and had a noon broadcast on KVOO radio in Tulsa.

The first thing Bob said—told one of the boys—"Take Dan down and get him a uniform and a pair of boots."

Bob Wills and His Texas Playboys, 1941-42. L to R (standing): Red Agnew, Louis Tierney, Darrell Jones, Bob Wills (on "Punkin"), Gene Tomlins, Woody Wood, Eldon Shamblin, O.W. Mayo (manager). Kneeling: Leon McAuliffe, Benny Strickler, Alex Brashear, Wayne Johnson, Tommy Duncan, Al Stricklin, Don Harlan, Danny Alguire. Courtesy of the Estate of Bob Wills/ OKPOP Museum Collection.

We played dances every night, except Sundays, and I loved it. The band was a joy—knocked me out. Fine musicians. Bob later said it was, by far, the greatest band that he ever had in all his years. We packed them in!

Bob was a great fiddle player—beautiful tone—and his sense of rhythm was perfect. He wouldn't let the band get off the beat one hair, and if he detected it, he had a finger snap like a whip that you could hear across the bandstand. A few of those finger snaps would straighten out the band in a hurry. The beat very seldom missed being right on. And what a beat! If you couldn't dance to Bob Wills' band, you couldn't walk. There was no one better at "calling" a dance than Bob Wills. He could sense a crowd's needs and change the music accordingly.

When I was interviewed for the book *San Antonio Rose*, by Dr. Charles Townsend, I gave the following description of Bob Wills to the author:

One of his greatest assets—he had a sixth sense of knowing what the people at that particular dance that night wanted to hear, and I never saw him call a wrong tune. He just seemed to know what to play and when to call it, when to call a horn tune, or when to call a fiddle tune, or when to call a vocal, or when to call a guitar special. And listen, even today, years later, working in the Firehouse Five like I am now, I have taught the guys in the band the tricks of the Bob Wills era of how to call tunes for people. I learned; I used to watch Bob like a hawk and watch him call the right tune at the right time. And I figured out he had a system. He never called the same tempo or the same key twice in succession. In other words, the tempo would either be a faster or a slower tempo. It would either be slower or faster so that you have an undulating type of dance which made for interesting music, you see. He would play a slow tune and then it would pick-up, then go faster, then drop down and play a waltz. You know, it was ever changing, and that was one of the beautiful tricks I learned from Bob Wills…and he used it very, very wisely.[3]

Although Bob had a few drinks occasionally, he found out he was not a drinker and as the years went on it became less and less of a problem.

Bob had a heart of gold and had very good manners. He was soft spoken, but you didn't crowd him either. He had a little Indian blood and sometimes he could be dynamite, especially with booze. He was generous: made a lot of money and gave a lot away.

When Bob was in Fort Worth, Texas in the early 1930s, he had a noon broadcast that covered the state of Texas on a special Texas network. It was a three-piece band called, "The Light Crust Dough-Boys," sponsored by a local flour company, "Light Crust Flour." I mean the whole state of Texas stopped at noon to hear them. They had a fiddle, guitar, and string bass.

After Fort Worth, he moved to Waco, Texas and started an eight-piece orchestra which he named, "The Texas Playboys." In 1934, he moved the band to Tulsa, Oklahoma. Bob tried to hook up with KOMA and later WKY radio in Oklahoma City, but his vengeful ex-partner from Texas, W. Lee O'Daniel, had the power to abort that effort. He went on to KVOO in Tulsa. They refused to buckle under to O'Daniel's continued pressure. After that, it was history.

In 1941 when Bob filed his income tax, it was said that he paid more income tax than any band leader in the United States, That's how well the band was doing.

We'd take to the road every night except Thursdays, Saturdays, and Sundays. On Thursday and Saturday we played at Cain's Academy in Tulsa, so I was home three nights a week. On Tuesdays we played in Oklahoma City. On alternate Fridays we'd play in Fort Smith, Arkansas and Seminole, Oklahoma. On Mondays, it could be different spots in Oklahoma, or Kansas. It was our wild card night.

Alguire pointing at Cain's Dancing Academy, Tulsa, Oklahoma, in 1941-42. Cain's was where Bob Wills and His Texas Playboys performed regularly when they were in the area. This photo may have been snapped by Alguire's section-mate Benny Strickler. Courtesy of Diane Breazeale.

A funny thing happened in Kansas. I hadn't been in the band very long, and we pulled into Hutchinson to play on a Monday night. The dance was in the armory, one of those ugly old dark red brick buildings, with vines covering the outside. We walked inside with our instruments, preparing to set-up. It had an old, musty smell complete with an elderly caretaker, probably in his seventies.

He had the rest of the lights turned up and then shuffled up to us and squinted. "Are you fellas a sitting-down or a standing-up band?"

"Mostly sitting," we said.

"Okay." He left to get some chairs.

Some of the guys walked out on the floor to test the acoustics—got out in the middle of the floor and stomped their feet. By listening to the echo you could tell whether it has a "live sound" or a "dead sound." A couple of guys were stomping their feet when this old caretaker walked back in and looked at us a bit curiously.

"What's the matter?" he asked. "Something wrong with the floor?"

"How are the acoustics here, Dad?"

He looked at us with a suspicious expression, brow furrowed. "Acoustics?"

"Yeah. How's the acoustics here?"

He thought for a minute. "We're not bothered with them. I've never seen one here in my life."

That broke us up.

I was getting accustomed to the band, and Bob gave me some songs to sing. Understand, I had never played in a Western band, not that this was too Western, but it was a mixture of everything. We had horn tunes, fiddle tunes, and so, not being what I call a Western singer, Bob figured out my singing chores in the band were to be the pop tunes like "White Cliffs of Dover" and "Chattanooga Choo-Choo" and all the popular tunes of the day.

Bob Wills and His Texas Playboys at the Trianon Ballroom, 1941-42. L to R (on bandstand): Leon McAuliffe, Earl Groves, Danny Alguire, Louis Tierney, Benny Strickler, Alex Brashear, Woody Wood, Bob Wills, Don Harlan, Gene Tomlins, Wayne Johnson, Darrell Jones, unidentified man, Eldon Shamblin, Al Stricklin. Courtesy of the Estate of Bob Wills/OKPOP Museum Collection.

On Saturday night, December 6, 1941, after the dance in Tulsa, I went to Oklahoma City to visit the folks. They were on Social Security by then. Betty had a cold and stayed in Tulsa. I stayed with Mother and Dad and slept until about noon on Sunday, December 7. My sister Bernice lived next door, and I was suddenly awakened when I heard Bernice rush in and start talking excitedly to Mother. I jumped out of bed, slipped on my pants and hurried in the front room to greet her. "What's new, Bernice?" I asked, happy to see her.

"Oh, Dan. I don't know, Dan. I just heard on the radio something about Pearl Harbor. The Japanese bombed Pearl Harbor."

To this day, I can remember feeling the blood drain from my face when I heard her words. "What did you say?"

"The Japanese bombed Pearl Harbor."

I flipped on the Philco on and began getting the news: "IN AN EARLY MORNING SURPRISE ATTACK, JAPANESE PLANES BOMBED THE U.S. NAVAL BASE AT PEARL HARBOR. CASUALTIES…."

When Bernice and Mother realized it in was Hawaii, they were pretty unnerved and I was in shock. "Thank God I got Betty away from California," was my first thought. The news commentator was warning of a possible invasion of the U.S.

Well, I cut the trip short and headed back to Tulsa to be with Betty. On the way, the car radio was blaring how they had begun blackouts in California, looking for the Japanese to invade the coast, which they could have darn well done, had they realized how badly they had crippled us at Pearl Harbor. Uncertain as to what would happen, we were in for some pretty tense days.

Nonetheless, the band continued and I learned some new songs. "You sing the pop songs," Bob said, "and Tommy Duncan and Leon McAuliffe will do the Western and Country songs."

At the 12:30 broadcast every day on KVOO, Tulsa, Monday through Saturday, people crowded in for the live show. Almost every day I'd sing a pop tune like, "My mama done told me, a woman's a two face...."

What a following Bob had. The band was terrific and I was so happy that for the first time I was in a good organized group. Being self-conscious about my lack of motivation and lack of progress, I thought, "Well, here's my chance. Maybe I can get somewhere." The war shadowed all my joy. The air was heavy with uncertainty.

But everything moved well with the band. Bob even bought me a new horn. I was fussing with one of my valves before a broadcast one day when Bob walked up. "What's the matter with your horn, Dan?"

"Oh, nothing, Bob. Just a sticky valve. I was just getting some oil on it."

"That looks like a pretty old horn."

"Yeah. I've had it several years."

"Tell you what you do, Danny. You go down to the music store and get a new horn. I'll pay for it."

The second trumpet player, Alex Brashear, got the same deal. Knocked us out! Bob was generous to a fault. And a helluva country fiddler, I might add.

Bob made good money. But he had a million relatives and every Thursday, on pay-day, they'd all show up, the cousins and nieces and nephews. They'd all get a check. Bob took care of his kinfolks. He was very loyal. After I left the band, he continued to make a lot of money and spend a lot of money. They had to throw a benefit after his stroke to raise money for him in Tulsa. But he began to get more royalties.

In 1942, the band went on. I'd already registered for the draft out in Los Angeles, so I wrote and told them where I could be reached. They wrote back, said thanks for letting them know and they'd notify me if I was going to be called up any time soon.

We went on playing through June of 1942. By this time, the heat in Tulsa began to affect Betty. She was raised in the state of Washington and never had been in heat like that. "I want to go back to California, Dan," she said one day.

"Well, I think the war is going to break up the band soon anyway. I'll drive you back." I asked Bob for a few days off and I drove her back to L.A. She moved back onto our old apartment (just happened to be available). I got her settled in, hopped a bus, and came back to Tulsa.

I hadn't been back in Tulsa two days until Bob suddenly announced, "Well, we're going to California! Do some recording." All my trip wasted, and costly! We loaded up the bus around the first of July, 1942 and went to California for a recording session. We made about eighteen sides. Some of them were never released, but we made some "horn tunes" and some Western tunes. It took about three days for the sessions, and each night we played dances, too.

At the old Venice Ballroom (on July 3, 4, and 5), we set a new attendance record. We did something like 15,000 people in three days which was absolutely amazing in those days. Now, of course, a 100,000 at a rock concert is nothing, but for those times, it was a hell of a crowd. The band went over like a million bucks.

On the second day of the recording session, Bob handed me a sheet of music. "Danny, I want you to sing this one."

I looked up, surprised. "This is a Western tune."

"Yeah. I know it is. I want you to sing it."

Now I think, personally, Bob just wanted me to have a vocal on a record. "All right," I said.

It was a simple song. And I walked over to a corner of the room and looked it over; memorized it, at least memorized the tune. I had to read the words.

"Okay," Bob sang out. "Next tune. Are you ready, Danny? You got that song down?"

"Yeah. I think so, Bob."

They worked up an arrangement, starting with fiddles. I came in on the second chorus. The tune was "Home in San Antone."

"Roll it," Bob said. "Let's go."

We made one take. While we waited for the playback, I walked over to Bob. "Gee, Bob, if you want to do another one, I'm sure I can do a little better. There was a little low note there that I didn't hit very clean."

"Well, let's wait and hear the playback. We'll see how it sounds."

They played it back and we all listened. "That's good enough for me," Bob said with his wry smile. "Good job, Danny. All right now, we'll get on to the next tune."

Twenty-eight years old, doing my first vocal recording, and that was the only time I heard it until over a year later. Incidentally, it was Bob that first called me "Danny" on that recording, and it stuck from then on. His unique voice and that "Ah-ha! Come on in, Danny boy," has been a wonderful memory.

After the session, I stayed in Los Angeles with Betty, because I was sure the war would break up the band, which it did. But Bob didn't go back to Oklahoma with the band just then. He stayed in Hollywood to make some "quickie" westerns for Monogram Pictures to stock up for the future. He kept three or four of the guys, because it was a western picture and he didn't need many musicians. I think he kept Leon on steel and a couple of standard guitars and a couple of fiddles and the string bass for the movies. I called Bob, told him I was staying in Los Angeles, and damned if Bob didn't start to book dance jobs, and I played four or five nice paying dance gigs with them out in California before the other guys left.

In 1941, Bob Wills had added so many fine jazz musicians to his band that when it was in California, it was being compared to Bob Crosby's Bobcats. We did play a number of tunes that were similar to the Crosby brand of Dixieland. Both bands played with a great Dixieland rhythm and could play dance music. They could both play sweet, easy listening music, as well. At times Wills sounded similar to Glenn Miller or Tommy Dorsey. But Bob Wills' music was more than just a combination of swing and Dixieland. It had its own uniqueness. Wills' band could do almost anything for an audience. It could give them swing, Bob Wills' fiddle tunes, or Dixieland jazz.

I always thought if the war hadn't broken us up, if there hadn't been a war, I'll tell you, this particular group would have been one of Bob's best. It would have been as popular as any band, Glenn Miller included. We had some great musicians; not only good Western players, but there were good horn men.

The war was accelerating and the band broke up. I reported to the draft board.

In the brass section we had Benny Strickler on first trumpet—just tremendous. (Sadly, Benny died in 1946 from tuberculosis in Fayetteville, Arkansas.) He was the guy that made me wonder, "why would he join a Western band?" I found out why.

We had Alex Brashear on second trumpet. Excellent. I was playing third trumpet. Playing with these two really helped my progress. We had a young kid from Fort Worth, Neal Duer, playing trombone. And a beautiful sax section: Don Harlan, George Balay, Woody Wood, and Louie Tierney, who also played fiddle.

When I went back to the fiftieth reunion of Bob Wills band members in 1984, I got to see some of them again. Many had passed away, about nine or ten. But I saw Darrell Jones again (bass) and Woody Wood (clarinet). A sad story about Woody: I didn't know until then that while in the Army, he was in a very bad jeep accident. It really busted him up. He was out of the war and home. He said that since the war, he had required twelve or fifteen operations over the years. I was sure glad to see him. I felt very sorry for him, because he was not a well man, but he still played great clarinet. Woody died in December, 1989. Of that group of fourteen, six of us are still alive.

At the Bob Wills band 50th anniversary reunion in Tulsa, Oklahoma on August 11, 1984. (L to R): Charlotte Bryant McCormack's son Joshua (lower left), Joe Frank Ferguson, Charlotte Bryant McCormack, Al Stricklin, Betty Wills, Danny Alguire, Bryant's son Ben. Courtesy of Charlotte Bryant McCormack.

Onstage at the Bob Wills 50th anniversary reunion. Alguire is seen at the microphone without a hat, perhaps singing "Home in San Antone" one last time. (L to R): steel guitarist Leon McAuliffe, Alguire, Al Stricklin (back to camera), bassist Joe Frank Ferguson. Courtesy of Charlotte Bryant McCormack.

I was playing in Oregon, about 1978, and I ran into a guy that found out I had worked with Bob Wills. "You know," he said, "I've written down programs from the old Bob Wills radio broadcasts from years and years ago. So you were with him in 1941, 1942?"

"Yeah," I said. And he flipped his pages. God, he had a mass of information. He got into the dates when I was with Bob. "Yeah. I got you here."

I had to tell him how to spell my name. He had it spelled "Olgyer" (that's the way he heard it over the air).

"You sang (so and so), by Danny Alguire."

"Right!"

Chapter Endnotes:

1. "Big Beaver" was recorded in 1940 and released on the OKEH label.
2. For an in-depth view of Benny Strickler and the southwestern trumpet style, see Hal Smith's essay in the Appendix.
3. Note from Alguire: "For a complete history of Bob Wills, read the marvelous book *San Antonio Rose*, by Charles Townsend; University of Illinois Press, 1976."

Chapter 12:

"Between The Devil And The Deep Blue Sea"

"Well, here I am, back in L.A." I gave the draft boys my new address which was really my old L.A. address.

"Gee," they said, "it doesn't look like we'll be calling you up for about six months yet. You're still married, aren't you?"

"Yes."

Bob Wills' band had dispersed. There was no reason to go back to Tulsa. "Maybe I can work some local jobs," I thought. Musicians were in short supply with so many going into the service. They even drafted Bob Wills for a while, but he got out shortly after.

When I was playing this job earlier in L.A. (1941), before I went back to join Bob Wills, they had a bouncer named Tiny (naturally), a great big guy; about 280 pounds. He was a uniformed special policeman. They had him because this joint was down by the railroad yards and a lot of railroad workers came in. Pretty rough crowd. But, Tiny could handle them.

He came up to me one night. "Hey, Dan, how'd you like to go to fingerprint school with me?"

"Fingerprint school?" I said. "Clue me in."

"I'm going to class now. There's a Lieutenant White from the police department that's teaching a fingerprint class, twice a week, in the afternoons."

I wasn't doing anything in the daytime. "Yeah. Sounds interesting."

So I started fingerprint class. I liked it. Best in the class. After I learned it, I promptly forgot about it when I went back to join Bob Wills in Tulsa in 1941.

So back in California in August, 1942, I had been playing around, just a few gigs, and I decided to call up this Lieutenant White at the L.A. police department. "This is one of your old students, Danny Alguire."

"Hey, Danny! What are you doing?"

"Been playing music, but with the war on and everything, I thought maybe I could get a fingerprint job somewhere. Help out the war effort."

"Where do you want to go?"

"What do you mean?"

"God, I get calls every day from air bases and police departments. They all need fingerprint men."

"What's the closest place?"

"Well, I got another student that I had before you. He's Chief of Identification at the Ogden Air Depot, Hill Field, Utah, and he's screaming for fingerprint help."

"I'll take it."

So I called this guy, G.B. Bates in Utah, and told him who I was.

"God, yes," he says. "I can use a fingerprint man. When can you get up here?"

"I'll take the first train out of here tomorrow."

So I took a train and left Betty in L.A. "Let me get up there and get the lay of the land and get a place to stay. Then you can come on," I told her.

When I arrived in Ogden, I located a rooming house, owned by a nice Mormon lady. All she had to do was rent me a room, but every morning when I got up to go to work, she'd fix me breakfast. I never forgot her hospitality, and her kindness.

Original description from Alguire: "About summer of 1943, Ogden, Utah. Taken in front of a stranger's house in the classier section of town (I borrowed the house for background). I went to Ogden after quitting the Bob Wills band (it was breaking up because of the war) in October, 1942 and worked there till October, 1943, when I was drafted into the Navy. I didn't have to go to war. I had two draft exemptions in Ogden, but turned down the third exemption because I felt I should go into the service and do my bit! Oh, what a terrible decision, but it turned out ok."
Courtesy of Charlotte Bryant McCormack.

I wasn't there long before I got an apartment and this same friend, Olan Grove, drove Betty up with the car to Ogden. He came up looking for a job, too, and was hired as a security guard. And the poor guy, up to then, had never done much of anything. Ran a filling station. A fly-by-night kid. Not too dumb, just couldn't seem to get hold of anything. Well, he ended up staying there twenty-five years. Pension and all!

I reported to Ogden Air Depot in October, 1942 and saw Bates' secretary. "I'm Danny Alguire."

She turned around and shouted, "Hey Bates, he's here!"

He rushed out of his office and introduced himself. Nice guy. Nickname was "Happy." "Boy, can I use you," he said.

"What do you want me to do?"

They were behind, and the poor guy really needed help. I taught soldiers how to classify prints and slowly, we began to catch up. Our fingerprint file was larger than the State of Utah, because we processed so many civilian and military personnel every day.

I settled in on the job, but I began to ask myself, "Wonder if there's any playing around town? I think I'll go down and see the secretary of the Musicians' Union."

I found his name in the phone book, went down to see him, and knocked on his door. Name was "Slim" Fleming—a piano player. He opened the door. "You Slim?" I asked. "I just got in town and I'm working out at the Air Depot and wanted to know if there's any playing around. Like to play a few gigs."

He looked at me, head cocked to one side. "What do you play?"

"Trumpet."

"Do you sing?"

"Yeah. I sing."

"I need a trumpet player that can sing."

"I'm your man."

I started that night and played three nights a week at a roadhouse called "The Old Mill." The owner (named "Fox") was the mayor of the town, and he had quite a business going. It was so big that he had three areas for bands: one downstairs, one upstairs, and one down at the other end of the building. And man, the guy was cleaning up! He had it all. Only decent place in town to go. The Air

Force (we didn't have any sailors) would flock in. I made six or eight bucks a night, plus tips. Slim played piano. We had a kid on sax and a local drummer. But, music was music in those days. All the good musicians had gone into the service. I was lucky that I played practically the whole time I was in Ogden. The extra loot came in handy.

Work until midnight, rush home, catch a little sleep, to work at the depot by eight the next morning.

And then the snow hit!

We had a hard winter. Snow. Snow. Snow. I had to buy tire chains. That was my first experience with a lot of ice and snow and cold since my Kansas City days, and I didn't have a heater in my car.

Bates moved up to Investigator and I was Chief of Identification with eighty people working for me. I felt myself a little motivated! (Like playing a tune better.)

One day, my boss, Captain Webber, the provost marshal, called me in. "Dan, ah, I've got a draft notice for you."

I groaned. "I figured it was about due."

"But I'm going to get you a deferment, because you're doing a good job here, and we need you."

I gave a sigh of relief.

"Great! I'll take a deferment."

Betty and I went out and celebrated that night, like "I got a few more months to live."

You know, music is so unpredictable that in the back of my mind the thought always recurred, "I've got to get into something that's got some substance to it, something to build on." So I worked harder at the finger-printing.

I got another deferment for two or three months. And I thought, "Oh, boy. I'm going to spend the war right here in Ogden, Utah!" Then, I began to make mistakes.

I came up for a third deferment, about September, 1943, and Captain Webber called me in.

"You know," I said, "I think I'll go into the service."

Bates almost fell out of his chair.

"Why? for God's sake!"

"Two reasons. Anyone that's not in the war is not going to come out with very much at the end. No benefits. Besides that, I have that crazy feeling that I should go into the service. Perhaps I can learn a new trade."

Captain Webber spoke up. "I'll tell you what you do, Dan. When you get to L.A. for your physical, tell them you want the Air Force. Go ahead with boot training, and after your boot's over, write me as quickly as you can and give me your service number and where you're stationed. I'll have you transferred right back here as a first sergeant doing exactly the same work, but you'll be Air Force."

"Sounds good. I'll do that."

So I left for Los Angeles.

Betty lived with a friend in L.A. until she could get straightened out. Shortly after I returned to L.A., I had to tell her a quick goodbye. I left the car and our money with her and took a bus at 6 a.m. downtown for my physical. Passed, of course. When I got to the last desk, it started: a comedy of errors—on my part.

This officer looks at me. "What do you want?" he growled. "Army, Navy, Air Force, or Marines?"

I should have said "Air Force" so I could have returned to Ogden. But, some guy had been talking to me earlier about the Navy schools, how good they were. "If you go into the Navy," he said, "and get into one of those schools, you can…." And I thought, "That's a good idea. I'll learn something new." (You wouldn't believe my stupidity.) "I'll take the Navy," I said quickly.

"Navy?" he grunted. "You got it!" He stamped "NAVY" on my papers.

In twenty minutes they had us all lined up in groups of eight or ten each. This big Petty Officer, bass voice, clopped down the line pointing out the training stations where we were to go. "This group—Farragut, Idaho!" Snarl. "You guys—San Diego." Growl.

"Great Lakes…." I was watching and waiting. He glared at our group. "And this group," pointing to us, "to San Diego."

"God! That's great," I thought. "Close to L.A. Come home on the week-ends after boot. Get me a good Navy school. Fine."

They crammed us into a bus and we rumbled off, just like that.

When the bus chugged into San Diego, it was dark. They fed us a meal and herded us into a barracks that held about 120 men (the number in a company). Boy, I was tired. I hit the bunk like a falling timber.

All we took was shaving gear. When we got our Navy outfits, they shipped our old clothes home.

So I was all set to have a good night's sleep and the Petty Officer yells, "Hit the sack! Don't want to hear a word out of you! Reveille at five o'clock!" These guys came in from everywhere. Half were from L.A. Half were wild Louisiana guys. And I mean a wild bunch of Cajuns. They were the most independent guys I ever knew in my life. And of course the first night, they weren't about to take any discipline crap. They were shouting, singing, and raising all kinds of hell.

The Petty Officer flipped on the lights. "Hey! What in hell is going on in here?" He stomped around, glaring. "If I have to come back here once more," he said, "you're all going out on the grinder and march!"

I thought, "Oh, God no! Why don't those bastards shut up?"

It happened again. He warned them once more. "Next time, out to the grinder!"

As he turned to leave, some Louisiana kid, way in the back, yelled, "Blow it out your ditty-bag!"

The Petty Officer turned and forced a smile that made me sick. "That does it. Everybody up. OUT!"

The first night we marched on the parade ground, called "the grinder"—for about an hour and a half!

When we finally got back to bed, they kept quiet. Not much sleep. Up at five. Boy they didn't waste any time, took us right over and cut our hair off and issued our clothes. We didn't even have lockers; kept all our clothes in large canvas sea bags, which we hung on the end of our bunks.

Boot camp! During those first few days my mind kept flashing back to Utah and the Captain and I wondered, "What have you done now, Danny boy?"

And I couldn't even play my trumpet.

Chapter 13:

"Anchors Aweigh"

Our first boot camp, Camp Decatur, a quarantine area, lasted three weeks. And then they moved us to Camp Lawrence. About this time, my sister's husband, Ed Chesnut, arrived. We took liberty together a few times.

But boot camp is boot camp. I wasn't prepared. I was flabby, out of shape and overweight. I lost twenty-five pounds in eight weeks. Thirty years old.

Several older guys like me, thirty and over, were also overweight. Everyone did the same thing: marching, training, ate the same food, did the same job. And at the end of an eight week boot camp, all the younger guys gained weight, and we older guys lost weight. But I never felt better in my life, physically. Mentally... uh, not so good.

About half way through boot camp, they brought me in for an interview, to see what I wanted to do. I had a real nice guy interviewing me. "What's your first choice?" he asked.

"Meteorology."

"Not a chance. One in a thousand."

"I've got a good IQ. Did you notice?"

A peculiar grin crossed his face. "Yeah. You got a good IQ. What's your second choice?" It was at that moment he noticed my music background on my record. "Christ, man. Get in the band! That's good duty."

"I want to learn something else."

"Okay," he said giving me a look of disbelief. "Second choice. Put down band. It's a good way to go!"

"Nope," I said.

Now this is the start of a succession of dumb things, and there's more to come.

I didn't get meteorology. I didn't get my second choice, either. My third choice was radio. And I didn't even know what that involved. They assigned me to radio school.

They put us over in some barracks waiting for the next radio class to begin, but until then, I had liberty every night. I was enjoying that. By this time, Ed Chesnut had finished boot camp and they sent him back to Norman, Oklahoma, eighteen miles from his home in Oklahoma City.

Now get this! A young Texan (a seventeen-year-old) was sitting with me on the barracks steps. I asked him where he was going.

"Well," he said, "I wanted to be a gunner on a destroyer, but they are sending me to meteorology school."

I almost fell off the steps! And that was only the start of my woes and disappointments.

Enrolled in radio class, I learned to copy code. I was knocking that stuff off like crazy, but after several weeks, doing great, the code speed began to pick up and I found I couldn't copy beyond a certain speed. These young kids were going like lightning—fifteen, sixteen, seventeen—and I couldn't get past fourteen words a minute!

So I went to my chief. "Hey, I'm having trouble increasing my speed."

"How old are you?"

"Thirty."

"Well, you see Dan, when you get past age twenty-five, you begin to lose that quick reflex that you had when you were younger."

"Well, jeez, what am I supposed to do?"

"Go to the classroom at night and practice—extra."

I finally made it. Got up to twenty-two words a minute, but that was it. The chief had promised I would get an instructor's job if I reached twenty-two words a minute.

When they began to hand out the assignments, here I was, second in my class, and I go to my Chief. "Okay, Chief. Now, do I get that instructor's job?"

"Well, Dan. I hate to tell you this, but there's so many radiomen coming back now from overseas duty, we feel they should have preference."

"You mean I did all that extra work with the class and I get nothing?"

"That's the Navy, boy!" he said.

After the war was over, and I took a fingerprint job at the L.A. Police Department until I could find something else, I ran into Captain Webber, my old boss in Ogden, Utah. He was a lawyer. I met him coming out of City Hall in L.A. one day. We recognized each other right away and shook hands.

"What in the hell ever happened to you?" he asked.

"I joined the Navy."

"Well, you dumb son-of-a-bitch," he said, "We had it all planned out. You were supposed to go into the Air Force. I waited to hear from you so I could get you transferred back to Hill Field in Ogden."

"Well, I went into the Navy, because I thought I could get into a good school."

U.S. Navy radio school graduating class in 1943. Alguire is visible in the front row, second from the left. Courtesy of Charlotte Bryant McCormack.

Man, I was really down. But that still wasn't the end of it.

They called us in and read off the assignments. "Okay, the following men will be stationed at…." say, "Point Loma," a land station close to San Diego.

"Oh, I'll get that," I thought. No. He even called the names of some of the screw-ups.

They kept going: "These next five guys go to San Francisco land base."

Good assignments.

"Long Beach."

"Close to L.A.," I thought. "Fine!"

My name was not called. And finally he ran out of all the specials.

"And the names that were not called, go to Coronado Amphibs."

Well, Coronado was an island, near San Diego, where they had the amphibian base. My job as a radio man in amphibs was to go in with the first wave on an invasion and set up ship-to-shore walkie-talkie communication—the worst duty you could possibly have! The first damn wave! With the Marines! "I'm dead," I thought.

I had made a rate out of school as a radio man, third class. Well, I ran into Frank Takach, an old musician friend of mine who was playing in the band at Coronado.

"What the hell are you doing here?" he asked.

"Man, I'm dead. I'm in the amphibs."

"Why didn't you get in the band?"

"Why didn't I get into band?' I wondered. "I was trying to get a Navy school, and I didn't get it. I turned band down."

"Turned down band!" he gasped. "I'll try to get you in our band. We need a trumpet. Come on, I want you to sit in. We're due for practice in a half-hour."

I had on my fatigues, so it didn't show my rank. I went over, borrowed a horn and sat in. They didn't have anyone that could take hot solos, but had good readers.

"God! You're great," said the lieutenant. "Give me your service number. I'll get you transferred to the band. Come around tomorrow." I slept soundly that night. Why did I ever leave my music in the first place?" I wondered.

For the first time in my life, I had a glimpse of something inside me, heard a voice within me that had been shouting all these years: "Listen to me, Dan! Listen! It's music for you. Music!" I said, "Ok, I'm listening now."

I went around the next day. "Jesus, Dan. You didn't tell me you had already made a rate in radio. They told me the Navy is not spending $20,000 to put a man through radio school, then let him go toot a horn in the band."

Too late for band.

We hung around the barracks, and finally I got assigned to a new outfit. Thirty of us lined up and the commander, Lt. Bill McDonald, marched up and returned our salute. "I'll be your division commander. You're in the small boat division. AKA-6, U.S.S. *Alchiba*. It's docked now for repairs in San Francisco. We'll be leaving in a few days."

"Boy, I'm going overseas to some bad duty. First wave. Dan," I asked myself, "what have you done with your life?" Finally, I cast away the self-pity. "You have put yourself in the war to test your courage. So face up to it!" I shaped up and got ready to "face the music," and to ship out.

Editors' Note: Below is the transcription of a letter written by Danny Alguire to his parents during his war service. Though the precise date is unknown, it is likely from the first half of 1943, when Alguire began his service in southern California, and before he went overseas aboard the U.S.S. *Alchiba*.

Dear Folks,

Got your nice letter. [...] Well I guess you noticed my new address. I dropped back to pick up Class Seven as their Class

Petty Officer—in charge of 200 men. Boy! What headaches are ahead.

I was top man for the first five weeks—99.3 average for my grades. And I can take twelve words a minute. Eight is all that is required for the first five weeks.

So now what happens is that I drop out of school for five weeks to get the new class started, then pick up school with them after five weeks.

With all the responsibility, it still is a good deal, as I can have more liberty, and am a cinch for a rate 'cause it makes my school five weeks longer.

Well, I finally saw Bob [Wills] and the boys. Only Bob, Tommy, and Louie left of my bunch. Alex left for Oklahoma City for induction five days ago. I sang lots of tunes with them out at Mission Beach [on] Sunday night. And naturally, being a servicemen, got over big.

Bob hugged me and said, "Dan, you were sure a loyal boy. And I want you to know you can work with me anytime, anyplace." [I] probably will never play professionally again, but it's nice to hear things like that.

[...] Must close now and get going. Will write when I can, but don't worry if I don't. I'll be busy.

Love to all,
Dan

P.S. Betty is doing fine. I sent her your letter. Sure hope you and dad could come out. We'll see.

Chapter 14:

"That's A Plenty"

The *Alchiba*!

When the war first broke out, the Navy didn't have many cargo ships or AKA's ("attack cargo") which carried the small boats. They leased several ships at the beginning of the war and mine was the AKA-6. You can tell by the low number that it was one of the first. It belonged to the old McCormick line, from Boston.

Back at the barracks, an old "salt" was bunking just below me. He had five red stripes on his sleeve, meaning he'd been in the service about sixteen years. Ornery guy. He'd been up to chief petty officer and now he was back at first class. He was a drunk, promoted and demoted several times, but real "salty." He rolled an unlit cigar across his lips, bit down on it and looked up at me on the top bunk. "Get a ship?" he grunted.

"Yeah."

"What'cha get?"

"The *Alchiba*."

"The *Alchiba*! That suicide ship?"

I turned my head from the pillow and stared down at him. "What do you mean, 'suicide ship'?"

"Hell, that ship took a couple of fish at Guadalcanal. They gave it up for lost at first, but finally beached her and hauled her back to Frisco. Been working on it. Don't run right." He rolled his eyes up at me and lit his cigar. "Damn ship's a wreck."[1]

Cigar smoke curled up around my head and I began to feel sick from that pleasant bit of information.

Well, when we got to Frisco and boarded the "suicide ship," it was under repair, and the repairs were extensive. Without a place to sleep on the ship, they had a couple of barges tied up alongside with bunks in it. That's where we slept and ate while they finished the repairs.

One day, when most of the other guys were on liberty, I was sitting in this barrack and there was a piano in there. I could play a few chords, a few old standards. I was sitting there at the piano by myself, just chording a few tunes and singing and whiling away time, when I looked up to see my commander, Bill McDonald, with a clarinet in his hand, followed by another officer, a lieutenant named Bob Hendricks. He had a trombone. I started to get up, you know, I was probably out of line.

"No. No," they said. "Keep your seat. We heard you playing. Let's play."

They were strictly amateur musicians.

The guy with the trombone shrugged his shoulders with a sheepish grin. "I'm really a guitar player but," he said, "when I came into this damn Navy I made up my mind I was going to learn to play trombone. I don't play it yet, but I'm going to learn."

And Bill, on clarinet, he played so-so; not too bad. So, he said, "Hell, we'll get a band together."

"Well," I said, "my instrument is trumpet. I don't really play piano."

"You play trumpet!?"

"Yeah."

"Great! Where's your horn?"

"L.A."

"I'll get you a pass."

He gave me a two week pass to go down to L.A. and get a horn! Music, giving me a break again.

While I had been at boot camp, my wife Betty got this job as an apartment manager on Fuller Street in Hollywood; salary and free apartment. The owner and his wife liked her. When I arrived in L.A. I was stunned at the place she had. Real swanky, just off of Sunset.

And just a block away, across an empty lot, was where the Ozzie Nelson family lived.[2]

Betty had these two little boys there (about eight and six). "Well, who are these little boys?" I asked.

"This is Ricky and this is David Nelson. Their parents are Ozzie and Harriet Nelson," and she said, "I'm babysitting."

Well, I hadn't seen her for about ten weeks, and it seemed like a year. Of course, we were more than happy to see each other and we spent some great days together, before I had to head for sea. I didn't know, maybe it would be the last days we spent together. I was so relieved that she had this nice set-up for herself. I made the most of my leave, a soft bed, home-cooked meals, and my dear wife.

Finally, with my horn in hand, I returned to San Francisco and the "band" started rehearsing.

The Navy band on the *Alchiba* had an accordion player aboard, Polish guy. All he could play was polkas. But we wrote out chords for jazz tunes. And then we had a bass player, a Marine lieutenant, and he was stationed aboard our ship as a transportation officer. He had a bass fiddle. He was from Okemah, Oklahoma; name was Scofus. And we had a drummer, Ensign Charley Sauers. (He is now a cartoonist, living in Great Neck, New York. Draws cartoons for *The New Yorker Magazine*. He recently sent me some of his stuff. Very funny.) We scrounged up a horrible set of drums. The executive officer played good guitar. So we started molding a band.

Finally one day, the *Alchiba* shipped out to sea. We were assigned to the Seventh Fleet, headed for the New Hebrides Islands. We crossed the equator and experienced the initiation for that glorious event. They almost beat the hell out of me. I ended up in sick bay.

The ones who had previously been across the equator, called "shell backs," the initiators, ran us through a long canvas tunnel filled with garbage. They made shillelaghs (canvas clubs), and put empty twenty millimeter shell cases in them and, like clubs, they beat on you as you crawled through the tunnel. Hell, I got hit on both kidneys and all over, even in the head. I was one of the first enlisted men through. It got so bad they sent some of us to sick bay.

The doctor looked us over. He was a good old country doctor from Wyoming. "That does it!" he said. He went up to the captain and told him to knock it off. He had that right. If anything aboard ship endangers the health of the men, a doctor can tell the captain to knock it off.

But, hell, I'd already been through it. A lot of them didn't have to go through that gauntlet. And I was glad for them.

In addition to crawling through the garbage, they painted our faces, cut our hair off, and put us in an electric chair, shocked us, and then we leaped into a tank of water and couple of big burly guys dunked you until you said, "Shellback, Shellback." They finally got through with me and dumped me out on the deck.

Another mate told me later that he hardly recognized me. "You looked like a drowned rat," he said.

"I felt like a dead rat."

I was in sick bay for three or four days, really beat up, along with a lot of others. I should have got a Purple Heart for that.

Someone turned the fire hose on one sailor. Broke his eardrum. He got out of the Navy on that. But I recovered and went back to my radio duties.

I was happy to just copy code. No outside watches. That was one break. They wanted me to strike for second class, but you had to tune transmitters and do a lot of electrical crap. I just wanted to get through this damn war and get out of the Navy. And all I did was copy code… and play in our band.

Chapter Endnotes:

1. For an extended history of the U.S.S. *Alchiba*, see the Appendix.

2. *The Adventures of Ozzie and Harriet,* starring the entire Nelson family, became a sensation on television and radio in the 1950s as one of the first American sitcoms.

Chapter 15:

"On The Good Ship Lollipop"

When our band got out and going—four officers, three enlisted men—we sounded pretty good. Lots of time for practice. I had been the only professional musician, so I was named the leader.

The best part about it was liberty. Instead of going to the enlisted men's liberty on Ulithi Island called "Mog-Mog," we would go to the officers' club where they had the good bourbon. The ship's enlisted men got terrible green beer, no Budweiser or other name brands. One time they gave me a beer called 'Green Mountain'—awful! So the band would go to officer's liberty and play. And it was great! You'd be surprised how a little live music is appreciated at sea.

The officers were tickled to death that we'd play for them while they danced with the nurses. And the funny part about it, I'd get stoned playing, then come back from liberty and usually, the way the liberty schedule worked out, as soon as I got back, I had to go on duty. Sometimes I was so "swacked" I could hardly copy code. It sounded like a covey of quail going by.

But the guys were good to me. They liked the music. They would help me until I got my head together. Good shipmates.

I was copying code one day and they were playing these "V disc" records over the intercom and, my God, I suddenly heard "Home in San Antone," the tune that I made with Bob Wills. "Hey, you guys," I said. "That's the record I'm on."

The guys looked at me. "Come on!"

"That's the record I'm on. That's me, singing!" And you know how a bunch of Navy guys are.

"Knock it off… Who are you trying to fool?"

"Okay. Forget it," I said.

It was the first time I'd heard the record, except for that one playback in 1942 when we recorded it.[1]

It was great to have music at sea. We molded this band together. The trombone player, Hendricks, would get me up in his room—officers' country—and have me go over tunes, show him the right notes to play.

One day, there was a knock on the door, and Bob said, "Come in."

It was a steward. "Begging your pardon, sir, but," he said, "the Captain's trying to get some sleep. He wants you to knock off the noise."

And, gee, I wasn't allowed up there anyway. So I started putting my horn away. This Bob Hendricks was the most independent Navy hater I ever saw in my life.

"To hell with 'em," he said. "Bastard. Come on. Now what's that note again?" But, I'm outa' there!

This Bob Hendricks, the trombone player, the Navy hater, chief engineer in charge of all the small boats, one time borrowed a boat somewhere, a small motor boat at some island, and we took our horns with us, got in the boat and buzzed around the islands playing to whoever would listen. And some of the natives were pretty wide-eyed! Hendricks was from Marblehead, Massachusetts. He didn't pay attention to Navy rules or regulations. It's a wonder they didn't throw him in the brig!

We got pretty good and it was not only great diversion from all the threats (and boredom) at sea, but it was satisfying to give a little relief to the poor guys stuck in this crazy war.

The *Alchiba* was a wreck. Like a car, you know, once they crash up.... The long propeller shaft was out-of-round and they didn't seem to be able to fix it. So every time we'd go over thirteen knots, the ship would start shuttering and shaking like an old washing machine and burn out the bearings. And we'd just float on the damn sea, in the middle of the ocean like a dead duck, until they repaired it. We didn't have an escort then; alone and dead in the water. This happened two or three times.

By this time, though, they'd pretty well cleared out the Japanese in these waters, so there wasn't a lot of danger, although one time later on, we picked up a Japanese sub on radar. We zig-zagged all night and got away. But when we joined the Seventh Fleet and went through maneuvers, we couldn't keep up—so they kicked us out of the Seventh Fleet, sent us back to San Francisco, which was a break for us. Liberty in San Francisco. Nothing better.

Instead of junking that old tub and getting another one—by this time they had lots of new ships built—oh no, not the Navy! They put us in dry dock to work on the ship again. It happened two or three times and was a good deal for me—because I could go play with all the good civilian musicians in Frisco. Some nights I'd sit in all night and get paid!

And it gave us a chance to go down and hear the jazz. That's where I met Turk Murphy. He and Lu Watters really started the revival of Dixieland, along with the Firehouse Five Plus Two, on the west coast after the war.[2]

The pattern, the common denominator in my life, continued to evolve and I began to finally recognize the value of music to my wellbeing. It took me long enough, but at last I knew, knew without a doubt that music was my life.

Because we had this band together (and they weren't about to lose their only trumpet player), my commander got me into ship's company which meant I didn't have to leave with the men in the landing division. Music now, I felt, had literally saved my life. They took all the small boats off, with the crew to man them. From then on the *Alchiba* was just "KA" (straight cargo) and all we did was haul "buttons and bows," food and clothing. Go out and anchor some place. Some island. All the other ships came to us for supplies. When we ran out, we would go back to Frisco and reload.

So, as it turned out, it wasn't bad duty. I got lucky. The band, music, was my break. I was on that ship until my discharge from the Navy. I guess everything evens out in life—some good luck and some bad.

We were at Manila in August, 1945 when they dropped The Bomb and, of course, we were elated. Guys said, "They dropped The Bomb!" And we would all yell, "Yeah!"

The scuttle-butt was very amusing. "You know this bomb is no bigger than a dime," one guy said.

And I thought, "That couldn't be right!" But we figured the war was over and boy, we felt good! No matter what size the bomb was.

The night before we were due to sail for Sasebo, Japan, they ordered the *Alchiba* back to San Francisco from Manila.[3]

It took us twenty-four days at ten knots. Three days before hitting Frisco, I reached my required number of points to get out. When that ship hit Frisco and sailed under the Golden Gate Bridge, I was home free of the Navy, where I got to keep playing trumpet and where my only wound was a bruised kidney![4]

Cover of *The Kingpost*, the onboard newspaper and magazine for sailors on the U.S.S. *Alchiba*. Coincidentally, this issue is dated August 6, 1945, the date of the first atomic bomb's use against the Japanese city of Hiroshima. At that time the *Alchiba*, with Alguire aboard, was in port at Manila, and nearly missed heading for Japan itself. Courtesy of Charlotte Bryant McCormack.

Chapter Endnotes:

1. Note from Alguire: "When I got back to San Francisco later in the war, 'Home in San Antone' was in all the juke-boxes and it was one of the biggest hits of all the eighteen songs we made at the Hollywood recording session. It's still considered a standard Western hit today. The Governor of Texas, in the book, *San Antonio Rose*, mentioned it at a presentation to Bob Wills. 'We're so grateful to Bob and his music,' said the Governor. It was 'San Antonio Rose' and 'Home in San Antone,' he mentioned. I felt proud about that, not being a Western singer."

2. Melvin Alton Edward Murphy was born in Palermo, California in 1915. He became fascinated with jazz music at an early age, following in the footsteps of his father and grandfather. He started on cornet, then switched to trombone. In high school, he acquired the nickname "The Terrible Turk." During the Depression years, he toured with dance orchestras led by Will Osborne and Mal Hallett. In the late 1930s he began associating with other musicians such as Lu Watters, Bob Helm, Paul Lingle, and Pat Patton, all of whom admired the older styles of jazz. When Watters organized the Yerba Buena Jazz Band in 1940, Murphy was an original member. The Yerba Buenans were a roaring success at the Dawn Club in San Francisco until World War II broke up the band. Murphy served in the U.S. Navy during WWII, then rejoined the Yerba Buena band at the Dawn Club in 1946 and stayed with them when the band moved across the bay to perform at Hambone Kelly's in El Cerrito. Murphy also formed a close friendship with Ward Kimball (future trombonist and leader of the Firehouse Five Plus Two). Murphy left the Yerba Buena Jazz Band in 1949 to form his own group. Over the next two decades, Turk Murphy's San

Francisco Jazz Band played opposite the Firehouse Five Plus Two—at the 1951 Dixieland Jubilee in Los Angeles, the Italian Village in San Francisco, and later at the annual "Dixieland at Disneyland." The Firehouse Five also traveled from Los Angeles to San Francisco to play at Murphy's "Earthquake McGoon's" nightclub until they disbanded in 1971. Kimball drew the iconic cartoon of Murphy wearing a Turkish fez and carrying a bent trombone in a bucket. Murphy used the cartoon in advertising his own band as well as Earthquake McGoon's. He continued to lead one of the top Traditional Jazz bands in the U.S. until his death in 1987.

3. After demobilization in San Francisco, Alguire participated in a session with Turk Murphy, Ellis Horne, Burt Bales, Bill Dart, and other pioneers of the Traditional Jazz "Revival." A privately-held recording of the session includes—in addition to jazz standards such as "Shake That Thing," "Canal Street Blues," "Dippermouth Blues," and "Fidgety Feet"—a few songs from the Bob Wills and His Texas Playboys songbook such as "31st Street Blues" and even "Take Me Back To Tulsa!"

4. Note from Alguire: "To this day, I correspond with Bill McDonald back in New York City. He was quite a successful journalist. Worked for *Time Magazine* and many business publications, and is still doing publicity writing. We correspond, and trade jazz talk. I got a few pictures of the band, some taken on the islands. Bill still plays jazz as a hobby." Editor's note: Sadly, the photos Alguire references have not been found.

Chapter 16:

"Baby Won't You Please Come Home"

Alguire in Los Angeles in the 1940s, likely after his return from Navy service in World War II. Courtesy of Charlotte Bryant McCormack.

Coming home from war is a funny experience. I'd been told what to do for so long, that I couldn't think for myself. I was befuddled. I'd lie on the sofa while Betty worked. She'd get up and go to work every morning. For several weeks I'd just lie there and listen to the radio or read the paper.

"What are you going to do?" Betty finally asked me one day.

My mind was blank. "I don't know."

"What do you mean, you don't know?"

'What was I going to do?'

"Well, why don't you go down to the Police Department and get a fingerprint job?"

"I hadn't thought about it, but that's a good idea." So I did. I went to work immediately for the Los Angeles Police Department, classifying and searching prints. I began to adjust. The Navy and memories of the war soon faded and the ache to get back into some real professional music begin to gnaw at me, stronger than ever. Never again would I turn away from music.

Alguire at the Los Angeles Police Department where he worked in fingerprinting after his return from Navy service in World War II. Courtesy of Charlotte Bryant McCormack.

Chapter 17:

"Love Is Just Around the Corner"

One night, listening to the radio, I heard a remote broadcast coming from the 97th Street Corral Dance Hall, not too far away. It was the Western band of "T. Texas Tyler," and I heard Tex mention Don Decker, a fiddle player in the band.

Well, I knew Don before the war. So, I thought, "I think I'll run out there and see my old friend Don."

Don was glad to see me. "You got your horn?" he asked.

"Yeah. Out in the car." (Just happened to have it.)

"Well, go get it, and sit in a few members," Don said.

I played the rest of the night and later Tex hired me.

I began playing music nights and working days on the fingerprint job. It got pretty rough. No sleep. By this time, we were working at the Riverside Rancho located near the valley, drawing good crowds. I was enjoying the playing so much, I figured, "I'm going to quit the fingerprint job, because I can always get that job back."

So, I quit. This time I quit the right job, for the right reason! But, believe it or not, the very next night, the Riverside Rancho burned to the ground!

Having no place to play, the band went on a road tour. In 1947, we took a long bus trip down through Texas, a town or two in Louisiana, and a little town in southern Arkansas; and three days in Houston, where I got some good gulf shrimp. "Order steamed shrimp," our manager said. "You get a little dish of mayonnaise and horseradish. Take a shrimp and dip it in both dishes." It's all I ate for three days in Houston.

Back in Los Angeles, we started making tours up north through California and the Oregon northwest. I made four of them and was the band manager for Tex, for which I got a little more loot. Before the tours, we made several recordings. Tex's biggest hit (and I wasn't on that) was "Remember Me." Then we made "A Deck of Cards" (which I was on) and it was also a huge hit, sold all over the country, and although Tex made some good money on the record, I'm not sure he got a correct count on the total sales. In all, I was on twelve of fourteen sides with Tex (on 4-Star label).

T. Texas Tyler later went into evangelical work, touring the states with a group, following the Lord's call. A few years ago, someone sent me a clipping from a Springfield, Missouri newspaper. "T. Texas Tyler died of cancer yesterday in a Springfield Hospital." Too late. Too bad. Tyler was known as "the man with a million friends." He was a decent man. I liked him.[1]

He was just a good old Arkansas boy that had a voice that caught on. Patsy Cline, one of America's greatest country singers, was also under a four-year contract with the same label (which she couldn't get out of) and it nearly ruined her career because she had to record only tunes that the record owner controlled; mostly bad tunes, too.

Anyway, Tyler and the band made several trips, one in the fall, one in the early spring, through the northwest. We played what we called the "grape circuit": Bakersfield, Fresno, Modesto, and on up the line into Oregon, playing Medford, Albany, Eugene, and Portland. And then after Seattle, Washington, we came back to Yakima, Washington, hit Boise, Idaho, and down through Salt Lake City, Reno, and back to L.A.

This Tyler band was a crazy bunch of guys, all good musicians, but they were a headache. I handled the payroll. We traveled in two cars and a trailer, and it was a rough chore to get them going each morning.

Finally, I gave up. "No more of this, boy! I've had it." Although Tex was paying me $100 a week, which was pretty good money, I couldn't take it anymore with that band. Oh, they were good musicians. I loved playing with them, but not nursing them.

And here I was back in Western music again. I grew kind of wary of that, because the band wasn't in the same class with Bob Wills. After the fire, the Riverside Rancho was rebuilt and we had resumed playing there following the road trips to Texas.

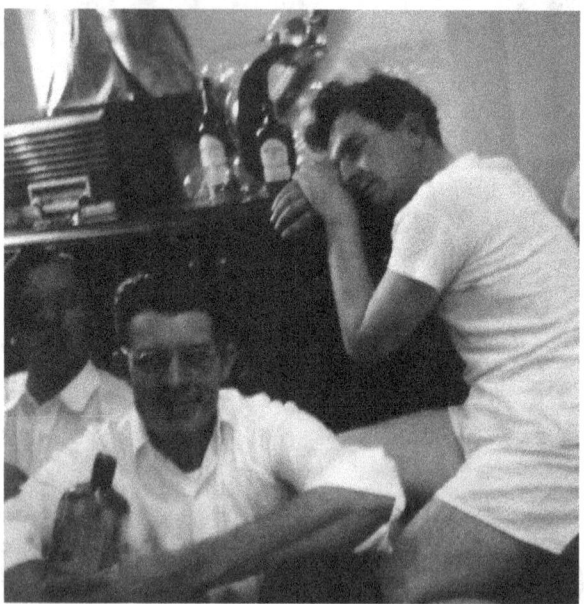

In 1947 and 1948, Alguire toured parts of the western United States with T. Texas Tyler and his western dance band. These photographs document those trips and the band's "recreational" activities along the way. Courtesy of Charlotte Bryant McCormack.

One night before I quit Tex in 1948, a red-headed guy named John Freeman, who worked at the Disney Studios and who liked Western music, came up to the bandstand at the Rancho. "Hey, Dan. There's a bunch of guys at the Disney Studios who get together every day at noon and play Dixieland. They need a trumpet player. Why don't you come out and sit in with them sometime? I've told them about you, and they said to have you out some noon hour."

"Sure, anytime," I said.

So we set a date and John got me a pass through the gate. I met Ward Kimball, Frank Thomas, and all the other guys: Jim MacDonald (drums), Ed Penner (tuba) and Clarke Mallery (clarinet). I started going out two or three times a week and sitting in. It turned out that I was just the guy that seemed to fit in best.

Meanwhile, T. Texas Tyler wanted me to go on another trip up north. I told him, "Just one more, then I'm staying in L.A."

On this last trip, we played Yakima, Washington. We had a broadcast at 8 p.m. on a fifty watter, half an hour before the dance started—to get the local people out. This announcer got up to the mike while we played the theme song. "And coming to you from," so-and-so ballroom "right here, live from Yakima, is the great band of 'T. Texas Tyler,' the man with a million friends. Come in, Tex, and say a few words."

Tex staggered up to the mike, drunk as a skunk. His voice slurred. "Ladies and Gentlemen. This is T. Texas Tyler. We're very happy to be playing here tonight for you in Yakima, Oregon," and it was Yakima, Washington! He didn't even know what state he was in. After that, I knew I was through.

Chapter Endnotes:

1. David Luke Myrick, "T. Texas Tyler," passed away January 28th, 1972. His band's hit record, "Deck of Cards," on which Alguire played, was released in 1948.

Chapter 18:

"Firechief Rag"

The Firehouse Five Plus Two started largely by accident. When I met them in 1948, most of the guys were working at Disney Studios and had been there since the 1930s. They all had musical experience in school—as a hobby. They met during the noon hour with Ward Kimball and listened to his collection of classic jazz records including King Oliver, Baby Dodds, Jelly Roll Morton, and Louis Armstrong. Pretty soon they began to play along with the records.

Well, one day during a thunderstorm over Burbank there was a power outage and when the phonograph conked out, they realized they sounded pretty good on their own. They agreed on strictly New Orleans style (Dixieland) and the favorites were Satchmo on the trumpet (always my favorite, too), Johnny Dodds on clarinet, and Kid Ory, trombone.[1] They were influenced, too, by Lu Watters who, before the war in 1940, organized the Yerba Buena Jazz Band in San Francisco, playing the good old New Orleans jazz. Watters composed some new tunes written in the same early style.

New Orleans jazz had always enjoyed popularity on the West Coast, particularly in San Francisco where Watters and Turk Murphy kept the Dixieland fires burning.

Watters' band played at a spot off Annie Street in Frisco called "The Dawn Club." They drew tremendous crowds who loved the music. Ward and some of the Disney guys had been to the Dawn Club and really liked the band, too.[2]

The budding Disney musicians kept on with the noon practice sessions and pretty soon, calling themselves the "Huggajeedy Eight," they began to play a few jobs and had jam sessions in Ward Kimball's living room in San Gabriel. Johnny Lucas had the trumpet job then.

After a name change to the San Gabriel Valley Blue Blowers, they were invited by the Horseless Carriage Club to play in San Diego for their auto tour. Ward found and restored a 1914 American LaFrance fire truck. Ward and his wife Betty had been members for years and often attended these caravans with linen dusters and goggles in their 1913 Ford. So this time a fire truck with musicians playing along the way would really be a hit. The LaFrance was bought from the City of Venice, California for $225.00. It took Ward six months to get it in shape, including workable firefighting apparatus. He created the uniforms of black pants, red shirts, blue ties and white suspenders and we donned our old white painted leather fire hats as the new Firehouse Five Plus Two. (Ward said he added the "Plus Two" to let people who hired us know that they were getting a *seven*-piece band!) The name would endure twenty-two years until we retired.

The Firehouse Five Plus Two at the height of their early fame, (L to R): Frank Thomas, piano; Ward Kimball, trombone; Danny Alguire, cornet; Monte Mountjoy, drums; Clarke Mallery, clarinet; Harper Goff, banjo; Ed Penner, tuba (posing with soprano saxophone). Courtesy of The Ward Kimball Family.

So after my last crazy Washington trip with T. Texas Tyler in 1948, Ward Kimball from Disney called me about the horseless carriage tour. "Hey, Dan. I got something you might be interested in. I belong to this antique car club and we're going to get thirty or forty antique cars together, make a little tour down to San Diego. We'll ride in the fire truck and play jazz along the way. It doesn't pay any money," he said, "but there's plenty of free booze, food, and lodging. It's just for kicks. Would you like to go?"

"Sure. Sounds good." And it was a fun thing. We were a sensation everywhere we stopped. People danced in the streets along the route to San Diego.

One of the guys who saw us on the trip was Bill Harrah, a recent antique car collector and owner of Harrah's Club in Reno and one at Lake Tahoe. He was just carried away with the Firehouse Five and invited us to come to Reno for his own old car meet in August, 1949.

And on our way back from the San Diego caravan, Ward told me, "There's a guy named Les Koenig that wants to record our band, start a record company."

Les was then associate producer with William Wyler at Paramount Studios. But Senator Joe McCarthy had those communist hearings in Washington D.C. and was investigating the Hollywood film crowd. In 1932 or so, Les was in college back east and joined the communist party. In those years, all the young students were joining, because that was the fashionable thing to do. He had a card and when they had the McCarthy hearings and all that crap, Les got fired from Paramount. McCarthy even hinted that everybody in Hollywood were communists, although Les Koenig had dropped out years before. Everyone was scared to death in Hollywood. "Hell, I'll start a record company," Les said.

So he came to Ward. "I want to make some records of the Firehouse Five Plus Two."

"I promised him we would," Ward said. "Listen, Dan. We've been using Johnny Lucas on trumpet. I told him that he could be on the first recording session, but after that, he wants to start his own band. He's against wearing the fire costume. Kind of a "purist." He dubbed our band a "funny hat band." It seemed like he doesn't want to play with us after the first record session. If so, we want you to take the trumpet job."

"Okay," I said. I'll tell you, things were happening fast. The Firehouse Five was starting to set the West Coast aflame.

With Johnny Lucas, it was a fair arrangement all around. He wanted to play pure jazz—no frills, no humorous things added to the music. Never having been into pure jazz, Ward Kimball looked upon the band as a "fun thing." When we had fun, the crowd did too. Lucas went on with his "pure" jazz, and did well. He was well known in L.A. for his talent.

On the first Firehouse Five Plus Two recording session, May 13, 1949, it was Ward Kimball, trombone; Johnny Lucas, trumpet; Clarke Mallery, clarinet; Frank Thomas, piano; Harper Goff, banjo; Ed Penner, bass sax; Jim MacDonald, drums. By the second recording session of October 8, 1949 (a singles session) I had replaced Lucas and Monte Mountjoy took over drums for MacDonald.[3] The final songs for the first album were recorded February 19, 1950 and included "Tiger Rag" and "The World is Waiting for the Sunrise." The latter was always a show stopping number, and featured Ward lighting a kerosene lamp on his washboard and duetting with Harper Goff on his banjo. This song was a big seller in Boston, of all places.

The first album was simply called the Firehouse Five Plus Two, produced by Lester Koenig, Contemporary Records, in Los Angeles.[4] The label was GOOD TIME JAZZ Record Company. (Les Koenig, the producer, always thought the band sounded like they were having a "good time," thus the "GOOD TIME JAZZ Record Company.")

The first place we played publicly was the Beverly Cavern in Los Angeles on Monday nights.[5] They specialized in jazz. And it was a crazy thing. I'll never get over it. I don't know what happened, but the first night we played, they had a big sign out: THE FIREHOUSE

FIVE PLUS TWO. And man, we had them stacked to the rafters. They came in droves, lined up outside. I don't know whether they'd heard our records or what, but from then on, every Monday night, it was total bedlam.

Members of the Firehouse Five Plus Two at the 1949 Dixieland Jubilee in Los Angeles. L to R: Harper Goff, banjo; Clarke Mallery, clarinet; Danny Alguire, cornet; Ward Kimball, trombone. Courtesy of the Ward Kimball Family.

We worked the Beverly Cavern in the spring and summer of 1949. We got so popular that one night Red Nichols came in and heard us. I didn't even know he was there. Red Nichols was a great cornet man and was playing on the Bing Crosby radio show. But as far back as 1925, he, along with Bix Beiderbecke and Louis Armstrong, were the top men on jazz trumpet. Red got such a kick out of hearing our band that one night, he brought Bing Crosby down to hear us. They sat over in a corner and pretty soon I saw them come up to meet the band. "Oh, God, what's going on?" I thought.

"You should put them on your radio show," Red told Bing. Bing agreed.

Here's what Frank Thomas, our piano player and a great Disney animator, had to say:

"Bing was at Disney Studios to record the narration track for *The Adventures of Ichabod and Mr. Toad* [released in October of 1949], and stopped by the room where the Firehouse Five Plus Two was blowing away at noontime. He commented to Perry Botkin, his ukulele-banjo-guitarist, that we didn't sound very good. But later on, Perry played with us on a couple of dates when Harper Goff couldn't make it, and told Bing he should get us to play at the Pebble Beach Golf Classic. Bing said, 'O.K.,' and we went. During our playing, Bing gets up in the middle of 'Yes Sir, That's My Baby' and takes two choruses with us. Imagine! Bing Crosby singing with us. We couldn't believe it. Later after two appearances on his radio show, he told the Andrews Sisters that he planned to have us three or four more times. I think we did five shows."

By this time we had signed with the Music Corporation of America (MCA). So Bing's agent called MCA and booked us on one of his radio shows. We did his CBS Chesterfield radio program in February, 1950 and we got a truck load of mail. We did four more shows during the year and Bing invited us to play for the Pebble Beach Golf tournament.

One night Bing had Ella Fitzgerald and our band as guests. It was Christmas time and was the first time I ever heard "Sliver Bells" by Ella. And Ella! What a great singer. After two rundowns on the new tunes, she had them committed to memory. We accompanied Bing and Ella, backed them up with our little band on the "Memphis Blues." All our shows with Bing turned out great. Bing said our band got as much mail as any guests he had on the show.

Before we started doing the Crosby shows, Charlie Morrison, manager of the Mocambo on Sunset Strip, contacted MCA, our agent, and wanted us to start playing every Monday night at the Mocambo in Hollywood. This was "the place" on the Sunset Strip for all the Hollywood stars to be seen and to socialize—let their hair down, etc. It was a big break.

Ward gave proper notice at The Beverly Cavern, and the owner had a fit, but we were off for the Sunset Strip. The Firehouse Five Plus Two was "going Hollywood!"

The first night we played, old Charlie Morrison played it safe. He had his own rhumba band there just in case we fell flat. The rhumba band played the first set. We got up and played next. He never let the rhumba band back on the band stand. The crowd went crazy! They started doing the Charleston, the Black Bottom, you name it! It was just one of those things that happened.

In their columns Louella Parsons, Jim Bacon, and Hedda Hopper gave us big write-ups about what a wonderful night it had been. Louella had us on her Sunday night radio show and suddenly reservations for Monday night at the Mocambo were booked two and three weeks in advance. Every Monday night, they had what they called "Charleston Night." Every celebrity you can think of in town was there. Ginger Rogers, Lucille Ball, Barbara Stanwyck, Ann Miller, Judy Garland, and many more were doing the Charleston to "Yes Sir, That's My Baby" and others. All of them came. It was the place to go on Monday night. World famous musicians sat in with the band—Benny Goodman, Dan Daley, Johnny Mercer, and others. They had Charleston contests, and it was wild!

One night I was out front playing a solo, when Harry James and his wife, Betty Grable, danced by right in front of me. For an instant I almost froze, and then I thought, "What the hell." I couldn't play anything Harry had never heard before, so I just continued, in my style.

The write-ups and picture spreads we got, *Time Magazine*, *Life Magazine*, local press, pictures and…almost overnight, The Firehouse Five was famous.

The media was saying that not since 1917 had there been anything like the Firehouse Five Plus Two. During 1950 we became a household word. Disc jockeys were playing our music and we were getting an avalanche of requests to play—from the Carson City Volunteer Fire Department to the exclusive Ocean House in

Santa Monica and Charlie Farrell's Racquet Club in Palm Springs. We were guest stars on Ed Wynn's Camel TV Show in April, 1950 and throughout the summer the Mocambo Charleston frenzy continued.

In 1950 we played the NBC National Convention at White Sulphur Springs, West Virginia, the Milton Berle Show, in New York, made an appearance on Make Believe Ballroom, did a Walt Disney Special on NBC playing "Jingle Bells" on Christmas Day and did our first Rose Bowl Parade New Year's Day. [6]

We played about three times a week—in our spare time! At Disney Studios, Ward Kimball, Frank Thomas, and Ed Penner were hard at work on *Alice in Wonderland* [released in the summer of 1951]. Our records were selling around the world and we felt like *we* were in wonderland. It was quite a year.

It was being said that the Firehouse Five Plus Two spearheaded the Great Dixieland Revival. Indeed the response to our music was so overwhelming, so sudden, that none of us were quite prepared. We were caught off-guard, and caught up in the frenzy of playing and working. Soon it began to wear on us. But we were having fun! Up until this phenomenal year we really thought that our only appeal was to jazz fans, but by the nature of our requests (civic clubs, private parties, dances, parades, benefits, and even high schools!) we soon realized that a broad cross-section of people liked our music. Most importantly, to us, our audiences always had fun. We were making people happy.

There was no one more independent than our leader, trombone player, Ward Kimball, and he didn't take anything off of anybody. He never played professionally, as such. Because he was a successful director and animator at Disney, he never went through the rigors of going without a paying job. All the other guys in the band had good jobs at Disney too. Ward was always just himself and if prospective clients for our band jobs didn't like our prices or whatever, Ward just said to hell with them. I admired him for it.

One night, they had too many people in the Mocambo and the fire inspector came in and told Charlie he had to get rid of about fifty people. Well, all these people were stars and friends, Charlie's "personal" friends. He was beside himself. He came rushing up to the band stand. The banjo player, Harper Goff, was playing a solo. So, Charlie rushed up and grabbed Harper's hands right in the middle of his solo. "Stop!" he screamed.

Ward quickly reached over and slapped Charlie's hand away. Remember, this was *the* Charlie Morrison! No one did that to Charlie. Except, Ward did. "Get your hands off the banjo," Ward shouted. "Wait until we finish this tune!" So, we finished the tune. "Now what do you want?" asked Ward calmly.

Charlie was livid. "The fire inspector is here," cried Charlie, "I've got to get some people out! Let's call an intermission and see if some of the people leave. I won't let anymore in. We've exceeded the limit the Fire Department allows here."

That kind of nettled Ward. "Okay. But don't you ever, *ever* put your hands on a musician's instrument. Just leave them alone. If you got something to say, you wait until the tune's finished, and then come to me."

Charlie was mad as hell, but he didn't know what else he could do, because he didn't want to ask any of his "Hollywood friends" to leave.

Charlie was the manager. But a syndicate allegedly owned the place. Charlie was supposedly the front man. This arrangement was true of most of the entertainment places in Hollywood in those days. Or, so I was told.

Anyway, we carried the Mocambo until it just seemed like it couldn't get any bigger or better. All of a sudden Ward said, "You know what? We ought to quit this job."

"Why?" we asked.

"Because it's going to run down pretty soon. Let's get out while we're on top." He knew Hollywood.

"Well, it's up to you, Ward," we said.

So he gave Charlie Morrison the band's notice and I thought Charlie was going to have apoplexy. Here he had a gold mine going. "You want to quit? Do you realize what you're doing to me?"

"Yeah. We're quitting," said Ward.

I thought Charlie was going to faint. But another thing that made it easier for us to quit was that Charlie refused to raise our pay when we hit it big. Also, his checks were always bouncing. Finally, Ward had to tell Charlie he had to pay *cash*, which Ward personally picked up at the cashier at the end of each performance. "It was easy to tell Charlie off," Ward said.

But we quit. It was probably a smart thing to do, because it would have eventually run down. Hollywood is like that; here today, gone tomorrow.

I remember the first night we opened the Mocambo. Walt Disney himself showed up and we were talking to him at intermission about how great it was going.

"Yeah!" Walt said. "But you know…this is Hollywood, boys. You're real high one day, and the next day you can be down on your tail. Don't take it too seriously."

I guess Ward acted wisely. We checked out while we were on top. Just checked out. And Charlie thought we were crazy. But if the tables were turned, and we played out, he would have gleefully fired us with no qualms at all.

After we left the Mocambo, Charlie Morrison thought, "Oh boy. I got a good thing going here," so he got together another band who dressed up like Keystone Kops and they tried to play like us. It was a Dixieland band and they had the siren and all that, but they didn't make it. Ward told me, "They won't make it."

"Why not?!" I asked.

Ward is a very slow speaking, very observant guy. "They won't make it because nobody likes a policeman, but everybody loves a fireman."

After about two or three weeks they folded. They just didn't do it. You got to be there first. The guy that gets there first with an original idea is the guy that gets it and imitators that come second, don't make it.

You won't believe how independent this Ward was, and remember Ward Kimball, Frank Thomas, and Harper Goff and the other guys in the band had big jobs at Disney. They were artists, animators, and background painters making very good money. About three times the money I was making, so they could be independent. The main thing—they had never worked professionally as musicians. That's what made it so funny, because they didn't take any of this music scene guff. They thought, "Well, I'm going to play the way I want and if they don't like it, to hell with them." And that was the attitude of the band. We played hard and pleased almost everybody, and we were a sensation. Not since Bob Wills had I gotten so much pleasure from playing music and watching people get happy; good wholesome, alive music. It was great medicine for a post-war society starting to hum again in the Fabulous Fifties.

A party or a night club or a big time ballroom in L.A. between 1949 and 1970, you name it, we played it. Anything that we thought was interesting. "I want to play where it's fun," Ward said. He didn't need the money. Of course, I did!

After 1951 we played more and more according to what we thought was enjoyable and good for the audience. We played Army, Navy, and Veterans Hospitals, and we turned down many lucrative jobs. Our largest audience was a hundred million for the televised opening of Disneyland in 1955, and we later played many summer weekends at Disneyland. Heck, anybody that liked jazz—we played for them—even the employees at Disney Studios during the noon hour!

But it was not all success and glory. We had some foul ups too. Remember, other than Monte Mountjoy, George Probert, and me, the Studio boys, although very good musicians, were still amateurs and were just learning to play together; you know, lots of enthusiasm (and nerve) but not everyone with professional know-how (musically, that is).

Coming out of the Mocambo with all our write-ups, we thought we were really sailing (and we were, because of the great press we had).

We were hired one Saturday night in 1955 to play for the annual Los Angeles Art Directors Ball in Hollywood. The place was packed with art lovers and friends, all wildly dressed in weird costumes, somewhat like the Mardi Gras in New Orleans, and all boozed up or on whatever their favorite "high" was—having a ball.

Now, for some unknown reason, a group of three gals were booked in for a floor show—certainly not needed, but a floor show for whomever.

George Probert on clarinet and I on trumpet were the only "pros" in the band who had played floor shows before, so I told Ward we'd better check on the acts to see what back-up music we would have to play for them. Ward, Frank, and I went down to the dressing room before the dance started and asked what the gals needed for music.

Two of the acts were a cinch. One, a dancer, needed just two and one-half choruses of "Yes Sir, That's My Baby" in her singing key. Okay. No problem. The other gal did a jazz dance to three fast choruses of some old standard. Took care of that okay.

Now the third act was our downfall. Basically it involved a routine featuring a scantily clad blonde in a see-through chemise who first danced with and then made love to her "partner," a full-size male dummy, all timed to a printed arrangement of the song, "Temptation." She insisted that we had to play the number exactly as written. The problem was that the well-worn sheet music was all scribbled over with a maze of arrows, crossed out changes, repeats, all done with a *RED* pencil! As her act started and with the folded four-page music sheets spread out on the stage floor, we started off all O.K., but by the time she had finished dancing a few bars and had ended up on a chaise lounge in front of the band to begin her love making pantomime with her dummy partner, things started to go badly with our band accompaniment, especially when the guy working the stage spotlight changed from a *BLUE* to a *RED* lens which naturally made all the red pencil changes on the song arrangement completely disappear! Unreadable!

I am playing the lead line of the song, but I know if Frank plays the correct chords, I can handle the lead line of "Temptation." Frank plays a four-bar introduction and boom! The stage lights go off. Total darkness!

The "half-and-half dancer" had briefed the light man, but she didn't tell us. I mean the stage is black-nothing!

Frank can't see the music so he's lost right away. I can't hear the piano chords, so I'm lost. All that's going is the drummer, bass, and banjo. Pretty bad. Probert doesn't know who to play with, so he doesn't play anything.

It sounded like everyone in the band was playing a different version of the tune. The soft red light came back on, but we were totally lost. It was then that the lady stopped suddenly in the middle of an erotic pose, turned her head back to the band and screamed, "ARE YOU GUYS KIDDING?"

This completely broke us up. Our rousing arrangement of "Temptation" shuddered to a stop. We started staggering around the stage laughing uproariously with real tears. By then, even the crowd watching was laughing. In the years that followed, a mere mention of this episode brought on a new laughing jag!

One time we were playing the International Ballroom, the top ballroom in Los Angeles. We played there several times, but this particular time, I don't know what the occasion was, but the crowd was in tuxedos and evening dresses.

Ward was on the stage getting set up and trying to hook up everything. He always had to have some electric outlets for his siren which was foot controlled. So he was fussing around in the back of the stage, having trouble because there was only one outlet and he needed two or three outlets for lights and other things.

I had gone through all this crap through my years from managers that told me how to play and fired me and bossed me around and told me I had extra hours, etc. I had no control over them. They just put you down. So here I was, and this incident just filled my heart with joy.

Here was Ward, concerned about getting three hook-ups. He needed a double plug. I just happened to be standing by Ward when this pompous, grey-haired, handsome, obviously very rich cat comes up; tall guy with a tuxedo on. "Where's Mr. Kimball?" he demanded.

"That's Mr. Kimball right there," I said. "Down on the floor working on a plug."

"Mr. Kimball?" he said.

"Yeah," Ward said, over his shoulder. "I'm Ward."

"Mr. Kimball, I am," Mr. so and so, "and I'm the chairman of the entertainment committee tonight and…." and Ward stopped him right there. The guy was obviously going to say something stupid like, "we'd like to have you play a waltz every fifth tune," or one of those crazy things like, "we hope you'll keep the music slow and not too loud, or play too many fast tunes and…." but he didn't get that far.

Ward turned to him, "Hey! Go get me a double plug. I need a double plug."

And the guy came apart. It was so sudden and unexpected. "Oh, ahhh, why, yes sir. You bet. We'll get…" and he took off.

Ward turned to me and, I'll never forget what he said: "That's the way you should treat those sons-a-bitches. Give them something to do."

The thing that got me, Ward was never afraid of big, affluent guys because he was a "big" guy himself. But no one knew it. Ward didn't take anything off anybody.

Born in Minneapolis, Minnesota, Ward lived in Parsons, Kansas and then finally settled in Glendale and Santa Barbara, California during the 1930s where he attended art school. Early in life he showed a remarkable talent in drawing and he started with Disney in 1934—twenty years old—and at $15 (Depression) a week! But he moved up the ladder quickly and became one of the better young animators on Disney's staff. He created the models for Lucifer the Cat and mice in *Cinderella*, Jiminy Cricket in *Pinocchio*, and many others. He was a producer for the Tomorrowland TV Series and on the films *Man in Space*, *Man and the Moon*, and *Mars and Beyond*. Ward also co-directed *Melody*, the first 3D cartoon, and *Toot, Whistle, Plunk and Boom*, the first Disney Cinemascope cartoon and his first of two Academy Awards. He also did the long sequence in *The Three Caballeros* which was considered a classic in imaginative animation. He animated on many Disney feature cartoons and, get this, he still had time to acquire a full size, 1881 Baldwin locomotive and antique passenger car which he restored and now runs on his track in San Gabriel, complete with roundhouse, depot, water tank, and windmill. He added another sugar cane locomotive in 1948. He has a collection of antique miniature toy trains which he displays and runs in a special building on his property, and he's an aviator and astronomer of some note using a sophisticated telescope at his home.[7]

All this and he played music too! At eighteen he was playing with the Santa Barbara Symphony. Ward was a "mover and shaker" and Walt Disney said he was a true genius. The late Walt Kelly (creator of Pogo) worked at the Disney Studios in the 1940s and was Ward's assistant, animating the famous crows in *Dumbo*.

Ward had immense creativity, always doing things a little different. To be sure, everything he did was original. And that is very difficult. I think it frustrated Ward's genius to be stuck with one simple character too long. His vision and imagination was too expansive for that. Unlike some other animators he could draw characters with any emotion and his real forte was caricature.

Ward Kimball, chief and first trombonist of the Firehouse Five Plus Two, poses with his instrument. Courtesy of The Ward Kimball Family.

I asked Ward one time, "Ward, how can you do so many things so well?"

"Well," he said with his usual dry wit, "some people spend their time bowling. I don't bowl."

Ward Kimball (left) and Alguire in the early 1970s. Both were nearing the end of their Disney careers, and had been playing jazz together for over two decades. Courtesy of Charlotte Bryant McCormack.

In our jazz band, Ward played trombone. We called him, "Chiefie." During our first two years, 1949 and 1950, MCA told Ward, "The Firehouse Five Plus Two is really going places! It's one of the hottest bands in the United States with all the publicity you've had. *Life. Time.* Newspapers! The thing to do now, as all bands do, once they get this publicity and all, is to take a tour. Cash in on all the publicity from the Mocambo, while you're hot."

"We're not taking any tour," Ward said calmly.

This MCA agent couldn't believe it. It had never happened this way for him before. He was dumbfounded. "What do you mean, you're not going to take a tour? I can book you a two or three-week tour in Las Vegas. You'll clean up. Big money!"

"We got our jobs at Disney," said Ward. "We can't let the band interfere with our Studio work. Besides we can't all get away at the same time. We work in different departments. No way we can do it."

This MCA guy flipped. But that's the way the band was. Independent. No band in the world, ever to my knowledge, was like it. But we had plenty of jobs. We'd play a lot of high schools (that was before rock and roll.) Ward had some funny business cards printed. "Ward Kimball and the Firehouse Five Plus Two plays for picnics, parties, funerals, and wakes."

"We never liked to do the same thing twice as far as casuals went," said Frank Thomas. "We got plenty of wild suggestions and ended up with several bizarre engagements. Two that never came through: a Las Vegas casino wanted us to play in their lounge every night for one week from 9:00 to 1:00. They would charter a plane, pick us up at the studio at 5:00, feed us on the plane, let us sleep on the plane after the job, fly us back in time for our studio work at 8:00." We asked, "When do we see our wives?" Their answer, "We'll put them on another plane and let them fly along beside you. We turned that down. The other was to fly over Burbank for two hours in a blimp with a broadcasting system, blaring a message about a shoe store opening. We liked that, but the city council wouldn't give their approval."

Chapter Endnotes:

1. Kid Ory and his Creole Jazz Band were the only of these to have a personal influence on the band in the 1940s (the Firehouse Five Plus Two would later meet Louis Armstrong in the 1950s). In particular, Ory's bandmates became close with the group, even subbing at times. They included clarinetists Joe Darensbourg and Albert Nicholas and drummers Minor "Ram" Hall and Zutty Singleton.
2. Ward Kimball's earliest visit to see Watters and Murphy play was in late November, 1946.
3. Mountjoy was another veteran of Bob Wills and His Texas Playboys, and it may have been through a connection with Alguire that he joined the group.
4. The initial Firehouse Five Plus Two recordings were in fact released as 78 rpm singles beginning in 1949. Their first 33 rpm album, a compilation of these singles, was released in 1951.
5. Kid Ory and his Creole Jazz Band had been successful headliners at the Beverly Cavern and helped open the door for the Firehouse Five at the venue.
6. *One Hour in Wonderland* (1950) was Walt Disney's first television special.
7. At the time of Alguire's writing, Ward Kimball still maintained his world-class collection in San Gabriel. After Kimball's passing in 2002, the collection was subsequently sold at auction per his wishes and most of his full-scale equipment was donated to the Southern California Railway Museum in Perris, California.

Chapter 19:

"High Society"

When I was playing with the Firehouse Five in 1951, (I had still not gone to work at Disney Studios), the banjo player, Harper Goff, was acquainted with some people at Treasure Tone Paint Company and they decided to put a float into the Rose Bowl Parade with our band. We were the first jazz band to play in the Rose Bowl Parade. I thought that was quite a distinction, but there was something else distinctive that happened on that float; something I'll never forget.

The 1951 float was gigantic with a huge yellow-flowered trumpet mounted across the full length of the float, made entirely of gold leaves—a beautiful gold trumpet; very detailed, very nice. We were to stand on the back part of the float, up high, each with his own separate microphone.

Our drummer then was Monte Mountjoy and old Monte and I took a drink occasionally. It was over in Pasadena, so to be sure that we didn't over-sleep, we spent the night with Ward and got up at five o'clock in the morning, still dark. Ward lived near Pasadena in San Gabriel. I'd picked up a pint of bourbon the night before. It's pretty chilly January 1, in the early morning, until the sun comes up.

We found ourselves at the line-up site for the parade. The parade forming ground was on Orange Grove Avenue, south of Colorado. God, the sun hadn't come up yet and we were standing in the cold, shaking and waiting on the parade to get going, so I walked up to Monte. "I got a little jug, out in the car," I said. We walked over behind a hedge of someone's home. I got out this jug and we both had a couple of nips.

Monte gave me and the bottle a smile. "Boy, that's great you brought that booze," he said. "That'll warn us up, make us play good."

I wiped my lips. "Yeah," I said.

So we had another little shot there behind the hedge, and, ahh… just fine.

Pretty soon, I heard Ward blow his whistle. "Hey! You guys. Come on. We're getting ready to move out."

"Oh," I said. "We got to go."

Here we were, two grown men hiding behind a hedge. "Wait a minute," he said, "gimme, ahhh, gimme a little…."

I gave him the bottle.

So we had another little nip and rustled back through the hedge. "That's fine. Gimme the…Monte, you got the stopper? The cap?"

"No I haven't got it. Have you got it?"

"No. I haven't got it."

We both searched our pockets. Neither one of us had the cap. "That's just great! I said. This was a pint bottle and we'd probably drank about a third of it between us. "God, I got to get something for a stopper." We couldn't find a thing. Maybe we can find something on the float. "Come on. Let's go."

So I put the jug in the front pocket of my dark pants and walked along with my finger stuck in it until we got up on the float. I started looking around for something, some paper or something, to make a stopper, because I was afraid this thing was going to slosh out in my pocket. And I couldn't find a thing. I turned to Monte. "Monte, have you got a, something I can make a stopper with?"

He looked around. "Geez, no. I can't find a thing."

"What the hell ever happened to that cap?"

"Boy, I don't know. Can you use a flower?"

(And I don't know to this day what happened to that bottle cap.)

All of a sudden the float lurched forward. All the way down Colorado Boulevard the float was bouncing and jerking, and every time it bounced that booze sloshed out in my pocket and, being alcohol, it was cold and running down my leg and my leg began to get cold. You can imagine—alcohol! I guess I could have dumped it on the flowers, but what a waste. The sun was up by then, but it was still chilly and my whole right pant leg was soaked. You couldn't tell it because they were dark trousers.

I'm telling you, at the end of that parade, I had to be helped off the float. My right leg had absolutely no feeling in it. I told Monte while we were in the parade moving, I kept turning around, "That thing is sloshing around in my pocket. My leg's wet and it's getting numb!"

And he just leaned back, laughing. Monte thought it was very funny. But I didn't. And I'll never forget that first Rose Parade with bourbon trickling down my leg. I'll bet that was a first for a Rose Parade.

Monte has been a good friend and played great drums for us. But I wouldn't put it past him to have had that stopper in his pocket the whole time.

By the way, Harper Goff, our banjo man, met Ward at a rail-fan vacation excursion on the old narrow gauge Denver & Rio Grande in Colorado and they got him into their sessions real fast.

Harper learned banjo on his own as a kid. He had it pretty rough growing up; had to get out on his own early in life, selling newspapers and whatever he could do to make a living. He worked his way through art school and became a marvelous painter and designer. At Disney he was the production designer for Adventureland at Disneyland and on one of Walt's first live action features, *20,000 Leagues Under the Sea*, released in 1954. (Walt won a television award for a behind-the-scenes look at that production.) Harper left the Firehouse Five Plus Two in 1956 and after leaving Disney he limited his work to painting. He settled in Palm Springs doing portraits and other artwork. Harper did art direction for several other movies including one we all remember, *The Thing*, at RKO Studios and for Disney's *The Great Locomotive Chase* (art direction). He did some acting, taught art, and painted magazine covers for *Collier's* and others. After Goff, our banjo player was Dick Roberts who had played professionally. He did several banjo recordings with Red Roundtree on the GOOD TIME JAZZ label. They called themselves The Banjo Kings. Dick was one of the few who did not work regularly at Disney. Later we picked up Bill Newman on banjo. But Harper got us into the Rose Bowl.[1]

Jim MacDonald, who also played drums, was an all-around man at the studio. He started out as a drummer and played a lot of dances aboard luxury liners for years. He came to the studio as a sound effects man in the 1930s. Now in his eighties, he worked at the studio forty-two years! Great talent. He made any sound that was needed—and for the animated cartoons and the live action movies. In *Snow White and the Seven Dwarfs*, Jim worked on the complicated sound effects involved in Grumpy playing the organ and even learned to yodel (for two years) to work out the structure and length of the yodeling scenes. Jim had a woodworking shop at home and made all sorts of gadgets for sound effects. For the exhausted dragonfly in *The Rescuers*, he used the whines and straining of a power saw! We used some of his sound gimmicks on stage with the band. He also did vocal effects. For many years he was the voice of Mickey Mouse. The first years of sound, beginning in 1928, Walt himself did Mickey's voice, but later Jim took over. Jim was the busiest man in the studio and was a big help to me when I started with Disney in 1955. He was on the first Firehouse Five recordings we did, but he was so busy with his many jobs at the studio that he had to drop out of some of the dances and the Mocambo job early on.[2]

And, as I mentioned, we had Monte Mountjoy with whom I played several jobs before the Firehouse Five Plus Two. He played with Bob Wills during the war. He was a pro on drums and played on some of our recordings. He also appeared in the two pictures we made, Universal's *Hit Parade of 1951* and MGM's *Grounds for Marriage* in 1950. No Oscars, but we had fun. We always had fun!

And then when Monte left town, we used Jim MacDonald again until Eddie Forrest joined and remained until the band stopped playing in 1971. Eddie was a very solid showman and old Vaudeville pit musician. He's retired now in Palm Springs. Interesting thing about Eddie: he made many recordings with Gene Autry in the 1930s and 1940s. In fact, he played at many studios in Hollywood, including Disney. Great all-around drummer.

Drummer Eddie Forrest (left) and Alguire. January 1, 1980 Tournament of Roses Parade. Courtesy of Charlotte Bryant McCormack.

Besides Ward, the other great animator in our group was Frank Thomas. He and Ward Kimball were two of the original "Nine Old Men," referred to by Walt Disney as his top animators; guys who did the *real* creating.

The phrase "Nine Old Men" originated around 1946 when an animation board was created at Disney Studios to help with management of the animation department. The nine supervising animators had great influence in the way Disney pictures were created. The expression "Nine Old Men" came about as Walt Disney joked about the judgment and wisdom these men possessed, comparing them to the nine justices of the Supreme Court. These men included Woolie Reitherman, Frank Thomas, Ollie Johnston, and Ward Kimball. I worked with these four a lot. The others were Les Clark, Eric Larson, Milt Kahl, John Lounsbery, and Marc Davis. Later, the press became enthralled with the title, "Nine Old Men," and the studio publicity department continued to use it as a symbol of the old guard—the original animators who had been there since the 1930s and 1940s. Under these nine men, there was a significant change in the method of casting animation. A supervising animator began to design and animate all the key characters in a scene. By doing this, they were able to get maximum emotional effect from the animation interplay. There were always problems and sticky decisions and the director was an arbitrator, but Walt always had the final word. All of the "Nine Old Men" either had learned their craft from the top animators in the early 1930s or were strongly influenced by their work. They all had one main desire: to put the finest possible entertainment out to the public and the system worked remarkably well for over twenty-five years.

So our little Firehouse band had two of the top nine animators. And the other members of the band were very talented artists and technicians too.

Frank Thomas was very intelligent. The son of a college president (Fresno State) he graduated from Stanford with honors. But Frank had been drawing since childhood for his own amusement. "I found out people paid money for drawing pictures, so," he said, "that's what I decided to do." Like Ward, he also started out at about fifteen bucks a week in the 1930s. Somewhere along the way, he learned to play the piano, especially jazz piano.

As with Ward Kimball, he moved up fast to drawing lead characters at Disney. He worked on most all of the animation classics including, in my opinion, the best one: *Snow White and the Seven Dwarfs*. He worked two and a half years on *Sleeping Beauty* and did Captain Hook in *Peter Pan*. *101 Dalmatians* was another film Frank animated. Some great scenes Frank created were Bambi and Thumper skating on the ice, Thumper teaching Bambi to say "Birr-d," Mad Madam Mim from *The Sword in the Stone*, the stepmother in *Cinderella*, the cute doorknob that talked in *Alice in Wonderland*, Robin Hood disguised as a stork, and the Seven Dwarfs sneaking up to attack the intruder (*Snow White*) sleeping in their beds. In *101 Dalmatians*, he even animated Pongo blushing. Impossible, but true.

Frank Thomas was one of the most sincere, honest men I have ever known and, like the other animators—perhaps even more so—he was intensely motivated in his effort to get the maximum emotional response from an audience. He had a great ability to draw characters in such a way to get emotional responses by the drawing alone. Frank never considered time restrictions in his work. He simply had to do the job right, whatever time it took. He was painstaking in his effort to pull out every drop of entertainment potential in not only the drawings, but in all aspects of scenic structure. He has been able to portray rather complicated personalities in characters and has done many memorable and complex scenes, such as the dwarfs weeping around Snow White's bier and the poignant spaghetti scene from *Lady and the Tramp*, among many others. I can say, having watched Frank and talking to those who know him, that he was never satisfied with his work. He was always striving for a little more. But in spite of Frank's obsession with perfection, he was always ready to help out others and his advice was often sought on all phases of animation, including music and storylines. Frank is a humble man. He expected the best of his colleagues, but did it with good nature and humor.

With the Firehouse Five Plus Two, Frank played great piano and was dependable; no nonsense. And he still had a great sense of humor.

In 1952, we had played so many places, some up until 2:00 a.m. Back at the studio by 8:00 a.m. We were exhausted and were all being threatened with divorces if we didn't slow down. Frank told Ward: "We're supposed to be playing for fun. Maybe we ought to quit for a while." We had a little meeting about the long hours and decided to slow down—at least until we felt like playing again! (And that didn't last too long.) But we did turn down a lot of offers after that. I would say in the summer of 1952 we turned down at least $200,000 in jobs, but golly, there were kids to play with, yard work to do, and some sleep to catch up on.[3]

During their hiatus in 1952 and '53, the Firehouse Five Plus Two musicians continued to enjoy music. This jam session gathered members of New Orleans musician George Lewis' band, the Banjo Kings, and Firehouse Five. (L to R): Slow Drag Pavageau, Joe Watkins, George Lewis, Lawrence Marrero, Frank Thomas, Tom Sharpsteen, Red Roundtree, Albert "Fernandez" Walters, Jerry Hamm (standing in back), Alton Purnell, Ward Kimball, Danny Alguire, Dick Roberts, Harper Goff, Monte Mountjoy (standing in back), likely Perry Botkin, Ed Penner, Jim Robinson, and Chloe Kimball (on the sofa). Courtesy of The Ward Kimball Family.

Erdman Penner ("Ed") on tuba was one of the leading writers at Disney Studio. He died suddenly in 1956 of lung cancer.... Originally from Canada and a saxophone player, Ed was also a concert violinist. That was his original ambition after music school in New York City, a concert violin career. But, he gave that up to draw cartoons!

After moving from New York City to Disney he said he quickly realized he wasn't good enough to make it with the kind of artists Disney had, so he got into the story department. He could write and draw sketches for the storyboards too. This was his niche and he became a leading story man. He worked on many films. His last was *Lady and the Tramp*. Ed was a magnificent screenwriter for twenty years. He received credits on *Pinocchio, Fantasia, Cinderella, Ichabod and Mr. Toad, Lady and the Tramp,* and *Sleeping Beauty,* among others. Ed was also into playing jazz. He even learned to play tuba (he had a good ear) for us. He started on bass sax, but switched to tuba on our request so we could have that old band sound. He was a good friend and it crushed us all to lose him so suddenly. Ralph Ball—who used to play for Turk Murphy—took his place until we got Don Kinch, about the time we made *The Firehouse Five Goes to Sea* album.

That was the album when Ward made his profound comment, "From the beginning of time, men have celebrated The Sea, the mother of all life. We, too, wanted to pay our tribute to the majesty of the oceans, the mighty force of the tides, and besides that, our tuba player was eager to see how low he could blow on 'Asleep in the Deep'!"[4]

Another great writer, musical director, and composer for Disney, George Bruns played tuba for many years when we needed him. "The eternal substitute" we called him, because George was a natural musician who could play almost any instrument. He had played with Turk Murphy and with the Castle Jazz Band in Portland, Oregon. But his real forte was composing movie and television scores for Disney. The "Ballad of Davy Crockett" was George's creation among many others. In *Sleeping Beauty* he adapted Tchaikovsky's music to the screen and he did a great job in *The Jungle Book*.[5]

Clarke Mallery was another animator at Disney and played clarinet with the early Firehouse Five Plus Two. He was an Artie Shaw fan, but came around to the Dixieland style which he grew to love, too. Clarke set some records in the high jump for the University of Southern California in his college days. He was on some of our first albums, but later dropped out of the band and studio for personal reasons.

We first heard George Probert on soprano sax in Frisco. Turk had taken over Lu Watters' band when Lu departed. The Firehouse Five Plus Two flew up there twice a year to play at Earthquake McGoon's. George was playing soprano sax with Bob Scobey's Band in Oakland, across the bay. We liked his style. I told Ward about him, and luckily, a week or so later, Scobey played a concert at the Pasadena Civic Auditorium. Ward and I went to the concert, and Ward liked what he heard. So after the show, we hustled backstage and talked to George. Ward and I both thought the soprano sax would go better with our raucous style than would a clarinet.[6]

As luck would have it, Scobey's band soon took off on tour back east, and George didn't want to go. So Ward asked him to come to Los Angeles, where he would arrange for a job with Disney.

George had graduated from Stanford the previous year and was a smart and talented guy! Things worked out beautifully. Ward featured George's solos a lot, and the crowds loved his playing.

The personnel changes in the band were so infrequent that the style never seemed to vary. Usually, it was almost impossible to not have dozens of changes in a band membership over a twenty-two year period.

Don Kinch took over the tuba chores from George Bruns in about 1962 or so. Don was a good trumpet man in Turk Murphy's band about 1957 and played several tours with Turk. But when Bruns got too busy scoring pictures at the studio, we brought in Don from Portland, his home after he left Turk's band.

It sounds like the band was playing musical chairs, but stretched over the twenty-two years that the band played together, there were infrequent changes, so everything moved along real easy and pleasant.

We all realized that there could just be one leader; Ward did all the talking, and we'd play the music. We never had any hassles on the bandstand, and everyone got along fine. The common love of music was the adhesive that held the band together when we played. Outside of playing, a few of us managed to chum around together.[7]

We made our last membership change during the last few years of the sixties. After Frank Thomas checked out of the band to concentrate on an animation book, *The Illusion of Life: Disney Animation* with another of the "Nine Old Men," Ollie Johnston, we brought in K.O. Eckland on piano and Billy Newman, a good banjo man, and a great guitar player.[8] We used the guitar instead of banjo for the first time on one of our numbers on the last album we recorded.

Finally, we used several great men as subs or "guests" over the years. Stan Wrightsman and Marvin Ash on piano, both fine studio musicians, who got a kick out of playing with our "have fun" band; George Bruns substituted for Ward on trombone when necessary, and Kinch could sub for me on trumpet when necessary. No matter what came up, we could make the job and still have the Firehouse spirit!

Don Kinch (left) and Alguire playing together with the Firehouse Five Plus Two at a jazz club concert in Southern California in the late 1960s. The band often utilized two cornets in the front line starting in 1955. Courtesy of Chris Tyle.

The Firehouse Five Plus Two marches down Main Street U.S.A. at Dixieland at Disneyland on September 30, 1967. L to R: Don Kinch, trumpet; George Probert, soprano sax; Danny Alguire, cornet; Billy Newman, banjo; Ward Kimball, trombone. Courtesy of the New Orleans Jazz Museum.

We rarely had problems, except for that famous "Temptation" act with the woman dancer, and the time we were in a jazz concert in Monterey, California and our fire hats were left on the plane, so we played bareheaded in the rain!

We recorded 144 tunes on twelve different albums. Probably the most interesting tune that the band composed was for the Los Angeles Obstetrical and Gynecological concert: "The Baby Snatcher Blues." But they were all great. All fun. I wish it was possible to bring the sound of our brand of Dixieland to these pages.

I told Ward one day, "We ought to make an album called *The Firehouse Five, the Band that Could Have Made a Fortune*." Because at one time, we were the hottest thing in the country. But maybe it was fortunate that we didn't do it.

Les Koenig, the Paramount Studio film writer and jazz fan, once noted on one of our albums: "Many explanations have been offered for the Firehouse Five's spectacular rise, ranging from 'sociological' analyses to notions of jealous brethren in other less successful bands attributing their success to the fact they wear fire hats and ride in a firetruck. One analyst appeared in print with the theory their popularity signifies a longing on the part of The Public to return to the happier days of The Twenties, before the A & H Bombs, and the Cold War. They have also been labeled 'a reaction to bop.' Perhaps the simplest explanation comes closest to the truth. They are in the unique and extremely fortunate position of playing only because they enjoy it. Their enthusiasm for jazz and enjoyment in playing are contagious and have been responsible for making a great many people for the first time aware of the vitality and gaiety inherent in the traditional jazz style. Perhaps a good part of their success in this connection comes from the fact they are not literal copyists of the past. They brought their own personalities, and a fresh, original approach to the jazz classics, taking them out of the museum and making them live again for new generations."

The Firehouse Five Plus Two atop Ward Kimball's 1914 LaFrance fire engine around 1959-60, likely for a GOOD TIME JAZZ publicity shoot. L to R: Frank Thomas, piano and bass drum; Eddie Forrest, drums; Danny Alguire, cornet; George Probert, soprano sax; Don Kinch, tuba; Ward Kimball, trombone; Dick Roberts, banjo. Courtesy of the Ward Kimball Family.

As Ward Kimball put it in the insert for a recently produced digital disc remastered from originals: "During the 1950s we played concerts, dances, weddings, parades, civic affairs, and benefits throughout the west. We made movies at MGM and Universal, played for Bing Crosby's golf tournaments and radio shows and appeared on national television with such diversified luminaries as the Disney Mouseketeers, Milton Berle, Ed Wynn, and Lawrence Welk, culminating with over fifteen years of summer appearances at Disneyland. By the time we decided to retire in 1971, we managed to record twelve albums which have sold worldwide. All this in our 'spare time.' And we did it for the enjoyment."

Members of the Firehouse Five Plus Two perform on July 4, 1957 during a caravan aboard the soon to be closed Pacific Electric "Red Car" trains in Los Angeles. L to R: Dick Roberts, banjo; Eddie Forrest, drums; Frank Thomas, bass drum; Danny Alguire, cornet; Ward Kimball, trombone; George Probert, soprano sax. Courtesy of the Ward Kimball Family.

The Firehouse Five Plus Two recorded twelve albums over twenty-two years because we never could seem to all get together at the same time. Guys married, had kids, PTA meetings, yard work. Crazy band, and, for me, it was a far cry from the 97th Street Corral Dance

Hall and T. Texas Tyler. But it was a continuation of jazz which I really started playing, in a unique sense, with the great Bob Wills.

At last I was entrenched in jazz. Often I thought back to the nights in Kansas City's black neighborhoods—the great jazz—and to the Bob Wills' special brand of jazz. And here I was. There is no other music so full of vibrancy. It's amazing how a few sounds from vibrating air can change moods or prod the body to dance. Some music is oppressive and some comes straight from hell. But Dixieland is happy music. It will live forever.

Chapter Endnotes:

1. Harper Goff was born on March 16, 1911 in Fort Collins, Colorado. The town's picturesque architecture would later serve as an inspiration in Goff's design of Main Street U.S.A. at Disneyland. His banjo skills were singled out in the Firehouse Five Plus Two's early years of popular success, and to this day, Disneyland guests can view a tribute to Goff in a window on the second story of the Adventureland Bazaar proclaiming "Prof. Harper Goff's oriental tattoo parlor and banjo lessons."
2. James MacDonald (1906-1991) had worked as a professional drummer before joining the Disney Sound Effects Department in 1934. His career at the Walt Disney Studios lasted 48 years, and included his succession of Walt Disney as the voice of Mickey Mouse in the mid-1940s.
3. In an additional fragment discovered with Alguire's manuscript, Frank Thomas would write that "we tried never to play every night in the same place, same tunes, same everything. We tried to play only on weekends because we needed the frustrations of a week at work to build up a head of steam for Friday night. We had seen other bands around the country who sat while they played, sometimes even

reading a book while another player was taking a chorus. We vowed that we would never play to that point of obvious boredom. We stood, we moved about, we enjoyed playing. Friday nights, the music 'had claws.' We tore into it with a savage response to the things that had gone wrong at work that week. Saturdays, we settled down to good, inventive jazz, traditional tunes and spontaneous gags. If we played again on Sundays, we felt we had already played every note on our instruments and were starting to repeat ourselves. The sparkle was fading and our playing was slower and more ordinary. I doubt we would have been so successful if we had to keep playing every night."

4. Original Firehouse Five Plus Two tuba player and Disney story writer Ed Penner passed away on November 10, 1956. The following year, the band released their album "Firehouse Plus Two Goes to Sea," and expressed their grief over the "heavy loss" in the accompanying liner notes. "[Ed] was not only a fellow musician," it continued, "but a colleague at the studio, and a good friend." In an additional fragment discovered with Alguire's manuscript, Frank Thomas would recount Penner saying, "Danny is a natural gentleman—he didn't have to learn his manners, or to be polite or helpful, he just is."

5. George Bruns (1914-1983) was a musical force at the Walt Disney Studios. The Oregon native cut his teeth in the west coast jazz community for years before his hiring at Disney in 1953 to assist in the adaptation of Tchaikovsky's ballet for *Sleeping Beauty* (1959). He contributed songs and musical scores to dozens of renowned films, television shows, and theme park attractions, including the national hit, "The Ballad of Davy Crockett." He became the Firehouse Five's virtuoso substitute player, taking over on multiple instruments as needed, primarily the tuba. He retired home to Sandy, Oregon, not far from where Alguire had retired

himself. Don Kinch, another Firehouse Five tuba player, was also an Oregon resident.

6. Ward Kimball hired George Probert *before* the Firehouse Five played at Earthquake McGoon's in San Francisco. They may have been playing at the Italian Village. Probert claimed that Kimball came to a party where the Bob Scobey band was playing, to pick up pianist Wally Rose – who was substituting for Frank Thomas. Kimball liked what he heard of Probert with Scobey and told someone—possibly Alguire—"Someday I'm gonna get that guy in the band!"

7. In an additional fragment that accompanied Alguire's manuscript, Ward Kimball would recount that "before Danny joined our Firehouse band he had played with quite a few Country Western groups like Bob Wills and had picked up a collection of cornpone stories. I remember one night we were on stage getting ready to play a concert when Frank Thomas, our piano man, said that his piano mike wasn't working. During this interruption while I was trying to fix the problem, Danny (an Okie) walked up to the front stage mike and said to the waiting jazz fans, 'While Ward is trying to fix the piano mic, I'd like to say a few words about *Texas*…you know, now that Alaska is the biggest state in the union, we've got a new name for Texas: *Baja Oklahoma!*' After the yucking died down a little, Danny quickly followed with, 'And I hear that they're going to black top Texas for the world's biggest *parking lot!*' The audience got such a big kick out of Danny's remarks that forever after, if there was any interruption during one of our performances, I'd tell Danny, 'Tell 'em about Texas, Dan.'"

8. Originally published in 1981 by Abbeville Press, *The Illusion of Life: Disney Animation* is among the quintessential works on American animation.

Chapter 20:

"I Can't Believe That You're in Love With Me"

For me, in the early years, the more playing the better. I wasn't making the money Ward Kimball and the rest were making with Disney, but Ward helped change all that.

"Dan, I'm going to get you a job at Disney Studios," Ward said to me one day, "so you can be with us. I want to get you in on the ground floor, a good position with good money. Now, it won't happen just yet, but Disney's expansion into television is coming, so be ready."

I enjoyed playing in the Firehouse Five, but there wasn't enough money coming in, and I wasn't feeling too secure. I couldn't be sure when Ward could get me a job at Disney and even though my wife Betty was working, the band didn't play enough. I needed more income.

Les Koenig had started this record company, and expanded by opening a big wholesale record distributorship. He took on more labels and they hired a guy named Jack Lewerke to run it. Jack really knew the wholesale record business.

I drove over to the shop one day. "Hey, Jack, what about giving me a job here? Day job."

"You want to work here?"

"Well sure. I want to do more than just play with the Firehouse Five. Besides, I need more income."

"All right," he said.

So I started to work and pretty soon, I began to learn the business, selling records. After all, I learned to sell clocks back in Texas in 1933! And I continued to play. Of course, being with the band and working for owner Koenig, I could get off work if I had to go out of town on a band job such as the Reno gigs.

Bill Harrah of Harrah's Club in Reno, who had flipped over us in San Diego, contacted Ward in early 1949 and in August, we played the first of his biennial old car tours in Reno. He paid our way ($100 a week) plus all expenses, and I mean all expenses—lodging, food, everything—to come up to Reno and play for these weeks on long antique car tours. We could take our wives and each time, it got bigger and bigger. We'd go every other year, on the even years, from 1950 through 1966. Each tour lasted a whole week. After 1966, the government would no longer allow a tax break for Harrah for this tour, so the bubble burst.

By 1954, I was making more money by playing with the band and working at the record distributor. So things were coming together. Betty quit working. I thought back to all the dumb decisions I had made before and during the war and figured maybe, at last, I was getting a little sense in my head.

So I told Betty, "Well, we're going to move over to the San Fernando Valley. We'll be closer to the Studio when I go to work at Disney's." I called a realtor to sell the house in Inglewood we bought in 1951 on a veteran's loan.

I thought, "Let's see: Owned this house about four years. Paid $10,000.00. Why not ask $14,000.000."

About then, my wife spoke up. "We want $16,950.00!"

"She is out of her mind," I thought.

The realtor looked around some more. "Well, it's a nice little house, but I'm afraid you're asking a little too much. But we'll list it for $16,950.00 and come down if we have to."

About a week later, I came home one night from work and Betty met me at the door. "Guess what?" she said.

"What?"

"We sold the house."

"You're kidding!"

"$16,950.00," she told me with a cute, but smug expression.

I couldn't believe it. We caught the right person at the right time. A couple bought it. The wife had her mother with her, and there was a little one bedroom house in back. It was the perfect spot for her mother. They say that for every man, there's a woman, and for every house, there's a buyer! Must be true. But they did all right too. They later sold it for a good profit.

When I first came to L.A. in 1936, I luckily ran into Bill Kernberger, an old friend from Kansas City. Bill was active in real estate, so I had him looking for a house over in the San Fernando Valley. I told him what we wanted, something near the studio in Burbank.

So, one day, Bill called me. "Hey, I want you and Betty to get right out here. I think I found a place that you'll like."

"We'll be right over." It was on a Sunday.

We met him in the Valley and he took us to this place in Studio City. It was only ten minutes from the Disney Studios. It was a cute little house; pretty yard, and a little white picket fence around it; two bedrooms, nice kitchen, big living room, fireplace, garage, and a perfect location. So, we bought it for $13,500.00.

I thought it was a pretty good deal, although it seemed like a lot of money. Of course, a lot depended on getting the Disney job.

Walt Disney knew he was going to start his television series in 1954. They were gearing up for hiring additional help. It was a pretty small studio at that time, only about 1200 employees, and they had just begun to build Disneyland.

Ward Kimball kept saying, "Well, anytime now, they're going to start adding more help. So hold on." Finally in April, 1955, Ward called me. "Get on out here. I think it's all set for your job."

So I went to my boss, Jack Lewerke, and told him I had a chance to work at Disney's. "God, yes," he said. "Get on out there, and good luck." Great guy and a fine friend.

Ward took me upstairs to vice-president, Bill Anderson.[1] Here I am, forty-two years old, and I thought, "Oh, boy. I don't know if they're going to hire me or not. At my age? Starting a new career?"

But Ward had plenty of influence, because he'd been there since 1934. By this time, he was one of the top animation directors. He had respect.

"Here's Dan," he said. "He plays in the Firehouse Five, and we want him over here where he can be close by, so we can practice at noon. Let's put him to work, Bill. How about it?"

I thought, "God! Pretty blunt. Here's Dan. How about it?"

"Yeah," Bill said. "We'll find a place for him." (The old thing, you know, "It's not what you know, it's who you know.") I've had my share of good luck! But again, it was music that got me in that position. You've got to go with your talent. It took me a long time to learn it.

Pretty routine. Filled out an application and went to work at the Walt Disney Studios.

They put me up in the music department, which was a good place for me to start, because Jim MacDonald (the voice of Mickey Mouse), who was the drummer in the Firehouse Five, was also the sound effects man and a helpful guy with everything in the studio. He could do almost anything. I began to learn sound effects and timing soundtracks. At the same time, they taught me how to time out a six-minute short cartoon on a moviola.

My first assignment was on one of the last cartoon shorts they made. I guess that's why Walt wanted to branch out and get into T.V., because by this time, due to T.V.'s influence, theaters didn't care for the short cartoons. They only wanted full-length animated features. In the old days, they'd show you the news, a cartoon, and then the feature. When T.V. came, however, the demand for cartoon shorts increased again. They stopped making the short cartoons at Disney for theaters. We were concentrating on full-length live action and animated features, which ran an hour and twenty minutes.

One of the last short cartoons they made was *Chips Ahoy* with Chip and Dale, the little chipmunks.[2] So they taught me how to time out the picture, indicating where the exact action would occur by the use of a footage counter, which would be set at zero on the first frame of the picture. I would just chart out the action by the footage counter: steps, hits, whistles, and any effects where sound was needed. We got the effects from a huge sound effects library, and cut them into the picture. If the exact effect wasn't on file, we would record a new effect to fit the new action.

With *Chips Ahoy*, at forty-two, I had set sail on a new career—because of music. And what a glorious career it would be. With the characters, the sounds and the music, we made a whole world a little happier. As I worked and observed the concerted efforts of so many talented and devoted artists and technicians at Disney, I gained tremendous respect for the organization. They put every ounce of effort into maximum entertainment. No shortcuts. No rush to make the dollar. They cared about quality and decency.

Who can measure the effect Disney features would have on so many lives—children and adults—all over the world? And I was part of it. The money really didn't matter. I was happy, and even got paid for it!

It was a start, but I had no idea how much more would come.

Chapter Endnotes:

1. Bill Anderson (1911-1997) was a production manager for the Walt Disney Studios when he hired Alguire in 1955. He had begun his Disney tenure in 1943 in the Production Control Department. He became an important figure in Disney's live-action production of both television and feature films, including *Zorro* (1957-59), *Old Yeller* (1957), *Swiss Family Robinson* (1960), and *The Happiest Millionaire* (1967). He

retired from the Studios in 1975 as a member of the board of directors.
2. Released on February 26, 1956, the short was directed by Jack Kinney and starred Donald Duck along with Chip and Dale. Alguire's colleague and bandmate Jim MacDonald was the voice of Chip.

Chapter 21:

"Fidgety Feet"

I was kind of slow at first, but Jim MacDonald was a big help. I worked about six months in the music department, learning the system.

By 1956, they set up another animation unit and each animation director had his own unit with a secretary, assistant director, a story man or two, a couple of sketchmen, two background men, a layout man, and eight or ten animators and their assistants.

When I got moved into the unit, *Sleeping Beauty* was being developed, so I became assistant director to the new director, Wolfgang Reitherman, who had been with Disney almost since the studio started—a top animator and one of the "Nine Old Men." He had been a directing animator which meant he had about ten animators under him. Each director was given a section of the picture. They had three feature directors working on *Sleeping Beauty* and they needed another one to push it along. It had been kind of slow getting off the ground. But Walt wanted it finished, so he set up this new unit.[1]

As the new assistant director, there was a lot I had to learn. Mainly, I had to keep track of the picture, know each scene and distribute scenes to the animators, along with many new duties that came up. I had plenty to do and loved every minute of it. I even looked forward to going to work on Mondays.

In the development of each scene of the feature, we recorded dialogue first; called in people for auditions until we found the right voices. The casting department lined up potentials. We might have thirty people; maybe two in the morning, two in the afternoon.

We looked for a certain type of character, like for the prince in *Sleeping Beauty*, a "macho," youngish voice—what you would imagine a prince would look and talk like. So, we would audition these voices, put them on a record and listen. "Naw, that's not him. That's not it." Finally, they would all agree. "Yeah, that's the voice!" Then we would check the selected voice with Walt. He usually went along with our selection, but not always.

The casting department was informed of the decision and casting made the financial arrangements with "the voice." These animation features would run three or four years in the making, so they set up a pretty firm contract. Disney would guarantee them so much money, then "the voices" had to guarantee Disney so many calls, like eight or ten, whatever we needed, with options for more sessions, because what they could record in a day would take three or four months to animate and there were often changes along the way, or the new character would be given more lines.

And sometimes, going for production, we would have, let's say, the voice of Sleeping Beauty and the Prince, and they would work together at the microphones.[2] Sometimes we would record them separately, and then put them together later on separate tracks. It was better to record them separately so you could maneuver. We might have five or six soundtracks running anyway, so we had room to spread them around. All would be evenly balanced in the final sound mix.

I'd always been a guy that liked detail. It's kind of like playing music. You play it right or you play it wrong. I always liked to play a tune right. We worked very closely with the film editors. Very important that we got along, as we worked a lot together.

Regarding the animator's actual drawing of a character's unique voice, Ollie Johnston had this to say:

"As animators we always closed our eyes and listened to the voice to see if it inspired us to see expressions and acting. We tried to avoid watching the talent and just listened. We listened for the guys who could project personality and most of all had a sense of entertainment—that ability to read the line like it was something you just thought of. That was what was so great about Phil Harris—he never sounded rehearsed."

At times it was better to record them separately because, like in the case of Phil Harris and Eva Gabor, he unknowingly dominated her so that she couldn't perform with any authority.

Some animators did use mirrors on occasion but most of the time we would just visualize the action as we listened to the dialogue. As you move your face around to get the expressions, you can feel what is happening to your mouth and cheeks and eyes without looking at the mirror.

The directors used a series of four-by-eight-foot storyboards where a continuous series of actual sketches were pinned up and dialogue printed underneath; in other words, a big comic strip. We got the pictures and dialogue right first. We then called in Walt for a meeting at the storyboard, before any voices were recorded. I was always in the meetings.

We never knew what Walt would say. He listened to everyone. "This part in here seems weak," he would say. "Anyone got any ideas how to strengthen it?" and maybe someone—he loved group talk—would say, "Well, we could have him do this and so…." Walt was a "chooser." He encouraged a lot of suggestions. And then, he chose what he liked.

Of course, Walt always had great ideas. And, strangely enough, sometimes Walt would be stuck, too. He would say, "Well, I just don't know how we can straighten that out. Let's let it stew." That was one of his favorite expressions. "When anybody comes up with some ideas, we'll have another meeting," he would say.

Of course, everyone came up with new ideas and sometimes even Walt would phone the director. "Hey. Let's have a meeting. I got some ideas on that sticky part." Walt wanted the right answer. He didn't care who it came from. But he knew when it was right. Boy, did he know when it was right!

No doubt, Walt was a genius. For years, I studied Walt a lot, in the trenches, where the real work was done, where the tough decisions were made. I watched the wheels turning in Walt's brain. And there were a lot of tell-tale signs. Walt's facial expressions and actions often would indicate whether things were going good or going badly.

His time was valuable. It seemed, strangely, that he never hurried, but he hated wasting time, too. Walt could be critical and demanding. He wanted quality, but he pushed to get the footage out. He had incentive programs, bonuses for fast work, but he didn't hesitate to cut out material he didn't like and start over, because quality was the priority, not cost. If something bored him or sounded "sticky," his hand would be on the arm of the chair, fingers drumming. We knew that sign.

One time on *Sleeping Beauty*, "This is going to be a good sequence here," Walt said. "We got it. Put it in production. I can't see any weaknesses." He was in a very jovial mood that day, and seemed reluctant to leave, which was unusual. We were all kind of laughing and joking because the meeting had been very productive.

And I must explain, everything we worked on had to be on our work card called a "charge card." I had to turn in a card once a week and account for each hour with a charge number. If I worked down in cutting for four hours, I'd put 60085 down, or whatever, so bookkeeping could account for the time and charge it to that department. A story meeting had another number, and so on.

At this particular meeting, Walt was laughing. "You know, you guys ought to get me down here more often." Of course, he was just kidding. "I'm a good story man. And you get me cheap. You know, I don't even have a charge number!" That broke us up.

One thing about Walt Disney, genius that he was, and I think all geniuses are this way, they can't come up with a perfect answer at any given moment. They are only human. But they would find the answer.

We might not see him for a month or so until another meeting. Oh, we might pass him in the hall or cafeteria. Everyone called him Walt. He didn't want to be called Mr. Disney. It was, "Hello, Walt." I often rode up the elevator with him. The building was four stories including the basement. My office was on the second floor, Walt's on the third. It made me nervous at first until I got to know him better. He would say, "Good morning, Dan." It was always hard for me to know what he would say next. Fortunately, it was only one flight up, so I wouldn't have to say more than, "How are you?" or "It's a nice day," or whatever. Although I always felt in awe of him, he made me (and everyone else) feel like one of the family.

And after a few years, he got to know me pretty well. But Walt was the type of guy who didn't want anyone to promote him; no "buddy-buddy" stuff. You wouldn't rush up and put your arm around Walt Disney and say, "Well, how you doing, Walt? How did you like the picture? How do you think things are going?" No way. Hands off. That's something you learned early. Well, of course, I wasn't about to put my arm around his shoulder, anyway!

One time, a new story man came to work at the studio. At his first meeting with Walt, he was going to "read" the new storyboard. When all had assembled, this guy picked up his pointer stick. "O.K., Walt," he said, "this is the way it's going to be." And he proceeded to go through the story. Next day, he was gone. No one, but no one, was going to tell Walt how it was going to be!

When I first started out, it was a one-man studio, and it remained so, until Walt's death. But Walt certainly knew and used his animators to the best advantage for all and, through his leadership, the film kept rolling. It was a wonder to behold: characters, voices, sound effects, music, and story all came together under the expert baton of the maestro himself, Walt Disney.

Chapter Endnotes:

1. For an in-depth view of Wolfgang Reitherman's animation units and Alguire's work as an assistant director, see the Appendix.
2. In this case, voice actors Mary Costa (born 1930) and Bill Shirley (1921-1989) respectively.

Chapter 22:

"Storyville Blues"

Born in Germany, Woolie Reitherman, my boss, moved to America as a child. He had that teutonic drive—a compulsive worker striving for the best, and he expected the best from all of his unit. If you did good work, he told you. If you "blew it" on something, he told you about that, too. But he was a fair man. He worked as hard as any of us. Day after day, he was so involved in his work we had to remind him that it was after 5:00 p.m. and time to quit. "Oh, it is?" he would say.

In his work, Woolie Reitherman stubbornly pursued perfection. He was probably the most physical and forceful animator of the group. His work reflected immense power, for example, with Monstro the whale in *Pinocchio*, the dinosaurs in *Fantasia*, and the dragon in *Sleeping Beauty*. He had enormous strength and stamina to keep track of all the people under him and a great ability to pull everything together near the last months of a feature.

One day, when only Woolie and I were in his room, he was running a reel on the moviola, running a scene back and forth, back and forth, to correct something. There was not a sound, but that of the moviola, and Woolie mumbling to himself. Finally, he stopped and turned to me. "That's it! That'll fix it. You got it?"

"Got what?" I asked.

He whipped his head around to me, irritated. "The way we're going to fix the scene!" he said.

"You haven't told me anything about the scene yet, Woolie." He stared at me a moment and then had to laugh. He was so absorbed in fixing the scene, so alive in that other world—the story world—that it took him a few moments to realize what had happened.

Wolfgang Reitherman. Everyone called him "Woolie." What a guy. He started out painting in watercolor, but somehow or another, he got to Disney in 1933 and into animation. He was one of the early men and was another of whom Walt called the "Nine Old Men." (Frank Thomas and Ollie Johnston, two more of the "Nine" with whom I worked, came aboard in 1934 and 1935 when Walt expanded in order to make *Snow White*. The first period at the studio was 1923 to 1928. The "early" period was considered 1929 to 1933. The "Golden Age" started in 1934 and continued to 1942.) These nine men got all the "juicy" scenes to create, or to hand out to their assistants. They'd do the main model setting and the majority of the "tough" action. They, along with Walt, did the real *creating*, the scenes and characters that make us laugh or cry or scream. They were largely responsible for the great moments in Disney animation that we all remember with a glow or a lump in our throats.

When Woolie became a director, he didn't draw anymore, except to make corrective drawings. On the moviola, the screen was about ten by fourteen inches, and it had pegs in it so that you could put a piece of transparent drawing paper over the screen and draw over a frame. He'd take a pencil. "Now, I want this mouth open wide! Ugly and mean." And he'd draw it correctly over the old drawing and indicate the change to his animators. He made the difference.

But he practically quit drawing. He knew what he wanted, and he got it. And Walt liked his work. Woolie was a good director because he could "move" a picture along. We were a pretty tight-knit unit that could turn out the footage.

The animators first made rough pencil drawings. They sent out their drawings by 3 p.m. to be photographed, frame by frame, and got them back the next day so the animator could run it (like a movie) for accuracy—timing, dialogue sync, action, etc. He might send out two or three tests, until he got the scenes drawn right *in pencil*. Pencil tests were cheap. When it was okay in pencil, it was to be inked and painted. If it worked in pencil, it would work in color.

That's how they got everything perfected. Once it got into color, the scene was rarely changed. This may be a little confusing. To simplify, essentially what we did with a "pencil test" was to watch part of the animated movie drawn in pencil only, and make sure it was right before it was inked and colored.

I remember some guys left Disney and went to work at Hanna-Barbera and other studios, doing *The Flintstones* and other cartoons. "Saturday morning quickies," we called them.

But Disney didn't do those. Our drawings had to be fully animated before they went to color. The only way the quickie studios could make money on those Saturday morning cartoons was by speed. The lips were never in "sync." They just opened and closed while the character was talking, but they didn't attempt to get lip sync or form perfect words like they did at Disney where both mouth and body movements were fully animated. And what a difference that alone made in emotional impact.

In the cheap cartoons, they'd draw the body one time and then just freeze it, put a piece of paper over it, and use the same body drawing while they changed the head movements and the mouth a little. They put that stuff out fast. A strong story and good voices carried it. But it was adequate only.

But not Disney. The average full-length cartoon, like *101 Dalmatians* or *Sword in the Stone* took about three to four years to do; about two million drawings per feature. ("It often took ten or twelve tries to get a drawing the way we wanted it," says Ollie Johnston. "There are many throwaways, so the actual number in final production is around 500,000.") It might have run three or $4 million to make, which seemed expensive then, but nothing like now, with inflation. Today (in the late 1980s), the cost is four or five times more to make a seventy-five minute animation feature like the earlier ones. Disney did it right. He cared about feelings more than profit. Disney sincerely wanted to entertain, to do the little things that brought a smile, a laugh, or a few tears. He knew human nature.

Whether it was a duck, a mouse, a cricket, or some other creature, the character had feelings and he would touch the human heart with joy or pathos.

In the old days, before *Snow White and the Seven Dwarfs*, animated movies and cartoons were formulated so that human emotions, other than laughter and joy, you know "zany stuff," were seldom evoked. With *Snow White*, animation reached new milestones in audience emotional response with sadness, fear, suspense, grief, and more. The scene where the Huntsman is sent by the jealous Queen to stab Snow White in the dark forest was one such innovation in animation art because they were *cartoon* characters (usually associated with laughs) in a serious, dramatic scene creating fear, suspense, and compassion. What a daring experiment it was. Walt was very worried about the audience reaction. But he gambled and left it in. Of course, it turned out to be very effective and had a monumental impact on the future of animation.

Disney grossed, in sales, about ten to $15 million per picture, and that was considered a good profit in the fifties and sixties. But nowadays, if they make one for twelve or fifteen million, they'd have to gross maybe fifty or sixty million to come out with a good profit.

One particular job I had with Woolie, and I had many, was trouble-shooter. I had to keep track of the picture. I had charts on the wall, reflecting every scene in the picture. I could tell Woolie on any given day where scenes were located, what stage of operation it was in, whether it was in pencil test, or whether it was being sent to be inked and colored, or whether the final drawing in color was on the work reel. Every scene, every sequence, organized.

My job, assistant director, was not like any other job. I should have been called a "Coordinator": work with film editors, keep the entire movie organized, cut in new scenes, put in sound effects, add music.

The final music wasn't written until the picture was nearly complete. But, we would begin to add sound effects, and, so the picture wouldn't drag, we'd add some temporary music which I thought was in the mood of the scene. I would take it from some old pictures or use some music from the classics. Later we replaced it with the final music. It was fun, and a challenge to match up music to a sequence. Called "tracking the picture" with music, it helped the sound while you were working on it.

For reactions, we called in a bunch of school students from elementary grades or high school and have them look at what we had done so far to see if they would laugh or react as we hoped at the right places. I used to have to run the picture for those trials. That too, had its problems.

We might have half of the picture done and, "Let's have a showing," Walt would say. And Walt remained alert for the kids' reaction.

The projection room we used was right next door to Walt's office. The minute he slipped in the room, he would sit right down beside me in the back, at a little console. I had control of the sound, so I would tell the projectionist to, "Roll the picture," over the intercom.

Here I was with about five, sometimes six, soundtracks. It hadn't been finally mixed yet, so I had to dial it for sound balance, keep the voices up over the music and not let the sound effects get too loud. Walt used to say, "If you can't hear the dialogue, what's it doing in the picture?"

I would be concentrating on running the sound, with Walt beside me. He would lean over and ask questions. "Has this bunch seen the picture before?" or "How old is this group?" And I'm concentrating on the dials! "This looks like a pretty young crowd," Walt would say. "What do you think, Dan? Huh?"

"Yeah. These are junior high school kids," I would say; little things he wanted to know. He kept up a running line of chatter, while I was trying to run the picture! I would come out of there in a sweat. A wreck!

I used to tell Woolie, "Boy, Walt sure is no help to me running that picture." Woolie would just laugh. Didn't bother him. He would say, "You did fine, Dan."

Of course, after I had been there for a while, Woolie Reitherman knew me quite well. "Hey, Dan, what you think?" he would ask or, "You got most of this in color yet?" Sometimes there would be lost drawings or lost scenes and I had to track them down. It was amazing how drawings got lost. Or maybe a scene was issued to this guy to animate, and he would come up to me and say, "I've lost one of my animation scenes." Ye Gads!

These young animators were almost like children. Not the old guys, but their assistants, not long out of art school, would come to me like a lost child. "I can't find my drawings. Dan, I've lost my...."

Or I might ask, "Why's scene five taking so long? You had it for quite a while. Where is it? Have you sent it out for test?"

And he might say, "Well, yeah. I think I sent it out."

And I would say, "Well, did it ever come back?"

And he would say, "Well, I don't know."

Things like that. So I would I find it in the craziest places, like on top of his desk!

On my wall charts, storyboards, every scene was numbered within spaces to the right of each scene which showed "rough test, clean up test, final test, sent to color, dates," etc. At any moment I could tell where any scene was. With several hundred scenes involved, close records were a must.

And then I had a "dope book" with each page reflecting a scene. It contained all the dialogue and sound effects in the exact place it was supposed to be, by footage. One page for each scene. On a feature, I would have several "dope books" to cover all the sequences.

The curse in making a picture was changes. Especially changes by Woolie, my boss. A perfectionist, he wasn't afraid to attack things and tear them apart. Just like Walt could do. I don't know which of the two could destroy a scene quicker.

A few years ago, Woolie Reitherman wrapped his car around a big tree and lost his life. Woolie was a pilot during the war. He flew cargo over the hump into China from Burma, and after the war, he kept up his flying. He drove cars fast, too. Maybe he just didn't make the right move that night. I used to see him roaring in to work in his old Packard Touring car with top down, hell bent, hair straight in the wind. "Never live scared," he once told me. He never lived scared.[1]

Making movies was not all easy. I once heard a guy say that most "geniuses" got that way by hard work. Maybe so. But working with Woolie Reitherman and Walt and Frank Thomas and Ollie Johnston on some of the greatest classics ever created left me convinced that they were both geniuses *and* hard workers. They inspired the whole team to do their best, because they were sincerely concerned about putting out the best possible entertainment to the public.

Chapter Endnotes:

1. Wolfgang Reitherman passed away on May 22, 1985 at the age of seventy-six.

Chapter 23:

"Over the Waves"

Walt had two daughters. The oldest one was Diane and that was his own daughter. And then they adopted a girl, Sharon.[1]

Now, the oldest girl, Diane, attended the University of Southern California, where she met and married a football hero, Ron Miller: big, tall, good-looking son-of-a-gun. He later played with the L.A. Rams after he got out of U.S.C. He didn't play too long because, by this time, he had married Diane, so he didn't have to get knocked around anymore. Of course, Ron went to work at the studio.

Walt couldn't resist testing Ron out. He wanted to know if Ron was a handsome guy or something else. Someone was supposed to have remarked to Walt, "Well, it's a good thing Ron got out of football before he had his brains knocked out."

And Walt said, all in fun, "I'm not too sure he got out in time."

The production job they gave Ron was an assistant director job in T.V., live action. In the early T.V. shows, Walt would appear first and make some opening remarks, something about what we were going to see that evening on T.V. So, he put Ron in as an assistant director on these (they called them "lead-ins") and Walt drove Ron out of his mind! I think Walt got a kick out of "needling" people.

For instance, Ron would say, "Okay, everybody set! You ready, Walt?"

Walt would say, "Yeah."

"Okay, let's roll the rehearsal."

And Walt would stop him. "Now, wait a minute, Ron. Ron, I have my part ready. I got my cue cards out there. We're wasting time. After all, film is cheap. Let's roll the picture!"

Ron would look a little hacked. "Quiet everybody!" he said. "This is the picture. Roll it!"

So, they would shoot the picture and most times it would work out fine. They wouldn't need a retake. Then they would set up for another angle, another shot. And this time, Ron was playing it smart. So, when they got all set for this second set-up, had the lights all set and everything, Ron would say, "Okay, roll the picture."

And Walt would say, "Wait a minute, Ron. This is a pretty hard scene. Every actor gets a rehearsal, you know. Let's rehearse this first before we shoot it."

Just anything to upset Ron. All the crew broke up about it, because they knew what was going on. But that was when Ron first started at the studio. It finally all worked out. And then, of course, they elevated Ron. He got a higher position, as he learned the business. He did his job. I got along fine with Ron. He used to come and sit near me while I was running a picture and I'd give him cigarettes. He was always trying to quit smoking, but bumming me for cigarettes. He finally quit smoking and I did, too. Later Ron became head of the production departments.

I could never figure out how Walt could handle everything like he did. But he did it. When they were shooting *Mary Poppins*, they were using an English director on the picture, Robert Stevenson.[2] He was a little wiry, nervous English guy but very good, very thorough. One time, Walt had to go to Europe and was gone for about ten days. When he got back, he just strolled down to the set where they were shooting *Poppins* and walked up and quietly stood beside Stevenson. Stevenson looked over to Walt. "Oh hi, Walt. Didn't know you were back! Well, Walt, everything seems to be just fine."

Walt just nodded his head.

"We're right on schedule, Walt. The cast has just been marvelous, and very cooperative, and we're making good footage, Walt." (Trying to make conversation.)

He would look at Walt, but Walt wouldn't answer. Just nod his head.

"The crew has been marvelous, especially the second unit," Stevenson continued.

Walt just looked at him. Finally, "I've been getting daily reports," Walt said in a monotone. So when Walt came back, he was quite abreast of everything.

I don't know how Walt kept up with everything, but one reason was that he knew every phase of the business. He was usually way ahead of everybody else. For instance, we might call him down to look at a new sequence. He would sit down and usually the story sketch man would get up with a pointer and read the dialogue and point to the pictures. Walt would read ahead and think ahead. I used to talk to some of these guys that would be telling the story and they would say, "I know Walt wasn't even listening to me. I didn't have to tell the story when he was way ahead of me, and not paying attention." Walt wanted to get on with it. But he'd wait patiently and then start tearing it to pieces or, perhaps, compliment the story. He had a habit of staring at one section, and he would go over to the storyboard and quickly rip off about five or six sketches and say, "We don't need that part. Take it out." Which he had already done himself. He knew what he wanted and usually knew it quickly.

I always sat behind Walt. Woolie used to tell me, "The main thing you want to get from Walt is when he says, 'Have this character say this....'" Whatever we did, we wanted to get the new dialogue that Walt gave us. Make sure we got that, because he would remember what he told us and you couldn't stop and say, "Now, what's that line again, Walt?" So we got it!

From way back, even on the early pictures, secretaries took notes in these sessions with Walt. He wanted the notes to remind him of every word that was discussed.

Walt had nothing against women and in addition to the secretaries, for years he had several in his story department. As for the meetings, he insisted that *every last word* be recorded so he and others could study what ideas had been offered and what reactions they had brought.

They used to tell us in the publicity office: "Now, if you hear Walt say some clever things, things that should be remembered, drop us a note and remind us of it." Several times, I turned in things that Walt said, for instance, Walt not having a charge number. I sent those things to the archives, among other things. They called me back on the phone. "Oh, that's good stuff." They saved things like that to be put in later write-ups about Walt, about the human side of Walt.

There, of course, was the "Disney style," the typical or usual Disney characteristics to all his features, but he was open to new ideas. Earlier I mentioned our band leader, Ward Kimball, who Disney called a true genius.[3]

In 1952, Walt Disney called Ward Kimball up to his office to discuss a couple of ideas he had for three educational short films he wanted Ward to do for the schools, dealing with music. The first film was to explain what melody was and the second film to be all about musical instruments and how man developed them down through history. At the time, Ward was between assignments and he looked forward to these music projects with relish. He would have Charles "Nick" Nichols helping out on the directing while Ward would plan the story line, design the characters and also animate some of the sequences.[4] *Melody* was finished first and Walt liked the picture and the new animation techniques he saw. Walt decided to have this picture finished as the first animation film in 3D for release in the theatres, then for the schools later. The musical instrument history film, *Toot, Whistle, Plunk and Boom* was made when Walt was on vacation in Europe and involved in early planning stages for the coming theme park at Disneyland.

When Kimball and crew were busy working on this picture, word got around the "rumor factory" that Ward was trying out some strange new animation designs and that when Walt saw what was happening, Ward, Nichols, and the crew would probably catch hell! "Walt won't release it with his name on it—Kimball has gone too far this time. It's so un-Disney," they all whispered.

Well, when Walt finally saw the completed film in its rough pencil form, he loved it! He said that it was much too good for school educational purposes. "Let's finish it up for the new wide screen Cinemascope," Walt said. On the night it was first shown for the Academy Award competition, it got a great audience response and good laughs. And, to the surprise of the envious disbelievers, *Toot, Whistle, Plunk and Boom* went on to win the Academy Award Oscar for the best animation film of 1953!

The regular size screen version of *Toot, Whistle, Plunk and Boom* has been shown in hundreds of American schools since about 1954 and Ward still receives letters from appreciative school teachers who thank him for making this instructive and entertaining music film.

Ward Kimball could do anything and after that, Walt thought, "Well, maybe this Kimball is a pretty good cat." So they started making a live action picture called *Babes in Toyland*. Walt cast the parts. He wanted Tommy Sands who then was married to Frank Sinatra's daughter, Nancy. Walt also wanted Annette Funicello in it. Both were weak actors to be cast in a major picture.

This was the first picture that Ward had ever directed in live action. He rehearsed like hell on it and worked it up and he finally went to Walt. "Walt," he said, "I can't make this picture with Tommy Sands and Annette Funicello. They're not strong enough characters."

And I guess they got in a hassle about it, so Walt took Ward off the picture. "Well, okay," he said. "That's who I want in it!"

But as it turned out, Ward was correct. It was a good picture and George Bruns, who wrote the music for it, did an excellent job and was nominated for an Oscar (for music) that year (he didn't win it, but he was nominated). It was a good show, but would have been much better with good casting.

Chapter Endnotes:

1. Diane Disney Miller was born in 1933 and passed away in November of 2013, just a month short of her eightieth birthday. For much of her life she was a strong proponent of her father's legacy and co-founded the Walt Disney Family Museum in 2009. Sharon Disney Lund was born in 1936 and adopted by Walt and Lillian Disney that same year. She passed away in February of 1993 at the age of fifty-seven.
2. Robert Stevenson (1905-1986) was a native of the United Kingdom and one of Walt Disney's most skilled live-action directors. He began his filmmaking career in the mid-1930s, worked with Frank Capra during World War II, and had moved into television production by the time Disney hired him. His first Disney credit as a director was *Johnny Tremain* (1957) followed quickly by *Old Yeller*. Other Disney features included *The Absent-Minded Professor* (1961), *The Love Bug* (1968), and *Bedknobs and Broomsticks* (1971). But perhaps Stevenson's greatest accomplishment for Disney was *Mary Poppins*, which received thirteen Academy Award nominations and won four.
3. Walt Disney famously called Ward Kimball a genius during a series of interviews with journalist Pete Martin in 1956/57.
4. Born on September 15, 1910 in Milford, Utah, Charles "Nick" Nichols lived in Chicago for several years prior to his joining Disney. From 1927 until about late 1934, he drew several comic-book strips including "The Adventures of Peter Pen" and "Just Supposin." Between 1933 and 1934, he also sold a cartooning course. Nick Nichols joined Disney in February 1935, probably as an inbetweener. By 1937 he was animating on many Pluto shorts and even on *Pinocchio*. His first directing job seems to have been on the short *Springtime for Pluto*, the first of a very long series of Pluto

cartoons that he would direct in the forties and early fifties. When the production of shorts started to wind down in the fifties, he handled hundreds of commercials produced by the Disney Studios for such outside customers as 7-Up (featuring Fresh-Up Freddie), Baker's Instant Chocolate (featuring Jiminy Cricket), Jello, Cheerios (featuring Donald Duck), Ipana (featuring Bucky Beaver), Derby Foods Inc. (featuring Tinker Bell), Nash (featuring Mickey Mouse and friends). He was also in charge of some cartoon "one-offs" like *Melody* (1953), *Toot, Whistle, Plunk and Boom* (1953), *Grand Canyonscope* (1954), *How to Have an Accident in the Home* (1956), *How to Have an Accident at Work* (1959), and *The Saga of Windwagon Smith* (1961). Nichols left the Disney Studios around the end of 1961 and was quickly hired by Hanna-Barbera, where he directed some episodes of "The Jetsons," "The Flintstones," and "Scooby-Doo" as well as the feature *Charlotte's Web* (1973). After a stint at Ruby-Spears, Nick Nichols' career ended at Disney where, in the 1990s, he directed episodes of the animated TV series "Darkwing Duck," "Goof Troop," and "Bonkers." He passed away at the age of eighty-one, on August 23, 1992.

Chapter 24:

"Who Walks In When I Walk Out"

When I became an assistant director, the first full feature I worked on was *Lady and the Tramp* (released in 1955). It had just been finished in English, but they wanted to make a Spanish version of it. We often made foreign language versions. So we had to re-use all the music and effects, but leave off the English dialogue track and substitute a Spanish dialogue track. That was my first experience in "dubbing." It was a great picture, in Spanish or English.

Ed Penner—who played tuba in the Firehouse Five Plus Two—had a little problem with the sequence where the dogs were locked up in the pound awaiting the gas chamber. To keep it light and even funny rather than morbid, he built a parallel with clichés from prison films using lines like, "Look, guys, they're takin' Jo-Jo."

The story of the "Cinderella" dog, as we called her, needs to be told. Ed Penner saw the dog on his way home one evening, but had no time to stop and find where "it" lived. The next day he combed the neighborhood but no one knew anything about the dog. The kids said it was a stray. It was a day or so later that they found it in the pound. The studio paid to bail her out on Ed's word that this was the exact dog the picture needed. Then to find out that she was a young female and the opposite of Tramp's personality was a bit of a blow. We photographed her for part of one afternoon, then put her in the kennels with the other dog stars of Hollywood.

We next worked on *Sleeping Beauty*. This picture had been lying around four or five years and they couldn't seem to get it into production. They kept rewriting the script for the story and it seemed like they would never make it, but finally they got a story that they could live with and the film was released in January, 1959.

The work was divided into three equal parts for the three animation units. The part that we worked on was the fight between the dragon and the Prince, the Prince killing the dragon, and the prince going to the castle to awaken Sleeping Beauty at the end of the picture. This sequence was perfect for Woolie's direction.

Our next feature was *101 Dalmatians* which was one of my favorites. It's the story of two Dalmatians (man and wife in Dogdom) who had puppies. The villainess was Cruella de Vil (translated, meant "cruel devil"). Her purpose was to find and kill all the Dalmatian dogs that she could steal in order to make Dalmatian coats.

Betty Lou Gerson, who played the part of Cruella de Vil, was a good actress. She had a great voice—kind of husky and mean like Tallulah Bankhead. She was well cast.

I loved to help write a little extra dialogue. Maybe my idea was rejected, but they would listen, and sometimes they'd use it. In *101 Dalmatians* there was a part where Pongo and his mate, Perdita, had found all their puppies plus the others which totaled ninety-nine (and counting themselves, made it 101). One got a first impression that they intended to take only their own puppies home and not the others. Pongo says, "Let's go home now."

So I went to the writer, Bill Peet, and said, "There's something that doesn't sound right here."

"What is it?"

"Well, you ought to have a line in here where one of Pongo's puppies asked, 'How about the others? What'll they do?'" It gave it more heart.

They agreed, and added the line. Pongo then said, "We'll *all* go! Come on, everyone!"

Speaking of Bill Peet: a real good writer and story sketch man. He preferred working alone and did his own sketching and wrote his own dialogue. Very dry and caustic (and funny) talker.[1]

There is a story about Bill. He was pretty moody and could get upset. Once he became so upset over Walt Disney's criticism during a meeting that he dashed back into his own office and threw ink all over his walls. Later, Walt would just come in, talk to Bill and never even comment about the splattered walls. It blew over. And when he thought the time was right, Walt said, "Bill, why don't you clean this stuff up?" And Bill did.

Bill Peet was a great storyman, but he got into it with Reitherman on *The Jungle Book*, too. He just hated to see his storyboard changed or messed up. Bill quit the studio, because he felt Woolie was changing his (Bill's) story too much. Bill turned to writing and sketching children's books, and is now a huge success. His stuff sells very well. Great talent, and he was a great character! He used to collect odd-sounding names as a hobby, (like "Clarice Box").

One day I was on my way to the cafeteria, and I passed Bill and invited him to go to lunch.

"I can't eat that food in there," he said, "It's terrible." It wasn't really.

"Well," I said, "Have a hard-boiled egg. They can't hurt an egg."

"Are you kidding? They can screw up a bottle of beer."

The Sword in the Stone was the story of King Arthur as a boy who later became King. It was before *The Jungle Book*. In the end they had the sword in the stone and an inscription that read, "Whomsoever shall pull this sword from the stone shall then rightfully become the King of England."

It was a beautiful scene. Everyone tried, of course, the big and the strong, but none could pull the sword out. Someone said, "Let the boy try it! Let the boy try it!" So the "wart," as they called little Arthur, pulled the sword out of the stone and became King Arthur. Good picture. I had a ball working on it.

And then we made *The Jungle Book*. It was a tough picture to get off the ground because Kipling's *Jungle Book* was kind of dull reading in a way. We had to do something to make it an entertaining picture. So, we started casting parts, and working over the story and dialogue. Good stories are critical. And we had to have some characters with good voices. We had a struggle getting the parts cast.

One of the parts that was holding us up was the right voice for Baloo, the bear, who at the outset was due only a minor role. It had to be a happy-go-lucky bear voice, and one who could sing.

We auditioned voices for the part; brought in three people in the morning and three in the afternoon and had them read dialogue, trying to find a "bear" voice. Frank Thomas, Ollie Johnston, Woolie, and I listened to all these people. Among them were some UCLA students from India who had British accents, but we couldn't get any acting into their performances. We finally decided on a comedian type. He wasn't too good, but we didn't think it would be a big part at the time. But Walt didn't like it.

And then, as always, Walt came through. "You know who I think would be good for that part? Phil Harris. He was a real carefree guy on the old Jack Benny Show. You know, like, 'Hi, Jackson. How are you doing?' Just a free-spirited guy."

"Yeah. He'd be great!" we agreed.

"I'm going down to Palm Springs this weekend," Walt said. "I think Phil is going to be there for a golf tournament. I'll ask him."

So he did. Walt kind of gave Phil a short description of the character and voice we wanted.

"Yeah. I'll try it," Phil told him, "but I don't think I can do a bear." He was very hesitant about the role. "I can't do voices. I could barely read to my daughters when they were little," he said.

He came in for an audition. And he turned out to be just the right voice. The writer, Larry Clemmons, told him not to read it as written, but just to read it in his own way (with his own personality), and to just do it the way that he felt it.[2] And when they let Phil do Baloo his own way, that bear just came alive. Ollie Johnston, who animated Baloo, knew he had a major character emerge.

Phil was in the habit of meeting some pals in a bar. They would have a few belts. Often, without phoning his wife (Alice Faye) Phil would go hunting or fishing with a buddy. Then he would show up in a couple of days. Of course, Alice would get mad at his excuses.

Well, this day after he auditioned at Disney he got home late as usual, and Alice asked where he had been. "Doing a bear voice for Disney," he said.

"All through the years you've given me some flimsy excuses," she said, "but this really takes the cake!" The next day, Phil's agent asked for a recording of the tape to take home so she would believe him. We got that to him in two hours!

Ollie Johnston, who created Baloo for *The Jungle Book*, was struggling somewhat with the dance scene Baloo was to do to the "Bare Necessities." Walt happened to come by one day while Ollie was working on this scene and, out in the hall, Walt showed Ollie how he thought the bear should dance. But still Ollie couldn't get the right rhythm to it so he asked me what I thought about how a bear should dance. I used a little different approach and had a hand clap on certain beats of the song during the dance. After I acted out the dance at Ollie's office, he said, "That's it! That's what I'm looking for."

From Ollie Johnston: "I'd just like to add that the hand clap that Dan suggested not only did something special for the rhythm, but more than that, gave Baloo a personality trait that added immensely to his entertainment. Little things like that bring a character to life and make him memorable. In the end, it made Baloo more fun for me. Danny helped me get what Walt was looking for because when Walt first suggested Phil as the voice he said, 'You know how Phil is—he's always snapping his fingers and doing everything in rhythm.'"[3]

Later, in Ollie's backyard near the tracks of his miniature train, Frank Thomas used a sixteen millimeter camera from the studio to take a movie of the entire dance along with the recorded sound track from the "Bare Necessities," a song written especially for this movie, and Ollie used the film action to animate the entire dance sequence.

After Walt saw the work, he became very enthused with not only the dance scene, but with Phil Harris' voice and Baloo's role was enlarged from that of the originally planned cameo to "star." In fact, Baloo became a major force that carried *The Jungle Book*.

Ollie often stated that he loved doing Baloo, that he could have kept drawing "that bear" for years. Ollie was so adept at expressing feeling in the characters because of his sensitivity and imagination. And he was an expert at arranging scenes for the very best effect. He also knew what voice was needed for the various characters and those decisions were often very difficult. He hit everything perfect with Baloo. It was one of his all-time favorites.

Ollie, by the way, worked on all of the major animated features. Ollie not only drew accurately with great emotion, but he could really put out the footage. He was one of the greatest animators and another of the "Nine Old Men."

Ollie Johnston and Frank Thomas met at Stanford, both ended up at Disney, are neighbors, have done books together (including a new one in the works on *Bambi*), and are, of course, great friends. I think their work on *The Jungle Book* rates right up there with *Bambi* and *Snow White*.[4]

One key element in the success of *The Jungle Book* was the bond of love between Baloo and the boy, Mowgli. The old axiom, characters make the story, was never more true than with these two. Their relationship carried this movie by making the audience care.

After Baloo, we cast Sebastian Cabot as the black panther Bagheera and George Sanders as the tiger voice, Shere-Khan; again—superb voices.

We finished *The Jungle Book* and it was such a success, it just tickled Phil Harris to death. He would come in and watch the animation. "That bear," he would say. He wouldn't say, "That's me," or "*My* voice." He would say, "That bear just knocks me out."

The Jungle Book was the last picture that Walt had anything to do with. I mean, he guided this picture all the way because he felt it would be very good. And it was good. One of the best.

Walt had done some preliminary work on *The Aristocats*, okaying models, etc., but no story yet. In 1966, we were just starting to cast the parts when…Walt died.

The Aristocats was about a white, pure-bred Persian cat (voiced by Eva Gabor) who hooked up with an alley cat who had befriended her. And we needed the voice of the alley cat. "Well, let's get Phil Harris again. He was so good in *The Jungle Book*!" everyone said. So, we called Phil and asked him.

"Gee, I don't think I should," he said. "I did Baloo, so I don't think that people would like my voice as a cat, but," he said, "I'll get Dean Martin. He's a loose guy. He'd make a good alley cat voice. I'm going to play golf with him next week. I'll get him to come over and read the part."

He later called us. "You know what? I was out with Dean and I told him, 'Dean, they're making an animation feature over at Disney and…. Listen, Dean. I know it's a cartoon, but it's an animated feature and Disney films always do well. It'll put you in history. They'll never forget you. After *The Jungle Book* came out, I could walk down Broadway in New York City and everyone recognized me as Baloo. I'll tell you, it gave me a whole new image.'"

"Naw. No cartoon voices," Dean said. And that was that!

We were getting desperate for a voice for an alley cat, so finally Phil called back. "You know, I can't get Dean to do this. So, what the hell! I'll do it myself."

And happily, we agreed. We told Phil, "If you see a bear up there on the screen and hear the voice of a bear, the audience will accept it as a bear. If you hear the voice up there as an alley cat, people will accept the voice of an alley cat."

As far as I could learn, we never received any letters about the voice of the cat conflicting with the bear's voice.

And, by this time, Phil was in love with Disney and vice-versa. We all liked working with Phil.

We even used Phil Harris as the voice of Little John in *Robin Hood*. And he did a great job in that picture, too!

The Aristocats and *Robin Hood* were the first two feature-length cartoons that I got title credit for at the beginning of the picture. Up to then, my union wouldn't allow assistant directors to get screen credit, but before *The Aristocats* they changed the ruling. When they finally hooked all the *Winnie the Pooh* features together, (I worked on all three), I got name credit on that also.

Alguire with wife Irene on the evening of *The Aristocats* premiere in 1970. Courtesy of Charlotte Bryant McCormack.

At *The Aristocats* premiere in 1970, (L to R): Disney composer and Firehouse Five Plus Two musician George Bruns, Danny Alguire (back to camera), voice artist Phil Harris, Irene Bryant. Courtesy of Charlotte Bryant McCormack.

We did *Winnie the Pooh and The Honey Tree*, *Winnie the Pooh and the Blustery Day*, and *Winnie the Pooh and Tigger, Too*. The second one, *Winnie the Pooh and the Blustery Day*, won an Oscar for best cartoon for that year.

When our crew at the studio had their picture taken with the Oscar, I was down in the cutting room. Nobody called me.

Chapter Endnotes:

1. Artist Bill Peet was born in Indiana in 1915 and had attended Herron Art Institute before he joined Disney in 1937. Peet soon moved into the Story Department where he rose to prominence on many feature and short projects. After leading work on *101 Dalmatians*, *The Sword in the Stone*, and beginning work on *The Jungle Book*, Peet left Disney to begin a successful career as a children's writer and illustrator.
2. Larry Clemmons was born in Chicago on November 25, 1906. He graduated from the University of Michigan and began his association with Disney in 1932 in the Animation Department, where he worked as an animator on shorts that included *Mickey's Man Friday* (1935), *Mickey's Circus* (1936), *Hockey Champ* (1936), *The Practical Pig* (1939), *The Autograph Hound* (1939), *Sea Scouts* (1939), *The Volunteer Worker* (1940), *Mr. Duck Steps Out* (1940), *Billposters* (1940), *Donald's Vacation* (1940) and *Tugboat Mickey* (1940). During a brief leave from the company in the 1940s and early 1950s, he wrote scripts for Bing Crosby's radio program. Returning to Disney, he provided his animation and story services in short cartoons, animated features, and in television. Among his numerous animated feature credits as storyman are *The Reluctant Dragon* (1941), *The Jungle Book* (1967), *Winnie the Pooh and the Blustery Day* (1968), *The Aristocats* (1971), *Robin Hood* (1973), *The Many Adventures of Winnie the Pooh*

(1977), *The Rescuers* (1977), and *The Fox and the Hound* (1981). For many years, Clemmons also wrote Walt Disney's introduction dialogue for the weekly anthology series. He retired from Disney on October 31, 1978 and passed away on July 22, 1988 in Friday Harbor, Washington.

3. In an additional fragment discovered with Alguire's manuscript, Ollie Johnston would recount that "one other important thing Danny did for me on [*The Jungle Book*]: a fellow named Cappy Lewis played the trumpet in a recording session we had for the sequence I did of Baloo scratching himself on the palm tree. Walt had suggested we should get some music to give that section added excitement. Cappy did a real nice ad-lib of 'Bare Necessities' so when I started on my last scene in the picture where Baloo and Bagheera dance away into the sunset I wanted some music to make the whole ending real upbeat so that the audience would go out happy. I asked Danny if he didn't think that ad-lib trumpet would work good there and he agreed with me so I asked him if he thought he could get George Bruns, the musician doing the score, to use it. He said he'd talk to him, which he did, and George said OK and I thought it worked out great and I've always been pleased that Danny did that for me. It was a sad time around the studio with Walt having just died and this put an upbeat ending onto his last picture."

4. "Walt Disney's *Bambi*: The Story and the Film" by Frank Thomas and Ollie Johnston, was published by Stewart Tabori and Chang in 1990.

Epilogue:

"Stranger On The Shore"

I often thought the Firehouse Five Plus Two was like an animated scene from a Disney movie. We played the roles of happy firemen—playing tunes and having fun. We were visual: the fire hats, the siren, facial expressions. Everything contributed to the total effect on a crowd—whether it was a high school dance, the Hollywood "in crowd," or ordinary folks at Disneyland. We knocked them out. Every summer we won the contest for "Favorite Band at the park" at Disneyland.

Danny Alguire with the Firehouse Five Plus Two at Earthquake McGoon's, San Francisco in April, 1970. Courtesy of Leon D. Oakley.

People would say, "It's great to watch your band playing. You look like you're having such a great time!" I can tell you, we were. In hundreds of engagements, we never failed to enjoy our music. The crowds knew that and it was contagious. And that was exactly the effect we were striving for. It was the secret of the Firehouse Five Plus Two and we carried it out to perfection.

It was the most unique band in the history of jazz. This bunch of firemen—characters on stage—who looked like they just tumbled out of the screen, yet played great music, were a total entertainment package.

It was a shame that the entire nation—the whole world—did not have the opportunity to see and hear the Firehouse Five Plus Two. We changed a lot of attitudes.

Ward Kimball on trombone (left) and Danny Alguire on tambourine during a performance of the Firehouse Five Plus Two in the late 1960s. Courtesy of the Ward Kimball Family.

I could name several bands that musically (and technically) were better than the Firehouse Five Plus Two, but no one could make people feel good about themselves like we could.

I met this young dentist at an affair in Phoenix. Near the end of the dance he came up to me nearly in tears (we talked to everybody). I guess he had tossed down a drink or two. "I never danced in my life—until tonight," he said. "But this music…you guys…."

He could hardly talk. "You guys are having such a good time." He didn't know any dance steps—not by the book—but with our beat, he did fine and enjoyed it. And that's what is important.

We were professionals, but we all had great jobs with Disney. We didn't have to play. We did it to have fun and to see the joy it created. To see people like that dentist, and thousands of others, kick off their shoes, forget all their problems and just have fun, was a reward more satisfying than any amount of money.[1]

Here we were. We could have played every night somewhere, taken a national tour, even played in Russia. And we were absolutely assured of a great reaction. We had seen it too many times to think otherwise.

In Ward Kimball, Frank Thomas, Harper Goff, Jim MacDonald, and George Bruns we had a bunch of high-salaried men. Why did they do it? For the love of jazz and to watch people turn on to jazz. And it was therapy for our mental strain, too, after a hard day of drawing, creating, or composing at Disney Studios.

Maybe it would have changed us. Maybe, if that band had taken a full-time status—our only source of income—it would not have been the same. If our only focus had become money instead of great entertainment, I believe our band would have changed for the worse. Ward Kimball was right: do it for fun. That's Hollywood and that's entertainment—go too far, give them too much—and it's over.

The Firehouse Five Plus Two broke up in 1971 when I suddenly had to have emergency surgery. We had been playing for over twenty years (1948-1971), so after making twelve albums (144 tunes)...we quit. The music stopped.

We got together one more time, December, 1979, and played our "last dance" before the Rose Bowl Parade. We played at the old Wrigley Mansion in Pasadena for a group of Rose Bowl officials. The band sounded surprisingly good after several years apart. And on January 1, 1980, we played the Rose Bowl Parade on the top of a huge fire wagon, pulled by six black Percherons (sponsored by

Western Airlines), swinging away on "Tiger Rag" (no booze sloshing down my leg this time!).

The Firehouse Five Plus "Three" reunite for the 1980 Tournament of Roses Parade, seen here at the Grizzly Flats Depot in the Kimball backyard. (Back row, L to R): Don Kinch, George Probert, Frank Thomas, Danny Alguire, George Bruns. (Front row, L to R): Ward Kimball, Harper Goff, Eddie Forrest. Courtesy of Charlotte Bryant McCormack.

Reunion lunch at the Kimball home for 1980 Tournament of Roses Parade. Seated around the foreground table (clockwise) are Danny Alguire (center, back), Irene Alguire, Frank Thomas, unknown, Billie Forrest, George Bruns, Flossie Goff, Harper Goff. Seated around the background table (clockwise): Betty Kimball (left), Don Kinch, Nathan Lord (a Kimball grandchild), Theodore Thomas, John Kimball. Courtesy of Charlotte Bryant McCormack.

Jazz inspired my life. I made my share of mistakes and it took me long enough to listen to the music voice within me, to follow my talent. When I did so, music carried me all the way from the dust bowl days in Oklahoma to the glamour of Disney Studios. I believe good music was crucial to my emotional well-being. In fact, I think good music saves a lot of people in this rather negative world.

My advice? Keep jazz alive. Loosen up and don't take life too seriously. Follow your talent, whatever it is. And support your local firemen!

After Walt Disney's death in 1966, we faced the task of starting production on the next full-length cartoon feature, *The Aristocats*, the first animated feature to be made without Walt, who had always showed us the way. Our "pillar of strength" was gone.

The burden fell on Woolie Reitherman, who became our "Producer and Director." No one heard him say what was on everyone else's mind, "Can we do it without Walt?" We did it. We moved right into production.

Disney Studios continues now with the same excellence. Guys like Ward Kimball, Woolie, Frank Thomas, Ollie Johnston, and, of course, Walt left a mark on the now giant Disney Productions. The new faces carry the same burden and challenge: to produce the very best in entertainment. That is what it is all about, the focus on quality.

Bob Wills also strived for excellence, the Firehouse Five Plus Two did it, and other great organizations in America always demand the best. But the ranks are thinning. Excellence starts with sincere people and proper motivation. If quality is there, the rewards will follow. I'm concerned that many American industries, including entertainment, in their push for the quick buck, are losing that focus on quality and decency. It is a dangerous trend. I must believe, however, that Disney animation will live forever. Don't let the cynics get to you. Keep Bambi and Thumper and Baloo alive for your children and for yourself. One could do a lot worse nowadays.

In 1968, tragedy struck. My wife Betty began to lose weight. Cancer of the pancreas. She had no warning. I lost her June 18, 1968. Almost two years alone, I dated no one. Just working at Disney and playing jazz wasn't enough. I met Irene Bryant and later married her on November 23, 1969. She and her daughter Charlotte and son Bob became a wonderful family to me.

In 1974, Irene, daughter Charlotte, and I agreed that we should all move to Oregon. We sold our home in Studio City, and departed Southern California…and Disney…and the Firehouse Five Plus Two.

Oregon was Irene's home, and she and Charlotte were so glad to see their lush, green beautiful state again.

In the 1980s with grandsons Ben (left) and Joshua.
Courtesy of Charlotte Bryant McCormack.

Two old and dear musician friends had also moved to Oregon from California sometime earlier. One, Don Kinch, had played tuba with us in the Firehouse Five Plus Two from 1957 until 1969 when he moved to Portland. Then George Bruns also moved back to Sandy, Oregon.

Well, I hadn't been in Oregon very long until I was playing jazz again! I joined up with Jim Beatty, a fine clarinet player who played with that real good New Orleans tone. We also had Norman Domreis, piano; Pete Pepke, trombone; Dave Weirbach, banjo; Delane Guild, drums; Dave Gentry, bass; and, of course, I was on cornet and sang a few old "goodies." All were good jazz musicians. We recorded two record albums, which came off very well.

The last band that Alguire regularly played with was the Jim Beatty Jazz Band in Portland, Oregon. They released two records in the 1970s on which Alguire played: "The Joys of Jazz" and "Salute to the Bicentennial." Courtesy of Hal Smith.

In 1980, I put away my horn.

After all, I'd been hearing music since my "in utero" days and playing and singing music since I was five years old. I had so much reading I wanted to do I never had time for through the years. My mother read until she died with a book in her hands at ninety-five.

I can say I miss Disney and the jazz, but I can also look back to the rough times—the depression days in Kansas City, the broomcorn in hot dry Oklahoma, the telegraph clocks, the Navy and that old tub, the U.S.S. *Alchiba* that barely stayed afloat, and the late night dances with Bob Wills—and I can smile to myself thinking where music got me: teaching a bear how to dance! [2]

Chapter Endnotes:

1. In an additional fragment left with Alguire's manuscript, Ward Kimball would recount, "During the twenty-two year life span of the Firehouse Five Plus Two, the personnel of the band changed but little. Even so, we were always an interesting group of characters who were dedicated to a simple style of playing old time jazz, or, Dixieland. Sure, we had at one time or another a few egocentrics, prima donnas, extroverts, and air heads, but we always had a good time playing together and this half insane, very relaxed musical comradery seemed to be a great infectious joy to our audiences. In looking back it becomes obvious to me that Danny Alguire playing his steady cornet was the glue that held the band together. Danny was a walking encyclopedia who could remember most every popular tune or old time jazz classic that was ever written, and the lyrics, to boot! Very seldom was he ever stumped on a request, and if he was, he'd say to the person, 'Hum the bridge, I think I know it.' Danny was no slick trumpet virtuoso, but he had a simple, no frills style of playing that always stuck to the melody whether it was a straight lead first chorus or a more jazzed up solo. This helped give the Firehouse Five its friendly sound and made people bounce in their seats or want to get up and dance. As the saying goes, 'You can't go wrong playing the melody.'"
2. When Alguire passed away in 1992, Irene Bryant received letters from more than one of his Disney colleagues. Animator and Firehouse Five Plus Two bandmate Frank Thomas wrote that "Danny was surely well-loved and left quite a mark both as a musician and a man wherever he went. I think his influence was greater than he realized, but being modest and practical, he never seemed to

think much about such things. But those of us who are left behind have so many wonderful memories of him." Story artist Vance Gerry, who started at Disney around the same time as Alguire, would explain that "Danny was, of course, an especially friendly man, and helped me with music even though I had very little musical ability. He had the patience to teach and encourage me nevertheless. We worked closely together in the making of story reels for Woolie and he was the accomplished assistant director in the business. He trained many of the young people who are in the business today." Firehouse Five Plus Two bandmate Eddie Forrest would also write that "the years I spent with Danny were most enjoyable. We used to ride together, at times, to our jobs with the Firehouse Five, recalling pleasant times we had experienced. [Danny] was the main one I always listened to while playing our jobs together."

Afterword: Remembrances

Theodore Thomas (Trumpet)

Recording sessions, gigs, band trips—the Firehouse Five Plus Two was always in my life. My father, Frank Thomas, played piano in the band, and their music and Danny Alguire had an outsized impact on me from my earliest years.

I don't think Danny ever set out to be a role model, and he might be surprised to hear me call him that—but, as I reflect on it, that was what he was to me.

My sister studied some piano, my older brother picked up tuba, and when I turned eight my father asked me what instrument I might be interested in learning. There was no hesitation—none at all; it was trumpet. When Frank told Danny, Danny went to Bert Herrick, the go-to guy for LA brass players at that time, and had him machine a mouthpiece for me, and then he loaned me one of his horns for about the first six months I was getting started—an Olds Ambassador cornet.

During the years that the Firehouse Five Plus Two played summers in the Golden Horseshoe in Disneyland, I was there almost every Saturday night, in the box, stage left, that was reserved for the band. It wasn't so much that I yearned to play *like* Danny, it was that I thrilled to the *way* he played—the way he phrased, the way he led the band through a tune with his simple, melodic, and *always* rhythmically solid playing. Nothing high and showy, but with an unstoppable swing and punch that energized the whole band. I guess maybe that was the most valuable lesson that I was learning from Danny—he was so comfortable on stage, performing, sharing, exchanging ideas with his bandmates *and*, significantly, the audience. Frank, Ward, and the other guys who had started the band while animating at the Disney Studios certainly understood storytelling with their art, and they brought that to their music. Danny, I think, had always done it through his horn; it was in his bones.

As I started to learn how to play jazz, I jammed with Frank, and with George Probert who played soprano sax in the band, but I never really got to play with Danny until I started working summers at the Disney Studios in 1969. The noontime jam sessions that had started the band two decades earlier were still going, with several of the studio employees relaxing on their lunch hour, and I was allowed to bring my horn and join in. Danny, it was quite clear, was the musical director of what was going on, and he was a fairly stern taskmaster in terms of who would play, when, and even coach *what* to play during ensembles. We were there to make music, and it wasn't going to be a free-for-all. There was a discipline and rigor to that easy-going swing that he created onstage.

There were two horn players that he idolized, one was Louis Armstrong, and the other was his bandmate from the Bob Wills band, Benny Strickler. In the weekly sessions where I got a taste of playing second trumpet to Danny, I suppose that I also got to absorb a little of the inspiration that Danny had picked up from those two masters. Then the summer was over and I was off to college.

The pattern repeated itself in the summer of 1970, and a little of 1971, but Danny was having some health problems, and I think that the joy he found in the weekly jam sessions pretty much ended together with the death of Louis Armstrong, July 6, 1971. I recall that moment having a big impact on Danny, and after that he'd sometimes call a tune, saying seriously, "Let's play this one for Louis." Of course, this wasn't simply admiration from afar—Armstrong and Danny had played together when the two bands shared a stage at Dixieland Jubilees, a Horseless Carriage tour, and on the television show "Stars of Jazz." At the end of the summer I went back to college, and by the time I returned the following summer, Danny had retired from the studio.

The Firehouse Five Plus Two and Louis Armstrong All-Stars at the Horseless Carriage Club tour in South Lake Tahoe, September 13, 1956. L to R: Ralph "Zulu" Ball, tuba; Dick Roberts, banjo; George Probert, soprano sax; Frank Thomas, piano; Edmond Hall, clarinet; Billy Kyle, piano; Velma Middleton, vocals; Trummy Young, trombone; Ward Kimball, trombone; Barrett Deems, drums; Louis Armstrong, trumpet; Danny Alguire, cornet; Eddie Forrest, drums; Dale Jones, bass. Courtesy of the Ward Kimball Family.

By the end of the decade, when the Firehouse Five Plus Two came back together for the Rose Parade, the old spirit was back for a few days, and I recall Frank returning from the dance they played on New Year's Eve, bubbling over with how, when the band hit the downbeat on the first song, it was as though they'd never stopped playing together.

It was a good way to put a capper on a musical life. It's quite amazing to realize that the library of Firehouse Five recordings are still available and being listened to today, all the way from 1949 through 1970. Danny is an essential part of that sound and, to me, an essential part of what I've always tried to bring to music. And now, thank goodness, we have his autobiography to round out that musical life. It reveals, so beautifully, how Danny's gift was not only how he played that horn, but who he was. Of course, I have many musician friends, especially in jazz, who claim that those two are one and the same. In the case of Dan Alguire, you'd be hard pressed to argue otherwise.

Hal Smith (Drums)

For want of an ice cream cone, I might not have become a jazz musician....

In the summer of 1962, my parents offered to take me to Disneyland to hear the Firehouse Five Plus Two. Eight years old, I was already addicted to their GOOD TIME JAZZ records, and jumped at the opportunity to hear them in person. We arrived at the "Oaks Tavern" gazebo in Frontierland about a half-hour before downbeat and anxiously waited for the music to begin. When the musicians finally mounted the small stage, bright lights illuminated the colorful firemen's costumes, the bright red-sparkle drum set and the large fire bell at the center of the stage. In just a couple of minutes, leader Ward Kimball stomped off the tempo and the band launched into a high-flying version of "At The Jazz Band Ball."

I was transfixed for the entire set—my first experience with a *live* jazz performance. As the final number of the first set came to a close, I hoped for a chance to tell the band how much their music meant to me, and to acquire their signatures in my autograph book. But most of the musicians were already huddled together behind the stage, smoking their cigarettes, cigars and pipes. Only Danny Alguire stood apart, enjoying a vanilla ice cream cone in the late-evening July heat. I was having second thoughts about approaching any of the musicians, but my mother took my hand and said, "Come on. I'm sure they would like to know how much you enjoy their playing."

Danny had a friendly smile as we walked up to him. He stuck out his hand and said, "Howdy. How are you? Enjoying the music?" Wide-eyed, about all I could do was stammer "Y-yes! Can I please have your autograph?" Danny said, "Sure! Where do you want me to sign?" As soon as he autographed the page he said, "Come over here. Let's get the other fellas to sign your book." And just like that I was introduced to Dick Roberts, Eddie Forrest, Don Kinch, Frank Thomas, George Probert and the chief himself—Ward Kimball. All of them were wonderful to talk with, and treated a young fan and his mother with courtesy and, sensing my nervous state, a little good humor. I left the backstage area not only with treasured autographs, but with the great feeling that a fantastic group of musicians would take their valuable intermission time to make me feel appreciated.

Subsequently, my family made numerous trips to Disneyland to hear the Firehouse Five Plus Two. We always enjoyed their performances and I was happy to be able to talk with the musicians between sets—especially Danny. My interest in their music inspired me to start playing music, with the thought in the back of my head that someday I might be good enough to perform in a band like the Firehouse Five Plus Two. The Firehouse Five musicians encouraged me, and recommended records that I should listen to. Their kindness and support put me on the path to playing jazz for a living.

Years later, I accepted Danny's kind invitation to visit him at the Disney Studios in Burbank—to talk about his mentor Benny Strickler. Danny identified Benny for me in a couple of microscopically-small photos and told me about his playing style. I even got to jam with Danny and several other Disney musicians in one of their lunchtime sessions!

Danny moved to Oregon in the 1970s, and I also lived there briefly. My friend, Chris Tyle, was also acquainted with Danny as they had played together in some local bands. Knowing of my appreciation for Benny Strickler's playing, and Chris' newfound interest in it, Danny invited us to his house in Beaverton. There, we recorded an interview with him and we were able to find out even more about Strickler's music, his family and his personality. Not long after the interview, Chris, my wife, and I attended Danny's birthday party at his house in Beaverton. His famous Texas Chili was served to the guests. That was one of the highlights of the party, together with a jam session which included Danny, Don Kinch, and George Bruns!

During the 1990s, I made some CDs with Chris Tyle, where he played cornet in the Alguire style. After hearing the recordings, Danny responded by letter, with warm praise for Chris' cornet playing and appreciation for the band's approach to Traditional Jazz. 30 years after meeting him for the first time, Danny Alguire continued to inspire me to be a jazz musician. But if he had been in the group of smokers that first night, instead of standing off to the side with an ice cream cone, I might never have gotten the courage to talk with one of the most important people in my musical career!

Chris Tyle (Trumpet)

I unfortunately don't recall exactly when I first met Danny Alguire. It was definitely in the Portland, Oregon area, after he had relocated there from years in Southern California. I'm pretty sure he came to play at one of the meetings of the Oregon City Traditional Jazz Society—a newly-formed group of jazz fans that held monthly meetings in Oregon City—a suburb south of Portland.

I do remember the first time I played cornet in public, in 1975, was on a gig which Danny was playing, again in Oregon City, in a little tavern called McAnulty and Barry. He was working there with a band led by clarinetist Jim Beatty. Danny welcomed me to the bandstand and I got to play a few tunes. At that time I wasn't much of a player, but Danny couldn't have been nicer to me. He was very encouraging and said I was on the "right track."

Sometime later, he and I were again at a meeting of the traditional jazz society, and when I was playing the tune "Fidgety Feet" with the jam band, I played trumpeter Benny Strickler's half-chorus from the GOOD TIME JAZZ recording made when he was a member of the wartime, San Francisco-based Yerba Buena Jazz Band. I had known the record for years (my father Axel had the 78), but what I didn't know was that Danny and Benny had been in the Bob Wills band. When the jam band went on a break, Danny came up to me, a big smile on his face, telling me, "Wow, man—you played Benny's solo!" At that point he explained to me their connection.

Fast-forward a couple of years, when I was playing in a group led by Danny's band mate from the Firehouse Five Plus Two, Don Kinch. Don, a marvelous trumpeter, string bass and tuba player, had been in touch with drummer Hal Smith, who had been enthused by Kinch's band and eventually moved from La Jolla to Portland. I got to know Hal quite well, and he introduced me to Danny's work with Bob Wills and also to his work with the Firehouse Five. Although my father (who played drums in Kinch's band) had a large record collection, he only had a few of the Firehouse Five records, but I vaguely remembered as a small boy seeing the group on television.

During the late 1970s and eighties I occasionally saw Danny, but we basically lost touch. When I moved to New Orleans in 1989, I recorded a tribute album to his Bob Wills band mate, Benny Strickler. Fortunately Hal Smith sent a copy to Danny just a short time before he died, and he was very pleased with our efforts.

I will never forget Danny's kindness and encouragement to me when I was starting out, and his cheerful attitude. So much of that comes through with the words in his autobiography. His playing was always a joy to hear, very straight forward and direct with an emphasis on the importance of knowing the correct melodies to the tunes, and when taking a solo keeping it uncomplicated— much in the style of his Bob Wills section mate, Benny Strickler. I don't know how Danny played before he met Benny, but he was a huge influence on him—and on their other section mate, Alex Brashear.

I do recall two little anecdotes about him. One time he went up to my dad and said, "You know, you're the luckiest guy in the world!" My dad was a bit taken aback, and replied, "Oh...why is that?" Danny responded, "Because you never have to work with a bad drummer!" The other is the little speech Dan said at the end of gigs (I think appropriated from Firehouse Five trombonist and leader Ward Kimball): "Now folks, when you get in your car, and you're on your way home, just remember one thing...GIVE 'ER HELL!!!"

Tribute to Benny Strickler by Danny Alguire (precise date unknown)

Danny Alguire's comments throughout the book confirm that Benny Strickler was a profound influence on his musical outlook as well as his playing style. When Alguire realized that the only article about Strickler was Floyd Levin's (in the British Jazz Journal), he received a green light from publisher Paul Affeldt to write this heartfelt tribute to his friend for Jazz Report *magazine.*

I recently asked Paul Affeldt if I could write an article for *Jazz Report* about Benny Strickler, one of the great trumpet men I knew and admired—both as a musician and as a person. As far as I know, only one article was ever written about Benny—a short piece by a Mr. Levin, which appeared about 1950 in an English jazz magazine. The article was well done, and adequately set down Benny's musical ability. But, to me, there was more to be written about Benny.

It was my great pleasure to have played with Benny for eight months in what is now referred to as the first "big band" of Bob Wills and His Texas Playboys (1941-1942). Now, before any reader mentions "Hillbilly Band," let me hasten to assure you this was a great, swinging band, consisting of four brass, four saxes, four rhythm, plus steel guitar, and two fiddles. Sure, we played Western tunes and fiddles hoe-downs (and no one played them as well as Bob Wills). Particularly, if we played the smaller Oklahoma and Texas towns, the people got more than a few of the country tunes (and most of these really swing, if done right!). But more than half of the dance numbers were filled with good big band and small band jazz and the great driving force of the band was spearheaded by the solid, spirited trumpet of Benny Strickler.

Benny Strickler at San Francisco's Dawn Club in 1942.
Courtesy of Diane Breazeale.

Benny had joined Bob Wills in Hollywood in the summer of 1941, when the band was in California making a picture. The story goes that Benny stopped Bob in the lobby of the Plaza Hotel in Hollywood and said, "Bob, my name is Benny Strickler. I play trumpet, and I want to play with your band." Benny had just heard a record release of the Wills' band on "Big Beaver" (OKEH label) and had been gassed by the beat of the band on this tune, so Benny just decided that's who he wanted to play with.

Well, Bob Wills is a great judge of character, so without even hearing Benny play, Bob said, "Okay, you're hired." And he never regretted it. Later, Bob remarked, "Hell, I could tell by looking at him that he could play good!"

I'll never forget the Tuesday night in Oklahoma City in November 1941. I had come from Los Angeles to Oklahoma City to visit my folks. Well, I read in the local paper that Bob Wills was playing that night at the Trianon Ballroom. I had met Benny in California and as I had heard he had joined the Bob Wills band, I was curious to know what Benny was doing in a Western-type band. So I dropped down to catch it. What a crowd! It took me at least fifteen minutes to work my way up to the stairs and through the crowd to the bandstand. But all this time, I was hearing the band, and particularly Benny, blowing great!

Well, it wound up that I joined the band that night too. It just happened that Bob Wills had decided to start his big band, and was augmenting. That same night Alex Brashear on trumpet and Woody Wood on clarinet and sax also joined the band. Both good jazzmen.

At this point I should list the personnel of this great band, for here was a musician's dream of a band, a "one in a million" coincidence that brought a bunch together that thought and played alike. On trumpets were: Benny Strickler, Alex Brashear, and Danny Alguire; on sax: Don Harlan, George Balay, Woody Wood, and Louis Tierney; on trombone: Neil Duer; piano, Al Stricklin; drums, Gene Tomlins, later replaced by Bob Fitzgerald; steel guitar, Leon McAuliffe; standard guitar, Eldon Shamblin; string bass, Darrel Jones; vocals, Tommy Duncan; fiddles, Bob Wills and Joe Holley.

This band could play anything well. Alex Brashear made some wonderful big band arrangements. And for variety, many "head" arrangements were worked out, featuring Benny on trumpet, Woody on clarinet, and Neil on trombone playing the traditional small group things. This was Benny at his best, a delight to hear. Here was Benny playing with such a good taste, warmth, but still with a swinging drive. And in this connection, here, too, was an insight into Benny himself. His concern always was the general overall sound of the band. Many times I heard him say, "Now, let's just make the tune sound good!" What he meant, of course, was to listen to each other, and play with the thought of *contributing* to the sound, not just what one person could get out of it for himself.

This, to me, is the essential thing in jazz, the striving for a meeting of the minds. Benny often said, "If you don't think together, you can't play together." And he proved it by his mental approach to his playing. He brought to the bandstand each night an enthusiasm that actually permeated throughout the band. It was a feeling that we were all going to play good. And we did. I never heard Benny play badly. He just didn't have an "off night." I recall a night that Benny had a split lip from a cold sore. Alex and I felt concern for him and wanted to trade parts with him to help him. But he said "Oh, it's okay. It only hurts when I take the mouthpiece away from my lips."

Benny was born in Fayetteville, Arkansas about 1917. I never knew just when he took up the trumpet, but presume it was at a fairly early age, because he loved to play. Benny was an excellent sight-reader, a talent I envied. I asked him once where he learned to read so well. He said, "I don't know. I just never thought much about it." Probably it came as natural as did his improvising. He never questioned it, just accepted it.

Benny told me he learned jazz by listening and playing with records of Louis Armstrong, Bix Beiderbecke, Red Nichols and others of his day, but then went on to develop his own style. I can't remember that Benny played like anyone else, although he could mimic any style. One night on a job he suddenly turned to me and said, "Here is the way Bix would play this," and played a chorus so close to Bix I almost fell out of my chair.

Benny married his wife Frances, and they came to California sometime in 1935 or 1936. They had two daughters, Diane and Janet. Times were pretty rough then, and Benny had his ups and downs making a living for his family. But music was his life and he was determined to play. I must mention Bob Logan, a wonderful trombone player and one of Benny's closest friends. They worked together almost constantly through good bands and bad bands from 1936 through 1941 in California.

About 1937, Seger Ellis got together a group including Benny and Bob Logan, which he called "The Choirs of Brass," consisting of four trombones, four trumpets, one clarinet, and four rhythm. They made several sides on Decca. I never heard any of these records, but I understand Benny played several solos on this session, the best one on a tune called "Bee's Knees." Someone should track these records down. I've tried but without success.

Benny also played in Wingy Manone's big band, Rube Wolfe's Paramount Theater pit band, and with Joe Venuti's band. Times got rough enough that Benny even took jobs with certain nameless hotel-style bands to provide a living for his family. One such job got so bad that he quit. He came home to his wife and simply said, "I'm sorry; I just couldn't play in that band." Frances answered, "It's all right, Benny, I understand," and then wondered how they would get groceries the next day. But Benny always provided, some way.

Money, to Benny, was the curse of his life. To him, it was a necessary nuisance. He knew he needed a certain amount of it to provide for his wife and children, whom he loved dearly, so he was forced to be concerned with it. But, money, as such, meant nothing to him. Here was a human with a horn who wanted to play. It was his life, and to have to be governed by monetary worries was to him an imposition on his time. He would turn over his checks to Frances, and let her budget the money, which she did—somehow!

The big trouble in Benny's life was that he lived at the wrong time. Too late for the flash years of the 1920s and too soon for the more secure years that followed the last war. I often think how far Benny would have gone had he lived the full life he deserved!

In the summer of 1942, the Bob Wills band left Tulsa to come to California for playing dates and recordings. As I recall, about eight sides were recorded for Columbia records (OKEH label) with the big band. Three or four of these were never released (and I never knew why). The ones released were: "My Confession," "Ten Years," "Let's Ride With Bob" (blues), and "Whose Heart Are You Breaking Now?" Unfortunately, Benny never took a solo on any of these sides except for a little Dixie chorus on "Ten Years." Some collectors thought the trumpet solo on "Let's Ride With Bob" was Benny. But this is not true. Alex Brashear played the solo on this. But Benny's horn is certainly there on first trumpet, swinging the band on all the releases listed above.

The Wills band began to break up in August 1942, because of the war. About this time, in San Francisco, Lu Watters joined the Navy, and they were desperately looking for someone to replace Lu. At last, here was the perfect spot for Benny, and the best man they could possibly get. Now, Benny would be where he could play as he wanted to play, so Benny came to San Francisco and joined the band. In later years Burt Bales (Watters piano man) said to me, "What a talent. Benny was playing just great. He was an inspiration to all of us!"

Fortunately, about the first week in S.F., the band made an air check, and four tunes are preserved. They were released on GOOD TIME JAZZ: "Cake Walkin' Babies," "K.C. Stomps," Dipper Mouth Blues," and "Fidgety Feet."[1]

But it wasn't to be. Benny had been in San Francisco hardly three weeks. One night on the bandstand, Benny suddenly became ill and started hemorrhaging. Doctor's verdict: tuberculosis. Benny returned to Fayetteville to enter a sanitorium, where he remained for over two years. Then he began to get better, even started to play a little on his horn. I talked to him by phone Christmas, 1945. He told me then he felt good, and that he was starting to play again. But this, too, was not to be. A few months later, he had a relapse and died. Everyone lost a great musician, and I lost a wonderful friend. Benny Strickler! A fine musician, a warm, human soul, a gentleman.

The End

Original Editor's Note: After reading the story above, there is only one comment I could make: "I wish I had written that!" This is the kind of story no jazz critic could have written. It is just a simple story about a warm, friendly musician, by a warm and friendly musician. It was written, not with a typewriter, but with a heart. You can't help but know when you read it, that Benny and Danny were friends, and that Benny's death hurt Danny a lot more than he'd ever say. I have an idea that knowing Danny is very much like knowing Benny, because the only possible way to dislike him, is to never meet him. Anyone who can read the above story without being moved, just can't read properly, and may as well quit. Thanks, Danny, it really "swings."

Section Endnotes:

1. To clarify, Alguire incorrectly identifies "Cake Walkin' Babies" as one of the songs from this session, when in fact "Jazzin' Babies Blues" was recorded.

Danny Alguire Remembered

By Chris Tyle, *The Mississippi Rag*, September 1992

Danny Alguire, cornetist and vocalist, died July 8. He was seventy-nine years old.

Alguire is best remembered for his long association with the Firehouse Five Plus Two, from 1949-1971. His tenure with that band is available on many GOOD TIME JAZZ recordings. In addition to his work with the Firehouse Five Plus Two, he was a member of Bob Wills and His Texas Playboys in 1941-42, during which time he recorded "Home in San Antone," a hit record during World War Two, which is now available on a Rhino compilation of Wills' material.

Born in Chickasha, Oklahoma, August 30, 1912, Alguire grew up in a musical family, his father playing drums professionally as did his brother. He began playing mellophone at age five and joined the Ft. Worth (Texas) Rotary Club Boys' Band. His family moved to Kansas City, Missouri where young Alguire heard Bennie Moten's band and the Coon-Sanders Nighthawks. He was 16 when he got his first trumpet, and played in the high school band, playing stock arrangements, including Red Nichols' arrangement of "Ida, Sweet As Apple Cider." During this time he listened to records by Nichols, Bix Beiderbecke, and Louis Armstrong, and live radio broadcasts from Chicago by Earl Hines' band. By 1935 he was working professionally in bands in Oklahoma City, and the next year he moved to Los Angeles to work in bands there.

On a visit to his parents in Oklahoma City in 1941, Alguire went to the see the Bob Wills band, as a good friend and fellow trumpeter, Benny Strickler, had recently joined them. Although the Wills band was erroneously thought by many musicians to be a "hillbilly band," Bob Wills' favorite music was jazz and his band was becoming well known as a fine jazz group in addition to playing "Western Swing."

Wills was riding high on a crest of popularity; his band frequently packed ballrooms, and this was the case the night Alguire went to hear them—it took him 15 minutes to reach the bandstand! Alguire was very impressed with the band. That night, Wills hired him, trumpeter Alex Brashear, and clarinetist Woody Wood.

The effect of trumpeter Benny Strickler on both Alguire and Alex Brashear was immense. Strickler influenced both men's playing for the remainder of their professional careers (Brashear died in 1983 after a brief comeback playing with Merle Haggard). In a written tribute to Strickler, Alguire recalled Strickler emphasizing a cooperative band spirit, which he termed a "meeting of the minds for a meeting of music." Strickler stated, "If you don't think together, you can't play together." Alguire commented that Strickler "brought to the bandstand each night an enthusiasm that actually permeated throughout the band. It was a feeling that we were all going to play good—and we did."

The Wills band broke up in 1942 due to the war, and Alguire joined the Navy as a radioman, stationed in the South Pacific. During his stint, he and his shipmates heard Wills' recording of "Home in San Antone" played on a radio show. Although his shipmates didn't believe it was Alguire singing, the fact was confirmed by the radio announcer! No doubt Alguire was very proud to know that Wills' record was a hit.

Following the war, Alguire spent time in San Francisco, playing "dime grands" (dance hall jobs where a dance with a female employee cost ten cents) with Harry Mordecai (banjo) and Burt Bales (piano). He also visited Hambone Kelly's to hear Lu Watters' band—sometimes sitting in, but more often just listening. Alguire also played a session with Turk Murphy (trombone), Bob Helm (clarinet), Burt Bales, Bill Dart (drums) of which private recordings exist.[1]

Returning to Los Angeles, Alguire played for a while with T. Texas Tyler's Western Swing Band, but eventually left full-time music to work as a fingerprint expert with the Los Angeles Police Department and later as a distributor of classic and jazz recordings.

Alguire joined the Firehouse Five Plus Two in 1949, and played and recorded extensively with them. Through the band's association with Walt Disney Studios he secured a job as an assistant director of Disney films (mostly cartoon work). He stayed with Disney until the mid-1970s, when he retired and moved with his wife to Beaverton, Oregon. While in the Portland area, he continued to play music occasionally, with Monte Ballou's Castle Jazz Band, the Jim Beatty Jazz Band and pick-up groups. He made frequent appearances at meetings of the Oregon Traditional Jazz Society, even after he quit playing (for medical reasons) in the early 1980s.

During the time Danny Alguire lived in the Portland area I had the pleasure of getting to know him, and the first time I played cornet in public was in a band with him in 1975. Alguire was a consummate musician—he knew exactly what he wanted to do and played everything from the heart. Personally, he was a down-to-earth man, and he had an infectious sense of humor. Although he loved and lived jazz, he knew how to entertain, and his version of the 1930s radio theme "Little Orphan Annie" was an oft-requested favorite.

Although the Firehouse Five Plus Two has been criticized by some writers for the occasional use of various sound effects (a tongue-in-cheek approach that was actually used sparingly), the band was totally dedicated to playing good jazz, and Alguire's input regarding tempo and pacing, based on his experience with Bob Wills, was invaluable. Alguire's recorded work with the band illustrates his style—simple, direct, no-nonsense approach to playing jazz—which worked perfectly. Standout performances can be heard on his solo on "San Antonio Rose," and his ensemble work on his own composition "Fire Chief Rag" (based on the Bob Wills composition, "Beaumont Rag").

Firehouse Five Plus Two pianist K.O. Eckland commented in the NOJC News, "Danny Alguire played a straight-ahead lead and the front office did little circles around him, all this set to a firm boom-chick beat. In reviewing Danny's sound, I realized that he probably never played anything past a quarter note. He didn't have to. He was relaxed. And what the relaxation brought about was time for fun."

In a letter to Hal Smith two years ago, Alguire stated his intention of "just riding it out to the coda"—an appropriate sentiment from a former Texas Playboy.

Section Endnotes:

1. Ellis Horne, was in fact the clarinetist for this recording.

Danny Alguire and the Southwestern Cornet Style

By Hal Smith

Occasionally, the sound of the Firehouse Five Plus Two threatened to descend into chaos. On the outchorus of "Tiger Rag" or "Anvil Stomp," the combination of Ward Kimball's acrobatic trombone glissandos, George Probert's relentless triplets on soprano sax, hard-scrubbed eighth notes from the banjo, busy tuba lines and loud cymbal crashes—and, many times, the wail of the siren—could almost overwhelm a listener. However, there was always one calm, stable instrumental voice amid the wall of sound: cornetist Danny Alguire. Danny's concept of the beat, regardless of the tempo, was always relaxed and his phrasing unhurried; a reflection of his personality and his Oklahoma roots. In the early 2000s, this writer talked with clarinetist Bob Helm regarding similar characteristics in the playing of trumpeter Benny Strickler—Danny's main inspiration. Helm, who had worked with both men, said: "I think [the cornet style] might be native to the Southwest."

As usual, Bob Helm was correct. And the "Southwestern Style" can be traced back at least to the 1920s recordings of Bennie Moten and his Kansas City Orchestra. (Danny heard the Moten Orchestra in person in Kansas City and without a doubt he heard their top-selling VICTOR record of "South" from 1928.) One of Moten's trumpeters, Ed Lewis, was a fellow Oklahoman (born in Eagle City). On "South" he plays a jaunty but laid-back lead on the ensemble choruses, (including a triplet figure that Danny later used). On the repeat of the chorus, Lewis played a cornet break that is totally unlike anything being played at that time in New Orleans, Chicago, or New York. There is a definite hesitation in the phrasing—like a Southwesterner ambling along, pausing to hitch up his trousers.

The "hitch" turns up on recordings by a number of well-known Southwestern hornmen—such as Missourian Yank Lawson's playing on Bing Crosby's 1942 version of "When My Dreamboat Comes Home." Another good example of the peculiar phrasing can be heard on Bob Wills' 1938 record of "Big Beaver" where Texas trumpet man Tubby Lewis tempers his Harry James and Bunny Berigan-inspired solo with some well-placed "hitches." New Mexican Alex Brashear plays a similar hot chorus on Wills' 1949 record of "Boot Heel Drag." The relaxed phrasing can also be heard occasionally on recordings by Kansas-born Nate Kazebier and even in the playing of outliers like Harry James, Sterling Bose, Bill Graham, Manny Klein, and Billy Butterfield.

Perhaps the most influential Southwestern hornman after Ed Lewis was the Arkansas trumpeter Benny Strickler. As a young jazzman during the Depression years, Strickler would have almost certainly heard the Bennie Moten record of "South." (Perhaps Ed Lewis' unique phrasing made a lasting impression?) Strickler worked with several Territory Bands before emigrating to Los Angeles in the mid-1930s. There he worked with orchestras led by Ben Pollack, Joe Venuti, Wingy Manone, and Vido Musso. He also played and recorded with Seger Ellis' "Choirs of Brass"—an orchestra with unusual instrumentation for the Swing Era: four trumpets, four trombones, four rhythm...and *one* clarinet! Though the Choirs of Brass only existed for about a year, Strickler was the star trumpet soloist. His chorus on a transcription recording of "Copenhagen" shows just how effective the easygoing Southwestern phrasing could be in a big band setting.

In 1941, Strickler joined Bob Wills and His Texas Playboys. About a year later he was briefly featured on one of their finest records: "Ten Years." This side includes a chorus by a band-within-a-band that was obviously influenced by the sound of Bob Crosby's Bob

Cats. Strickler's trumpet lead drives the ensemble, but with a relaxed down-home feel, which Danny Alguire called "the wide beat." He heard this kind of playing night after night sitting with fellow trumpet man Alex Brashear next to Strickler in the Texas Playboys brass section. When the Playboys recorded for *Columbia*, Danny recalled that even though Strickler was the strongest soloist, he was generous in sharing lead and solos with the other hornmen. As a result, we are able to hear Danny's first recording playing lead in a small band— the "Bob Cats" chorus on Bob Wills' "We Might As Well Forget It." The Strickler influence is undeniable in Danny's playing (although it takes a considerable amount of effort to filter out Wills' hollering, which nearly drowns out the ensemble).

When World War II broke up the Texas Playboys, Strickler moved on to San Francisco. He took over for trumpeter Lu Watters at the Dawn Club with the Wartime version of the Yerba Buena Jazz Band. Unfortunately, rapidly-worsening tuberculosis cut short his stay in the Bay Area. But before he returned to Arkansas, several transcriptions were made of Strickler with the Yerba Buena band. Despite the illness, his playing on "Fidgety Feet" and "Kansas City Stomp" shows the same kind of "relaxed heat" as Ed Lewis in 1928. Trombonist Bill Bardin, who played on the sessions with Strickler, described the trumpeter's style as "bouncy."

Danny Alguire never hesitated to name Benny Strickler as his major influence. He used the same kind of phrasing and many of the same licks throughout his musical career. After World War II, Danny played and recorded in Southern California with Western Swing bandleader T. Texas Tyler and Country Music guitar wizard Merle Travis. Danny is also seen and heard onscreen in three Snader Telescriptions with "Merle Travis and his Westerners," from 1951. His wonderful, loping cornet solo on "Sweet Temptation" is a perfect illustration of the style that originated in Kansas City in the twenties.

When Danny joined the Firehouse Five Plus Two in 1949, the band was still a novelty. On the recordings for GOOD TIME JAZZ and various radio and television performances, the band concentrated on sound effects, noisy ensemble passages, and tempos that often were too fast for comfort. As the only professional musician in the band, Danny's presence helped to tamp down some of the wilder elements, while still retaining the excitement. He also added immeasurably to the *jazz* content of the Firehouse Five Plus Two performances, as the band continued to evolve into one of the premier Traditional Jazz bands of all time.

By 1951, the Firehouse Five began turning out records such as "Fire Chief Rag" (Danny's composition)—totally free of gimmicks that were so prominent on the earlier discs. Though some of the band's later records might teeter on the edge of burlesque, "Fire Chief" is an excellent jazz performance. Another side from the same era is "San Antonio Rose," with a magnificent cornet bridge and ensemble lead on the outchorus. Danny's playing on "Rose" is in a class with the best Traditional Jazz hornmen: Lu Watters, Bob Scobey, Don Kinch, and (of course) Benny Strickler.

When soprano saxophonist George Probert joined the Firehouse Five in 1954, the sound of the front line changed drastically. Probert played aggressively, both in ensembles and solos. His tone could be piercing, and on occasion it nearly drowned out the cornet. But Danny resolutely continued to blow at a moderate volume, and sometimes simplified his already-uncomplicated melodic lines to accommodate the cascade of notes from the soprano. A good example of this is the Firehouse Five's 1959 version of "Ballin' The Jack" from the GOOD TIME JAZZ "Goes to a Party" album. Danny plays the melody on the first chorus, with the beautiful "wide beat" he admired so much, and keeps the melody going with just a few well-placed decorations on the last two choruses. He played the same way in person. If the other horns were filling up all the available space, Danny might start an ensemble chorus by holding a whole note, then easing into a simple improvisation on the melody. On solos he often played a pickup phrase, then five even quarter notes before improvising. Danny's choruses were never crowded with *too many* notes. He instinctively played just the *right* notes, and placed them where they would have the best effect. His phrasing always ambled along with a "wide beat" and almost always included a well-placed "hitch." The Southwestern cornet tradition reached its pinnacle with Danny Alguire as the hornman in the Firehouse Five Plus Two. Ed Lewis and Benny Strickler would have approved.

For Whom the Brass Bell Tolls: A Personal Appreciation of the Firehouse Five Plus Two on Their Fiftieth Anniversary

By Hal Smith

Originally published in the Spring 1999 issue (no. 8) of the Frisco Cricket, *the publication of the San Francisco Traditional Jazz Foundation.*

On May 13, 1949, a group of traditional jazz musicians gathered at Radio Recorders' Studio B in Hollywood. Though this GOOD TIME JAZZ session was made at the height of the West Coast Traditional Jazz Revival, the first number recorded was not played in direct imitation of Lu Watters, Turk Murphy, Kid Ory, Bunk Johnson or George Lewis. The selection was not a long-neglected composition by King Oliver or Jelly Roll Morton; rather, it started with a brass firebell and fire siren, ushering in a banjo solo based on "Under The Double Eagle." The reaction to the first four sides by the band was instantaneous and, thankfully, mostly favorable. One prominent critic called it, "The happiest band I have heard in a long time."[1] Though the band also suffered detractors (who continue to criticize it even to this day), those early recordings helped to launch the band's career, making it one of the most famous and successful traditional jazz groups of all time. The band's story is well-documented—in the liner notes of their recordings, in the pages of *Record Changer* in the forties and fifties and in the Southern California jazz club publications of the sixties. Still a capsule description of the band's accomplishments is called for....

In the mid-1940s, a group of Walt Disney animators, artists, writers and musicians who loved jazz would gather around a phonograph and play along with records during lunch breaks. One day, when the phonograph broke down and the musicians kept playing, they decided that the results were good enough to take to the public. With leader Ward Kimball, trombone; Clarke Mallery, clarinet; Frank Thomas, piano; Ed Penner, bass sax and Jim MacDonald on drums, the group billed itself as the "Hugageedy Eight" and later as the "San Gabriel Valley Blue Blowers." Eventually they picked up a trumpet man—Johnny Lucas—and a fine banjoist: Harper Goff. The final evolution came about when the Kimballs discussed the idea of taking the band along on a Horseless Carriage Club caravan from Los Angeles to San Diego. The only vehicle Ward Kimball could locate which was large enough to hold the band and old enough to qualify for the caravan was a 1914 American LaFrance fire truck. Keeping with the "fire" motif, Kimball acquired genuine fire helmets and red fireshirts to outfit the band. The newly-outfitted band was rechristened as the "Firehouse Five Plus Two."

To no one's surprise, the Firehouse Five Plus Two was the hit of the Horseless Carriage caravan.[2] Soon they were playing jobs, including a benefit for Kid Ory's guitarist, Bud Scott. Ory's clarinetist Joe Darensbourg recommended the Firehouse Five to the owner of the Beverly Caverns nightclub and the Firehouse crew began a series of successful appearances at "The Cavern."[3] They also attracted the attention of screenwriter and jazz fan Lester Koenig, who had helped start up the JAZZMAN label in the early forties. Koenig launched his own GOOD TIME JAZZ label with those first four sides by the Firehouse Five. The rest, as they say, is history.

Soon after the first recording session, bass saxophonist Ed Penner switched over to the more resonant tuba. Scheduling conflicts caused Lucas and MacDonald to bow out of the band. Their replacements were cornetist Danny Alguire and drummer Monte Mountjoy, both of whom had worked with Bob Wills and His Texas

Playboys. This lineup soon became the toast of Hollywood, playing the Mocambo nightclub, where Ginger Rogers, Lucille Ball, Judy Garland and other stars danced at the Monday night "Charleston contests." The band appeared several times on Bing Crosby's Chesterfield radio program, on television with Ed Wynn, Milton Berle and a Walt Disney Christmas special. In addition, the Firehouse Five was seen in the movies *Grounds For Marriage* and *Hit Parade Of 1951* and was the first jazz band to play the Rose Parade in Pasadena.

The Firehouse Five held tremendous appeal to the general public, but they were also a hit with jazz fans, playing to huge crowds at the Frank Bull-Gene Norman "Dixieland Jubilees" at the Shrine Auditorium in Los Angeles. In the early fifties they made several journeys north to play at Hambone Kelly's, Club Hangover and at the old Opera House in Virginia City, Nevada.

Contacts made in the Bay City produced enduring friendships and a mutual admiration society. This resulted in several San Franciscans donning firemen's gear during the ensuing years. Musicians such as Wally Rose and Bob Short guested with the band on occasion; Don Kinch, George Bruns, K.O. Eckland and Billy Newman had longer stays. And the band gained an admirer for life in Turk Murphy, who imported the Firehouse Five to the Italian Village and, later, Earthquake McGoon's. In addition, the Firehouse musicians became friendly with many of the pioneer New Orleans jazzmen, such as Albert Nicholas who, Ward Kimball explained, "gave us an awful lot of the do's and don'ts."[4] At various times, Zutty Singleton, Joe Darensbourg, Minor Hall and Nappy Lamare were featured guests with the band. (The "New Orleans" association worked both ways, when Ward Kimball was called on to substitute for an ailing Kid Ory).

The lessons learned from the New Orleans and San Francisco musicians helped to keep the jazz content high in the Firehouse Five's output. Their performances—live and recorded—were a high-energy combination of well-played traditional jazz, sound effects and novelty vocals saturated with an infectious good humor and spirit. In later years, Ward Kimball described the major influences which shaped the Firehouse style: "Jelly Roll Morton for his imagination and humor; Lu Watters for his simplicity and beat and Guy Lombardo for his brother!"[5] Perhaps the best description of the Firehouse Five's music can be found in the name of the label they recorded for: GOOD TIME JAZZ. The band continued to play great jazz and to maintain their own sound, even with several personnel changes in the fifties and sixties. And except for a brief hiatus from the Spring of 1952 to the fall of 1953, the Firehouse Five Plus Two probably became the most popular and high-profile jazz band of the West Coast Traditional Jazz Revival.

Fast-forward to 1962: a transplanted nine-year-old Hoosier, newly arrived in California (who somehow managed to miss all those radio, television and film appearances and all the recordings mentioned above) was about to have his life changed through a magical musical experience. What could be a better place for such magic to occur than Disneyland? The setting was a hot July night at the long-gone "Oaks Tavern" in "Frontierland." A few minutes before the scheduled starting time, seven musicians mounted the small Oaks Tavern gazebo in the darkness. Suddenly the lights came on, revealing the bright red fire shirts, white suspenders and gleaming white fire hats. The trombonist looked left and right to make sure that the band was ready to go and quickly gave a loud count-off: "HEY! ONE-AND-TWO-AND-THREE-AND-FOUR!" And the Firehouse Five Plus Two lit into "At The Jazz Band Ball." As those sounds went clear through me, I literally shivered with delight and I don't think I have ever recovered! At the intermission, encouraged by my parents, I got up enough nerve to actually talk to the musicians. Friendly, polite Danny Alguire was my first contact. Without missing a lick on his ice cream cone, he introduced me to Ward Kimball, Don Kinch (helicon), Dick Roberts (banjo), Frank Thomas (piano), Eddie Forrest (drums) and soprano saxophonist

George Probert. The band generously gave up their intermission to talk to me and sign autographs, and they encouraged me to keep my interest in the music. When George Probert handed me a copy of the latest *Jazzologist* magazine, saying, "Here, man. I want you to read this," it was shades of Doc Souchon getting the nod from King Oliver. I had arrived. On the next set, Ward Kimball dedicated a number to me. "Magic" is indeed the only adjective I can think of that adequately describes this first encounter with live jazz.

After I discovered there were Firehouse Five recordings, the fate of my weekly allowance was a foregone conclusion, as were subsequent requests for birthday and Christmas presents. I stuck to the music of the Firehouse Five like glue, even as American culture embraced the Beatles, peace, love, dope and everything else that went with rock 'n' roll. I endured the "Old Weird Harold" label at school, listening to "Birmingham Papa (Your Memphis Mama's Comin' To Town)" instead of "She Loves You (Yeah, Yeah Yeah)."

As enjoyable as the records were, though, nothing could beat hearing the Firehouse Five in person at Disneyland. Thankfully, my parents indulged my newfound obsession, driving the long haul from La Jolla to Anaheim without complaint. They grew to enjoy the Firehouse Five performances almost as much as I did. We reveled in their music first at Oaks Tavern, then the Golden Horseshoe Saloon and finally at New Orleans Square. Ward Kimball gladly played my requests, eventually calling them as soon as he spotted me in the crowd. When I found that he was a rail fan, we had another subject to discuss besides jazz and even maintained a correspondence for a while. The other Firehouse Five band members continued to give freely of their precious intermission time to encourage a young musician and I can never adequately repay their kindness. I laughed, along with jazz fans and those who just enjoyed the Firehouse "experience," at Ward's droll humor on the microphone. I always got a charge out of the brass firebell introductions, the fire siren on the outchoruses, the boombass, washboard, tambourine, castanets, bird whistle, duck call, and train whistle. I loved Eddie Forrest's virtuosity with salad spoons on "Bye Bye Blues," the furious double-time outburst during a quiet passage of Sister Kate, the dog howls and "train wreck" on "Yellow Dog Blues" and Ward's "How do you like the opera so far?" on "Anvil Stomp."

The sound effects, colorful uniforms and well-done humor were enjoyable and no doubt helped the band put its music across to the public. But at Disneyland these elements were not overused and the Firehouse Five onstage was anything but hyper. The only movements that drew attention were George Probert's hypnotic head bobbing as he played and Danny's "Benny Strickler" position; leaning back, pointing the cornet slightly upwards to project better on solos and outchoruses. And the repertoire was remarkable. In the early days of the band, Ward Kimball was given several arrangements of "San Francisco" originals, which remained unplayed. When George Probert asked why the numbers were never added to the Firehouse repertoire, Ward replied, "The people wanna hear songs they recognize."[6] Certainly, the band played "Tiger Rag," "Muskrat Ramble," "St. Louis Blues," "Bill Bailey," "Sweet Georgia Brown" and the inescapable "Saints" with all the stops pulled out at nearly every performance. However, the Firehouse Five "book" also included many of the best traditional jazz compositions from the early years of jazz. The first versions I ever heard of "Milenburg Joys," "Panama," "San," "Doctor Jazz," "Memphis Blues," "Blues My Naughty Sweetie Gave To Me," "Come Back, Sweet Papa," "Storyville Blues," "Working Man Blues," "Copenhagen," "Mississippi Rag," "Tishomingo Blues," "Riverside Blues" and "South" were by the Firehouse Five at Disneyland. The band also played terrific vintage pop songs like "I Can't Believe That You're In Love With Me," "You've Got To See Mama Ev'ry Night," "Just Because" and "San Antonio Rose" with Danny Alguire's easygoing Southwestern vocals.

It was enlightening to hear occasional changes in the personnel. For a while, Frank Thomas and K. O. Eckland alternated on piano. Frank eventually left the band and K. O. was his permanent replacement. When Dick Roberts retired due to health reasons, Billy Newman took over the banjo chair. We heard Don Kinch sub for Alguire; George Bruns for Kimball; John Smith for Probert. But none of these changes—even the sharp contrast between Danny's and Don's cornet work—altered the band's basic sound. However, there was one edition of the Firehouse Five which sounded very different from all the others.... As I recall, we went to Disneyland one weekend in September, 1964 to catch the Firehouse Five Plus Two on their regular Saturday night job. The band may still have been at the Oaks Tavern, but I am not positive. What I do remember is my initial shock at seeing Don Kinch's helicon wrapped around George Bruns and Don standing next to Danny, both holding cornets. Ward stepped to the mic and rasped, "We're gonna play some Lu Watters style tonight." (Lu Watters? Ah, yes! That intriguing name on the GOOD TIME JAZZ LP sleeves. Well, now I'll find out how....) Four stomps and the augmented Firehouse Five sailed into "I Ain't Gonna Give Nobody None O' This Jelly Roll" and this writer was literally rocked back in his seat. Even at a remove of thirty-five years, I can still hear that first two cornet number as clearly as if it was just played five minutes ago. The band was rocking, literally, from the first beat. (By the way, that's "rock" as in "Annie Street"). Working hand-in-glove, Danny and Don traded off on the flawless lead and second parts. Their musical colleagues responded with even more of a stomp feel than usual and the resulting "two-cornet" jazz was one of the greatest musical evenings I have ever had the pleasure of hearing.

 I continued to follow the band even after the inevitable exposure to records by Lu Watters and Bob Scobey and live performances by Turk Murphy, the Bay City Jazz Band and the up-and-coming South Frisco Jazz Band. The "new" sounds and repertoire commanded my attention in the late sixties, though it was a delight to "go back to the roots" and to hear the Firehouse Five one final time at Disneyland in 1969. They were as good as ever and even played a couple San Francisco numbers I had not heard them do previously: "Auntie Skinners' Chicken Dinner" and "Beale Street Mama." By the early seventies, I had fallen in with a crowd of young musicians known loosely as the "Fink Street Five (Plus Two)." The original influence on this group should be readily apparent from the band's name. Though the individual musicians were also fascinated with the music of Oliver, Morton, Armstrong, Dodds, Ory, Beiderbecke, Venuti-Lang, Watters and Murphy, the Firehouse inspiration remained strong. (Despite the relatively broad musical tastes within this group, they were capable of pulling off Firehouse-like versions of "Anvil Stomp" and "You've Got To See Mama Ev'ry Night" without even a brief consultation beforehand). Finally, in 1971, one of our group got the word that the Firehouse Five was going to play its last job: a car show. On November 17, we gathered by the stage in the middle of the old Anaheim Convention Center to enjoy the Firehouse Five one last time. Danny Alguire had been sidelined by a stroke, but fortunately Don Kinch was flown in from Portland, joining Ward Kimball, George Probert, K.O. Eckland, Billy Newman, George Bruns and Eddie Forrest for the last time. I doubt that there was a dry eye anywhere surrounding the stage when the Firehouse Five Plus Two roared into "Tiger Rag" for the grand finale. For me, an era had ended and the jazz scene would never be quite the same, or nearly as much fun.

Now it's fifty years since the band's recorded debut, thirty-seven years after I heard them for the first time and twenty-eight years after hearing them for the last time. To Ward Kimball, Danny Alguire, Don Kinch, George Probert, Frank Thomas, K.O. Eckland, Dick Roberts, Billy Newman, George Bruns and Eddie Forrest I say: Without your dynamic performances and your kindness to a young listener, I would never have gained an appreciation for traditional jazz. Thank you for the great music, the good times and the friendship. You made a fan for life.

Section Endnotes:

1. George Avakian, *The Record Changer*, September, 1949.
2. Lester Koenig, notes to Firehouse Five Plus Two Story, GOOD TIME JAZZ CD-22055; Robert S. Greene, "The Firehouse Five Plus Two," *Record Changer*, September, 1949.
3. Joe Darensbourg, *Jazz Odyssey; The Autobiography of Joe Darensbourg as Told to Peter Vacher*, Baton Rouge, Louisiana State University Press, 1987, p. 118.
4. Greene, op. cit.
5. Ward Kimball, "Llabmik Draw Interviews Ward Kimball," *Southern California Hot Jazz Society Fanfare*, January-February, 1969.
6. George Probert, conversation with the author, 1994.

A Cinderella Story: The Firehouse Five Plus Two in 1950

By Lucas O. Seastrom

Originally published in the Hyperion Historical Alliance Annual, *inaugural issue, 2019.*

"One must approach [jazz] with an emotional awareness outside the bounds of traditional critique."—Dave Brubeck, January 1950[1]

On Monday evening, January 23, 1950, a seven-piece jazz band roared up Hollywood's Sunset Boulevard aboard an antique fire engine. Each musician was dressed in the garb of a fireman, albeit of some decades earlier: red shirts, white suspenders, blue pants with a red handkerchief, and a gleaming white antique helmet with the number "5" emblazoned on the shield. With a wail of the siren and screech of the brakes, the engine came to a halt outside the Mocambo, one of the biggest nightclubs on the Sunset Strip. Traffic congested to a swarm. Onlookers craned their necks for a view as the firemen ran inside with instruments in hand. Onstage, they looked onto a crowd overflowing with Hollywood elite. A sense of expectant curiosity hung in the air. Ward Kimball, the bandleader and trombonist, called the group to order, and they erupted with another siren wail into their first song. Feet tapped, hips swung, and bodies quickly moved to the dance floor. The crowd seemed in a trance, taken hold by the band's rhythm. It was the Firehouse Five Plus Two, and this was their spare-time job.

"Take 'em Away!"

The band that would take America by storm in 1950 had come of age in the late 1940s. Originating as a lunchtime jam group of artists and writers at The Walt Disney Studios, the Firehouse Five Plus Two had evolved into a part-time professional crew. They played gigs on nights and weekends whilst maintaining their full-time Disney jobs Monday through Friday. They played for fun, and it came across in their music. With grassroots origins punctuated by the inclusion of a handful of seasoned professional musicians, the Firehouse Five developed a loose, rhythmic style of playing traditional jazz, a musical form then experiencing resurgence in popularity. Capping it off was an innate sense of personality and showmanship, derived in part by their experience as Disney animation storytellers, and accentuated by their unmistakable uniforms. Audiences found them appealing. In 1949, they released their first recordings on the brand-new GOOD TIME JAZZ label and a contract agreement was made with the Music Corporation of America (MCA).

Ward Kimball on trombone was joined by Danny Alguire, a professional musician, on cornet, and Disney animator Clarke Mallery on clarinet. Banjoist Harper Goff, "the real high harmony spark plug" of the group, was at the time plying his trade as a Hollywood studio and commercial artist, though he'd later come to work for Disney.[2] Monte Mountjoy kept the beat on drums. Known as "the Beachcomber," he was another professional musician and friend of Alguire's.[3] Ed Penner had been a prodigy as a young musician on the violin and had developed into a multi-instrumentalist.[4] He learned the tuba specifically to play in the Firehouse Five, and spent his day job as one of the Disney Studios' core writers and story men. Frank Thomas capped things off on piano, and along with Kimball was one of Disney's most gifted animators.

The Firehouse Five Plus Two had grown used to performing on Monday nights. In 1949 the band took the Monday slot at the Beverly Caverns. The small Los Angeles club that had become a haven for jazz music was in a way the spiritual home of the Firehouse Five as a mature group. Ward Kimball would tell Los Angeles' *The Mirror* that October, "Our wives are Monday night music widows. And it's hard getting up the next morning. Aside from that we have a great time."[5] From the beginning of October to Christmas that year, the band wouldn't miss a single Monday at the Caverns, earning each man the munificent sum of $10.00 at each gig.[6] But if Kimball thought Mondays at the Caverns were taxing, he and his bandmates had little anticipation of the tidal wave which was to come.

Charley Morrison, owner and proprietor of the Mocambo—one of the Sunset Strip's two biggest nightclubs, the other being Ciro's—was looking to fill his Monday night slot. The Mocambo had become the stuff of somewhat dubious legend since its debut in 1941 as a South American-themed hotspot. For actors and talent, agents and producers, gossip columnists and other industry players, the Mocambo was the place to be, where Hollywood found its fun, and often rowdy, side.

It seemed strange enough for a Hollywood nightclub to open on a Monday night, but Morrison was following Ciro's lead and going with a seven-nights-a-week lineup. Stranger still was the prospect of hiring a traditional jazz band. But Morrison was onto something, some nostalgia-fueled energy gripping much of the country, and the idea of a Charleston contest came to mind. The Firehouse Five's success at the Mocambo was not guaranteed, however. *Fortnight* magazine would describe Morrison's backup plan that first Monday evening: "The first night he took no chances, stashed a trio of rumba players on the premises to take over should the jazzmen flop. After a few hot licks from the Firehouse gang, ecstatic guests were shouting, 'South America—take 'em away!' at the rumba men."[7]

Walt and Lillian Disney were present that opening night in January. Walt graced the stage at one point, giving a few brief remarks. He would return a handful of times to see the group play to the delight of the Hollywood society that had continued to keep his studio and much of the animation industry at arm's length. Perhaps Walt smiled with a hint of indignation, touched by the affirmation that his studio's lunchtime jam group could so enthrall the star-studded audience. Ward Kimball would later tell Michael Barrier, "[Walt] was so proud of that band for years that he went to all our openings at the Mocambo; he got up there on the stage, I remember, at the Mocambo, a place he'd never go. He said 'my boys' and made speeches in front of all the rest of the stars."[8] As Diane Disney Miller and Pete Martin would later describe, "People told [Walt], 'Aren't you afraid to let them do all that? They become so popular you'll lose them.' 'I think what they're doing is swell,' [Walt] said. 'It's not only good for them but it's good for their work at the studio.'"[9]

Sitting at the table next to Walt and Lillian that first evening was *Los Angeles Examiner* columnist Harry Crocker, who would serve as regular emcee of the band's fabled Charleston contests for the next three months. When Crocker "spotted a bright red, shiny fire engine outside Mocambo, it should have been a tip-off that there was something unusual inside. And oh boy was there!!!" Amidst the noise and energy of the nightclub, Walt and Lillian told the reporter about the band's work at their studio, about Kimball, Thomas, and Mallery's animation and Penner's story work. They spoke of the lunchtime jam sessions that had been an indelible part of the Studios' culture for a decade, sending music wafting through the halls of Disney's Animation Building. Together they laughed and cheered, that same music now blasting the Mocambo's doors practically wide open. "Ward Kimball signaled the commencement of each dance with the wail of a siren. They played red-hot blues. They played stomps and jazz and all in the most wonderful dance time."[10]

The next morning, the first review was already in from Florabel Muir of *The Mirror*, "Along about nine o'clock this morning seven guys from the Walt Disney Studio were chanting, like the seven dwarfs in *Snow White*, 'Heigh-ho, heigh-ho, it's back to work we go,' but it wasn't that way out on the Sunset Strip last night."[11] Brandy Brent of *The Los Angeles Times* would open her Friday column with a report:

> Night life has returned to Sunset Strip in full glory now that Mocambo has followed Ciro's lead and gone on a seven-nights-a-week basis. Charley Morrison was prepared to do a land-office business when he hired the Firehouse Five Plus Two. What he was *not* prepared for was the way traffic got tied up in front of his swank eatery when the unique band roared up in a real, honest-to-gee-whiz fire engine and parked it. Naturally, everybody passing by just *knew* that Mocambo was on fire and "took on" accordingly.[12]

The Firehouse Five Plus Two had arrived as Hollywood's new sensation, and the enthusiasm would not subside for nearly a year.

For many critics, the newest attraction on the Sunset Strip was a cause for bemusement. Florabel Muir attempted to explain the phenomenon at the end of January, calling it "That Old, Free Spirit." She continued, "there was a nostalgic reaching back for the wild days of the late twenties, when dance contests and marathon walking contests were the vogue...."[13] Nearly a month later, with the craze only intensifying, she again searched for an explanation. "It must be that an escape complex has gripped our townsfolk and sent them chasing back into the days when nobody had ever even dreamed of an A-bomb much less an 'H' one." In her same column, Muir would quote a Mocambo employee, "That kind of music makes everybody happy. I haven't heard of no fights here on Monday night. Nobody is mad at nobody." Pursuing her line on the bigger picture, Muir would add, "Maybe it would be a good idea to stage one of those Charleston contests at a meeting of the United Nations with Disney's boys playing. It might even put the grouchy Russians in a happier frame of mind."[14]

The apprehension of post-war American life was tinged with a sense of geo-political uncertainty. Americans were still getting used to the idea of being a superpower. The uncomfortable realities of a potential nuclear conflict seemed fertile ground for cultural nostalgia to take root. The wistful yearning seemed to come naturally for the days of 25 or 30 years earlier, before the crash of 1929 and before America fully stepped onto the world stage. Just in the week leading up to the Firehouse Five's Mocambo debut, headlines in *The Los Angeles Times* seemed dominated by news of diplomatic tensions with Communist powers like Russia and China. The Korean War would commence in June and escalate into a bloody, seemingly futile stalemate by the year's end.

The Firehouse Five Plus Two would play every Monday night at the Mocambo for the next nine months (barring just one night in February when the club was closed for a private party). Each band member brought home $18 a night at the start. Celebrities and stars became regulars at the Charleston contests, including Barbara Stanwyck, Bette Davis, Joan Crawford, Lucille Ball, Kirk Douglas, Van Johnson, and Jimmy Stewart, among countless others. Their repurposing of classic tunes like "Five Foot Two" and "Tiger Rag" into a rhythmic, dance-driven sound was striking a chord with the audience. And the Sunset Strip was only the top of the Firehouse Five's schedule. The band intended to stay busy, playing "Casual Engagements" at venues across Southern California on weekends. "This is undoubtedly the hottest combination in show business today and shows how a hobby can develop," Harry Crocker would say.[15]

"As Authentically As We Can"

Bing Crosby had first come into contact with the band in March of 1948 whilst recording narration and singing vocals for *The Adven-*

tures of Ichabod and Mr. Toad (1949).[16] He joined Walt and Disney Studios composer Ken Darby in a visit to Kimball's office to observe the jam group. "That's pretty good, boys," he would tell them.[17] By 1950, Crosby and the group had commenced a professional relationship. And only days after their Mocambo debut, the band was in the recording studio with Bing and the Andrews Sisters (themselves alumni of two Disney package features) laying down tracks for Crosby's nationally broadcast radio program sponsored by Chesterfield cigarettes.

The first show aired Wednesday night, February 22, at 9:30 p.m. Between songs, Ward held his own, bantering back and forth with Crosby like a seasoned entertainer. The band played fast and fun, and Crosby would join them on tunes like "Yes Sir, That's My Baby." Now, across the entire country, Americans were talking about the Firehouse Five Plus Two. National exposure—something similar jazz bands of the time could only dream of—was beginning to set the band apart. Fan letters began to arrive. New 78 rpm singles were released by the GOOD TIME JAZZ record company. Advertisements and profiles on the band now hailed them for both their success at the Mocambo and the Crosby program. By April, the Firehouse Five had appeared on two additional episodes. The band's "chief," Ward Kimball, was juggling it all without an official manager or press agent.

On the same Chesterfield program in which the Firehouse Five made their debut alongside Crosby, the crooner sang a brand new and soon to be smash hit song: "Bibbidi-Bobbidi-Boo." *Cinderella*, Walt Disney's first full-length animated feature in eight years, premiered in mid-February. Band members like Ed Penner, Frank Thomas, and Ward Kimball had been intimately involved in its creation. The Walt Disney Studios was, in short, relying upon the film's success for strong financial footing. As Thomas would later explain, "When [Walt] did *Cinderella*, he had to be sure it was a safe picture because his market was still uncertain. Well, it was solid…so now he was back in business, but he couldn't experiment as wildly as he had before."[18]

Cinderella's success to the tune of $8 million brought a new sense of hopeful opportunity for the Disney Studios. All of a sudden the boys in the Firehouse Five had a hit movie at their day job, and Ward would work references to the film into his emceeing at gigs. As Frank Thomas would jokingly remember to Michael Barrier: "[…] when Ward would introduce the guys and [tell] what they did at the studio, he would introduce me as the one who'd done the stepmother, and everybody would go 'boooo!' Then he'd say, 'I did the mice' [imitating sound of audience cheering and applauding]. He came off looking like a million bucks!"[19]

At the beginning of March, a photo in *Time* magazine showed Ward Kimball, dressed in fireman's garb, blowing his trombone on the Mocambo stage. The accompanying column profiled the Firehouse Five. "We try to play as authentically as we can," Ward told the magazine. "If we turned pro it might cease to be fun and the band might not have that good-time sound anymore." The *Time* columnist would conclude: "Playing to their first nationwide audience [on the radio], the Firehousers sounded like just what they were: topflight amateurs who can push some professionals when it comes to two-beat jazz."[20]

"Ain't Mad at Nobody"

In April, GOOD TIME JAZZ record producer Lester Koenig received two letters from Helen Lang of the Evergreen Record Sales Company in Seattle. Lang shared the recent excitement of their promotions for the Firehouse Five. Stores and radio stations in the area handed out countless red firemen's toy helmets. Elaborate window displays beckoned customers inside. "You should have been here yesterday," she exclaimed, "people came all day asking about the hats…." When just a day earlier she had hoped for a relatively modest hit of 20,000 records sold, she now proclaimed: "There isn't a reason in the world why the Firehouse Five can't sell a million...."²¹

The Firehouse Five were now setting their sights on television. Their appearance on *The Ed Wynn Show* made its debut on April Fool's Day. It was an ideal match. Wynn had starred in *The Fire Chief*, a national radio program in the 1930s, and his character remained well known. During Firehouse Five shows at the Mocambo he would join in on the fun and antics, sometimes donning a helmet himself.²² And Wynn was soon to join the Disney canon as the Mad Hatter in *Alice in Wonderland* (1951), the next Disney animated feature then in development. 1950 was the final season for Wynn's television program, which had been among the early pioneers in the new medium. This was most likely not, however, the Firehouse Five's debut on television. Rather, they first appeared on KTLA's *Bandstand Revue* just a few weeks prior.²³

Near the height of their demand, the Firehouse Five were earning their keep. April brought the band a raise at the Mocambo, which was nearly doubled a month later in May. By then each member was bringing home around $43 a night. In addition, they continued a bout of gigs beyond the Sunset Strip. They played everywhere from the Trianon Ballroom and the Hotel Del Coronado to the Palm Springs Racquet Club and a fraternity house near the University of Southern California.²⁴ The *Hollywood Reporter* noted, "The hottest band in the country, according to MCA, is the Firehouse Five.... But the boys won't move out of town because they value their Disney jobs more than the sudden and short-lived fame they're now having."²⁵

As acclaim for the band grew, the jazz community had continued to take notice and comment. *Downbeat* magazine, a leading jazz publication, had in general remained skeptical of the so-called "revivals" of the Dixieland and New Orleans styles of traditional jazz. One *Downbeat* columnist, Hal Holly, began reporting on a seeming divide in the community. With thinly-veiled disdain, he first wrote on what he considered a rather pedestrian fad in American jazz. Amidst a partially contrived debate on the merits and categorizations of the Dixieland and New Orleans styles, Holly quoted a series of "eminent authorities," among them Kid Ory, Pete Daily, and Ward Kimball. Sensing the ultimate futility of the discussion, Ward stated: "When you play 'Muskrat Ramble' like Jelly Roll Morton, it's New Orleans jazz. If you add a tenor sax it's Dixie. If you throw in a steel guitar, it's western. But if you add a fifth it's bop, I guess!"[26] The concurrent resurgence of traditional jazz and the rise of modern, progressive jazz remained a spark of conflict in music publications.

Competition was also intensifying. A series of "funny hat" bands, many directly in imitation of the Firehouse Five, were coming onto the scene. Doc Evans and his Six-Alarm Six released a recording in late March. A café pianist in Los Angeles reportedly billed himself as the Firehouse Five Minus Four.[27] Other groups donned uniforms, such as Turk Murphy's Circus Jazz Band, who seemed to be straight out of *Dumbo* (1941), and Bob Mielke's Fairway Five Plus Two, dressed in golf attire.[28] A popular group was Cavanaugh's Curbstone Cops, with whom Mocambo owner Charley Morrison had attempted to arrange a dual performance with the Firehouse Five.[29] Other reports, however, noted rumors of animosity between the two bands. Though this is difficult to substantiate, the Firehouse Five did indeed take a different gig that day at the Bel Air Country Club.[30] Most of these inspired groups were short-lived. Absent the Firehouse Five's distinctive appeal and unique sound, they conjured little more than laughter from audiences.

Other already established groups came onto the scene. Drummer Ben Pollack and his group, the Pick-A-Rib Boys had been making their break at the Beverly Caverns, the club that had seen both the Firehouse Five and Kid Ory bands to success before. Pollack and crew had then played a handful of Tuesday night gigs at Ciro's, though union complications kept them from taking a regular slot.[31] Nappy Lamare's Levee Loungers then tried their hand at a Wednesday spot. Hal Holly was by then calling it "the battle of the Sunset Strip," though Lamare's group reportedly fell out of favor within weeks.[32] All the while the Firehouse Five continued to overflow the Mocambo, at times turning away crowds at the door reportedly as large as 300.[33] Ciro's had been attempting to strike its own Dixieland lightning, even trying to lure the Firehouse Five away from their Mocambo stint. Ward and the band felt loyal enough to Charley Morrison to turn the repeated offers down.

Perhaps a little agitated by the Firehouse Five's continued success and his own group's failure to establish a footing at Ciro's, Ben Pollack did not mince words to Hal Holly in early May:

> The Firehouse Five Plus Two—plus seven funny hats! [...] This cornball conception of Dixie as played by the Firehouse Five and others will be dead within a year.... You have to play that way for these pseudo jazz lovers, like those movie stars who think it's smart to be seen capering around in front of the Firehouse Five at the Mocambo.[34]

With the risk of inciting an unseemly war of headlines, Ward intelligently kept his cool. He "decline[d] to be drawn into a verbal battle with Ben Pollack," as Holly would note. "The Firehouse Five ain't mad at nobody," Ward would tell the reporter,

> The fun we have playing New Orleans Dixieland jazz has proven infectious to the thousands of people in society drawing rooms, and dance halls who are now bouncing to our music. [...] The dancing public is starved for a good, obvious beat. They want to hear the tune and want to dance to an easy-to-get-with tempo. We are proud we have done so much toward taking Dixieland jazz out of the beer and ashtray joints and putting it back in the dance hall where it all started and rightfully belongs!

Holly remained skeptical of it all, but conceded what was by then plainly evident: "The one thing sure is that they are the biggest thing from the standpoint of impact and headlines that dance business has seen.... After several months, their Monday nights' sessions at the Mocambo are still strictly sellouts, with tables available by advance reservations only."[35]

In 1950, it seemed the traditionalists were winning the musicological battle on the commercial front. Americans were eager to buy Dixieland and New Orleans-style records and see their favorite groups perform on stage and screen. The record business took full advantage. By the mid-1940s, New Orleans legends such as Bunk Johnson, Kid Ory, and others had been brought out of "retirement" and played the same music which they had never really stopped playing since the 1920s. America was now ready to pay attention again in their post-war haziness set against a hard-fought musical debate most didn't bother to understand anyway. The music made them move, and for most that was enough.

With success on stage, radio, television, and records, it seemed only a matter of time before the band had a chance to grace the big screen. In early May, the *Hollywood Reporter* broke the news, "Firehouse Five Plus Two, jazz band that is current rage in the orchestra world, has been signed for its picture debut in Republic's 'Hit Parade of 1951,' starring John Carroll and Marie McDonald...."[36] It just so happened that John Carroll was married to Disney artist Herb Ryman's sister, Lucille. This connection may have helped open the door for the band at Republic.[37] A week later, another announcement came via MGM. The band would also appear in *Grounds for Marriage*, a comedy starring Van Johnson and Kathryn Grayson. Johnson had been a regular at the Mocambo. Filming for both pictures took place in June. It is in *Grounds for Marriage* that we can still glimpse the band playing "The Charleston," the tune with which they conquered Hollywood, but never officially released on record.

In case their appearance with Bing Crosby, mentions in *Time* and *Life* magazines, performances in television shows, and newly signed movie deals weren't affirmation enough, the band's honorable mention in a major *Look* magazine feature on June 6 solidified their place in American music history. A multi-page spread, "Dixieland Jazz is 'Hot' Again," covered America's new musical obsession, featuring a series of stunning photographs by up-and-coming filmmaker, Stanley Kubrick. The lineup of names and images now reads like a veritable who's who of traditional jazz legends: George Lewis, Eddie Condon, Muggsy Spanier, Pee Wee Russell, Louis Armstrong, and Jack Teagarden among others. And above two portraits of Sidney Bechet and Red Nichols were the Firehouse Five Plus Two, seen in a photo perhaps taken at the Mocambo, having been joined onstage by jazz greats Hoagy Carmichael, Johnny Mercer, and Benny Goodman. "They play a 'funny hat' Dixieland," the caption read, "but these Walt Disney sponsored semi-pros are [the] busiest sidemen in Los Angeles."[38] In one of the country's most-read magazines, amongst an Olympian collection of jazz icons, the "funny hat" band had carved out their place in the pantheon.

"It'll Blow Over"

In August 1950, Great Britain prepared to welcome the Firehouse Five on record via its own TEMPO label. "Next time you see a Walt Disney cartoon, and Pluto hurtles into a pile of saucepans, or Donald Duck is bombarded with everything but the kitchen sink—listen carefully for a Dixieland off-beat in the sound effects," the *Daily Mirror* exclaimed.[39] Meanwhile, "you still [couldn't] worm your way into Mocambo Monday nights," as the *Los Angeles Examiner* put it.[40] J. Edgar Hoover was spotted at a gig later in the month. Florabel Muir would comment, "The Charleston contests at the Mocambo every Monday night…have become so famous all over the United States the FBI is investigating the situation."[41]

During a gig at the Palm Springs Racquet Club later in the year, an old friend had reunited with Frank Thomas' wife, Jeanette. Unaware that she was married to the Firehouse Five's piano player, he confided to her, "They're real good, but they won't last… this thing's a fad, it'll blow over."[42] With such enduring popularity, it seemed to many only a matter of time before such came to an end. "I've got a terrible premonition of doom. Some forthcoming Monday night, I fully expect Mocambo's dance floor to give—pitching hundreds of café socialites to their untimely ends," wrote *The Mirror* with a touch of hyperbole.[43] Exaggeration aside, there was change in the air by the end of the summer.

The band played their last Charleston contest of the year at the Mocambo on Monday, October 23. A couple of days later, *Daily Variety* would report on the changes coming to both of the Sunset Strip's biggest nightclubs. Ciro's would "introduce community singing, with vaudeville vet Arthur Boran." The following Monday, composer and singer Freddie Karger would take over the slot at the Mocambo. The Firehouse Five were noted to be taking a "two-month plunge in TV and one-niters. If the community sings are successful, it's possible the Firehouse group won't return."[44]

The hours were catching up with the band. They were becoming disillusioned with the Sunset Strip and its star-studded intensity. With an MCA contract and ever-increasing demand, their independence suffered too. In short, the band was becoming a full-time job. They may very well have chosen to switch careers, but the members had little interest in doing so. The Firehouse Five Plus Two were in a unique position to put fun before finances. Post-Mocambo, they'd end the year strong. They had a new 78 rpm out for the holiday season, a rendition of "Jingle Bells." They had appeared on the Milton Berle television program in October, and a month after their last Mocambo gig, they were again in front of television cameras, this time for a special that would air on Christmas Day.

On November 21, the Firehouse Five performed their "Jingle Bells" recording in a segment for Walt Disney's own *One Hour in Wonderland*.[45] This would be Walt's first foray into television, a medium he'd later come to dominate. Journalist Bob Thomas—who'd later pen the first major biography of Walt—visited the production set of *One Hour in Wonderland* that autumn. His syndicated column appeared the week before Thanksgiving:

> For the first time, a topnotch movie producer was making a film for television this week.... Not only is he making a picture for television, but he is appearing in it himself. "I've got as much ham as anyone," he confessed on the set at his studio, while having his makeup applied.

Walt reassured Thomas that theatrical motion pictures remained his priority, but added, "We are not afraid of television. I think we can use television the same as we have used radio—to get people interested in seeing our pictures."[46]

Beyond the spectacle of a Walt Disney production, viewers on Christmas Day were lured with a preview of *Alice in Wonderland*, which came finally at the program's conclusion after the Firehouse Five's own sequence. The animation of the Mad Tea Party sequence previewed that day was fresh out of production. Drafts for the sequence are dated to early November 1950.[47] Kimball performed some of his best animation in the picture on the Mad Tea Party, handling much of the March Hare and Mad Hatter characters, the latter voiced by the erstwhile Fire Chief, Ed Wynn.

By the end of 1950, there was still much animation left to be accomplished on *Alice*. Among these sequences was that featuring the fabled Cheshire Cat, another iconic Kimball performance.[48] There was also Alice's encounter with the Doorknob, masterfully animated by Frank Thomas.[49] The piano player had work to do on the flamboyantly evil Queen of Hearts as well. A strong proponent of using day-to-day observation in the study and understanding of movement, Thomas found his unique position in the Firehouse Five of useful inspiration for the Queen. "The piano player is like the host," he'd explain years later for the *Disney Family Album*, "If you got a trombone you got something in your face and you can't really do anything…but the piano player sits there and smiles and nods and looks around. And I'm looking for characters that I can use in the pictures." It was during a Firehouse Five gig—perhaps one in 1950—that Thomas saw the woman who he'd adapt into the Queen of Hearts. "She was sitting at a table over there and she was very autocratic. She was the Queen but she was sloppy in her manners and sloppy in the way she ate, and there was just something about it that was funny."[50]

During the final week of 1950, the Firehouse Five played a few last gigs. Anticipation was building for New Year's Day, when the group would become the first jazz band to officially perform in the Tournament of Roses Parade. Rolling down Pasadena's Colorado Boulevard to a reported crowd of some 1.6 million people, they could look back on a year comprising some 110 performances, all the while having maintained their full-time work at The Walt Disney Studios. 1950 was their year at the ball, when they proved that passion, hard work, and a little good luck could still take someone to the big stage.

By 1951, the clock seemed to be striking midnight. Overworked and without their independence, the band was beginning to lose sight of the fun that so defined who they were. But when the glass coach of fame and fortune transformed back into its pumpkin form, the Firehouse Five Plus Two were only just getting started. Who needs an ornate, horse-drawn carriage when you have a fire engine, anyway? The incarnation of the band that was to emerge after this period was arguably the best of musical arrangements that Ward Kimball, Frank Thomas, and their bandmates had yet to assemble. But that is an adventure for another telling.

Section Endnotes:

1. David Brubeck, "'Jazz' Evolvement As Art Form," *Downbeat*, January 27, 1950, p. 12.
2. Harold Heffernan, "Shades of the 1920s: Now It's the Banjo Returning to Favor," *St. Louis Post-Dispatch*, August 13, 1950, Newspapers.com.
3. Bob Fallstrom, "Joyful Return: Jazz Drummer Monte Mountjoy Home After Longest Road Trip," *Herald and Review* (Decatur, IL), October 6, 1992.
4. Ted Thomas interviewed (e-mail) by author, August 31, 2017.
5. George Carlin, "Firehouse Five's Wives Monday Night Widows," *The Mirror* (Los Angeles, CA), October 19, 1949.
6. Ward Kimball, *Payroll Spreadsheets - 4th Quarter* 1950.
7. "Music: Dixieland Revival," *Fortnight*, April 14, 1950, p. 18.
8. "Interview with Ward Kimball from June 6, 1969," interview by Michael Barrier, *MichaelBarrier.com*, August 2003, http://www.michaelbarrier.com/Interviews/Kimball/interview_ward_kimball.htm.
9. Diane Disney Miller, *The Story of Walt Disney*, comp. Pete Martin (New York: Disney Editions, 2005), p. 199.
10. Harry Crocker, "Behind the Makeup: Round the Town," *Los Angeles Evening Herald & Express*, January 26, 1950.
11. Florabel Muir, "Reporting," *The Mirror* (Los Angeles, CA), January 24, 1950.
12. Brandy Brent, "Carrousel," *The Los Angeles Times*, January 27, 1950.
13. Florabel Muir, "Reporting: That Old, Free Spirit," *The Mirror* (Los Angeles, CA), January 31, 1950.
14. Florabel Muir, "Reporting," *The Mirror* (Los Angeles, CA), February 21, 1950.
15. Harry Crocker, "Behind the Makeup: Round the Town," *Los Angeles Examiner*, February 24, 1950.

16. Though not a member of the band at this time, cornetist Danny Alguire had played ensemble with Crosby as early as 1942 with Bob Wills and His Texas Playboys. See: Charles R. Townsend, *'San Antonio Rose': The Life and Music of Bob Wills* (University of Illinois Press, 1986).
17. Ward Kimball, *The Ward Kimball Journals*, March 1, 1948, Ledger Volume 3 - 1948.
18. Frank Thomas interviewed by Don Peri in Don Peri (ed.), *Working with Disney: Interviews with Animators, Producers, and Artists* (University Press of Mississippi, 2011), p. 8.
19. "Interview with Frank Thomas and Ollie Johnston," interview by Michael Barrier, MichaelBarrier.com, November 2, 2014, http://www.michaelbarrier.com/Interviews/Thomas Johnston1987/ThomasJohnston1987.html.
20. "That Good-Time Sound," *Time*, March 6, 1950, pp. 48-49.
21. Helen Lang to Lester Koenig, April 28, 1950, Evergreen Record Sales Company, Seattle, Washington.
22. Jimmy Starr, "Ex-Office Boy Wins MGM Second Lead," *Los Angeles Evening Herald & Express*, April 26, 1950.
23. "Hollywood Teletopics," *Downbeat*, April 7, 1950, p. 9.
24. Ward Kimball, *Payroll Spreadsheets - 2nd Quarter 1950*.
25. Herb Stein, "Rambling Reporter," *The Hollywood Reporter*, April 4, 1950, p. 2.
26. Hal Holly, "The Hollywood Beat: Coast Shaken By Dixie Versus N.O. Jazz Scrap," *Downbeat*, March 10, 1950, p. 9.
27. Edith Gwynn, "Edith Gwynn's Hollywood," *The Mirror* (Los Angeles, CA), April 10, 1950.
28. Hal Smith interviewed (e-mail) by author, August 31, 2017.
29. Louella Parsons, "Clark Gable Awaits Permission of MGM to Make Independent Film, 'Lone Star,'" *Los Angeles Examiner*, April 6, 1950.
30. Ward Kimball, *Payroll Spreadsheets - 2nd Quarter 1950*.

31. Hal Holly, "The Hollywood Beat: Says L.A. Deejays Unfair To 'Love Drunk' Warbler," *Downbeat*, March 24, 1950, p. 8.
32. Hal Holly, "The Hollywood Beat: Sunset Strip Club Sets Lamare For Steady Stint," *Downbeat*, April 7, 1950, p. 9.
33. "Around the Circuit," *Los Angeles Evening Herald & Express*, March 22, 1950.
34. Hal Holly, "Pollack Says Firehouse 5 Is 'Just a Cornball Crew,'" *Downbeat*, May 5, 1950, p. 12.
35. Hal Holly, "Firehouse Chief Kimball Scorns Pollack Hassel," *Downbeat*, June 2, 1950, p. 9.
36. "Jazz Band and Cleffers Set for Repub. Musical," *The Hollywood Reporter*, May 5, 1950, p. 10.
37. Jim Hollifield, e-mail message to author, November 1, 2017.
38. Joseph Roddy, "Dixieland Jazz Is "Hot" Again," *Look*, June 6, 1950.
39. James Asman, "Listen for the Firehouse Five Plus Two," *The Daily Mirror* (United Kingdom), August 9, 1950.
40. Cholly Angeleno, "Cocktail Parties Keep Smart Set 'Jumping,'" *Los Angeles Examiner*, August 31, 1950.
41. Florabel Muir, "Reporting," *The Mirror* (Los Angeles, CA), August 29, 1950.
42. Ted Thomas interviewed by author, January 11, 2016.
43. Paul V. Coates, "Well, Medium, and Rare," *The Mirror* (Los Angeles, CA), April 19, 1950.
44. "Next Week: 'East Lynne,'" *Daily Variety*, October 25, 1950, p. 2.
45. "Fire House 5 Plus 2 Record Disney TV Show," *The Hollywood Reporter*, November 22, 1950, p. 11.
46. Bob Thomas, "Walt Disney Is Making Movie for Television," *Mt. Vernon Register* (Mt. Vernon, IL), November 17, 1950, Newspapers.com.
47. Hans Perk, "Prod. 2069 (Alice) - Seq. 08.0 - Mad Tea Party (I)," A. Film L.A., December 18, 2007, http://afilmla.

blogspot.com/2007/12/prod-2069-alice-seq-080-mad-tea-party-i_18.html.
48. Hans Perk, "Prod. 2069 (Alice) - Seq. 07.5 - Cheshire Cat," A. Film L.A., December 9, 2007, http://afilmla.blogspot.com/2007/12/prod-2069-alice-seq-075-cheshire-cat_09.html.
49. Hans Perk, "Prod. 2069 (Alice) - Seq. 03.0 - Doorknob," A. Film L.A., November 24, 2007, http://afilmla.blogspot.com/2007/11/prod-2069-alice-seq-030-doorknob_24.html.
50. *Disney Family Album: Frank Thomas,* dir. Michael Bonifer (Disney Channel, 1985), Youtube.

Notes on the U.S.S. *Alchiba*

By Lucas O. Seastrom

Though it seemed to carry a dangerous reputation to some at the time, in hindsight the U.S.S. *Alchiba* and its crew are a model in resilience and commitment to duty. As Alguire notes in his text, the ship was originally built as a civilian vessel, and was acquired by the United States Navy in 1941. Converted to military service at the Boston Navy Yards, it was commissioned *Monnacdove* on June 15, 1941 but was quickly given a name change of *Alchiba*.[1] Though the Navy's motivation for the change is unclear, "Alchiba" is an Arabic word meaning "tent," and is the name of the Alpha star of the constellation Corvus.[2]

When the December 1941 attack at Pearl Harbor brought the United States into the Second World War, *Alchiba* was working in the Atlantic Ocean as a cargo vessel. It was quickly transferred to the Pacific Theater, and in August of 1942, *Alchiba* was among the fleet that transported the First Marine Division and their cargo in the invasion of Guadalcanal, the first American offensive campaign of the war.

Alchiba continued in its duty for over three months, until late November, when, returning to Guadalcanal with a critical supply of ammunition, fuel, and steel mats for airfield runways, a Japanese submarine torpedoed the ship's forward section. A tremendous fire erupted and the crew was forced to beach the vessel offshore. The servicemen worked tirelessly for several days to quell the fire and offload their desperately needed cargo. After they had seemed to contain the fires, they were struck again by another torpedo in early December. The Navy command considered the vessel lost, but its Captain and crew endured the catastrophe and were able to save the *Alchiba* from the depths.

Severely damaged but not destroyed, *Alchiba* was towed back to San Francisco and the repair docks at Mare Island Naval Shipyard. For their valiant courage under fire and commitment to supporting their Marine comrades, the U.S.S. *Alchiba* and crew were awarded a Presidential Unit Citation. The ship remains the only cargo vessel in U.S. Naval history to be so recognized.

Danny Alguire arrived on *Alchiba* during its three months of repairs at Mare Island between June 2 and August 13 of 1943. Though it had certainly seen better days, the ship must have carried some sort of rugged tenacity in its bulwark. Its story had reached the ears of many a sailor back stateside, as the old salt's warning attests, "Damn ship's a wreck."

In the late summer of 1943, *Alchiba* left again for the South Pacific, with Alguire aboard as a crewman. Over the coming two years, the ship served again at Guadalcanal and in the Solomon Islands, New Caledonia, and Bougainville among others. After the war, *Alchiba* was decommissioned and entered merchant service in 1948.[3]

Section Endnotes:

1. Alchiba (AK-23)," Naval History and Heritage Command, September 14, 2018, https://www.history.navy.mil/browse-by-topic/ships/modern-ships/alchiba--ak-23-.html.
2. Jim Kaler, "Alchiba (Alpha Corvi)," STARS, University of Illinois, n.d., http://stars.astro.illinois.edu/sow/alchiba.html.
3. "Alchiba (AK-23)," Naval History and Heritage Command.

Notes on Wolfgang Reitherman and Disney Feature Animation

By Lucas O. Seastrom

> "I was in a room once when Walt [Disney] was discussing certain things, and in the course of the conversation he started talking about Woolie [Reitherman]. [Walt] said, 'Whenever I want to know what the public thinks about a film I'm making, I ask Woolie, because in a way he's the All-American boy.... If Woolie approves of a certain thing, or makes a suggestion, I consider it very favorably.'"
> -Disney animator Bob Carlson to historian Michael Barrier[1]

In the late 1950s, Danny Alguire found himself assigned to Wolfgang "Woolie" Reitherman's animation unit on *Sleeping Beauty* as assistant director. Their primary task was to produce and animate the climactic battle sequence between the valiant Prince Philip and wicked Maleficent, the latter in the form of a terrifying dragon. In previous years, Reitherman had shown his adeptness at animating scenes with action, intense pacing, and forceful characters. His movement into sequence direction on *Sleeping Beauty* was, as Alguire notes, a pragmatic decision to shorten the film's production time. In hindsight, it was an eventful first step towards Reitherman's assuming creative direction of Disney feature animation.

Beginning with *Sleeping Beauty* (released in 1959), Danny Alguire was at Reitherman's side as assistant director for much of the period when he rose to the top animation chair at Disney. *101 Dalmatians* followed in 1961, and two years later, Reitherman became the first in Disney Studios history to receive sole directorial credit for an animated feature on *Sword in the Stone*. As Walt

Disney became increasingly busy with a diverse array of projects, he entrusted Reitherman to oversee the future of the division that had seemingly defined the company since the release of *Snow White and the Seven Dwarfs* a quarter century earlier. Reitherman, along with senior artists including Ken Anderson, Frank Thomas, Ollie Johnston, Milt Kahl, and John Lounsbery among others, had been part of that legacy since the 1930s.

Subsequent films included *The Jungle Book* (1967), *The Aristocats* (1970), *Robin Hood* (1974), and the assorted *Winnie-the-Pooh* short features which were later compiled together. As Alguire himself notes, due to union restrictions he did not receive screen credit until *The Aristocats* in 1970, where he shared the Assistant Director line with colleague Ed Hansen as "Dan Alguire." He again went by "Dan" for *Robin Hood* and the feature version *The Many Adventures of Winnie-the-Pooh* (1977).

Alguire's assistant director role in animation was different from its counterpart in live-action film production. Where the live-action role was mostly limited to on-set work during a film's principal photography, an animation assistant director took on a large portfolio of tasks spread across the entirety of a film's making, from pre-production to post-production. "I should have been called a 'Coordinator,'" Alguire wrote, as he would "work with film editors, keep the entire movie organized, cut in new scenes, put in sound effects, add music."

"I'd always been a guy that liked detail," Alguire continued. "It's kind of like playing music. You play it right or you play it wrong. I always liked to play a tune right." As an experienced pilot, Woolie Reitherman was also keen to the value of a multidisciplinary influence in the art of animation. Both veterans of the Second World War, Reitherman and Alguire made a successful partnership, the former with his tenacious, committed leadership, the latter with his open-minded, can-do attitude. When asked in 1982 about Walt Disney's value of his own perspective, Reitherman explained, "Yes, I think it was because I had been away [during the war]. Apart from a couple of the guys, the majority of the studio had been working throughout the war on shorts and training films. Walt always felt that I had an objective viewpoint and I think he valued that."[2] Alguire too had a well-rounded point-of-view, influenced by his diverse background.

Interestingly, Alguire seemed to leave his own mark upon his retirement in the early 1970s. As director Richard Rich later recounted about his hiring at Disney at the same time, "I had basically graduated in music at University and tried to get into the Music Department as a composer. They were looking for an assistant director as Danny Alguire retired. He had had a musical background; they were looking for the same. I didn't think I'd get the job and finally I did and was John Lounsbery's assistant director."[3] Rich went on to co-direct *The Fox and the Hound* (1979) and *The Black Cauldron* (1985).

Woolie Reitherman's own career extended well into the 1970s, as he directed the animated features *Robin Hood* (1973) and *The Rescuers* (1977). His leadership did much to sustain the endurance of Disney animation. The director could almost will the films into being from his own grit and determination. Animator and pianist Frank Thomas elaborated in 1987:

> [Woolie] was doing the best he could, and he was trying to remember—you know, it's a big job pulling off an animated feature film. God, the long hours he put in. Danny Alguire used to say, "Woolie can come back from flying around the world and stay there for ten hours and be ready for more, and the rest of us are all dead from an eight-hour day." Boundless energy.[4]

It's useful remembering that when Alguire was drafting his memoir, the names of individual Disney artists and their work remained generally unknown. As Reitherman noted later in his career, "We're trying to get those great talents out in front of people.... The names of our animators mean nothing to anyone except to more discerning people or people that have a real love for this thing."[5] Alguire's writing came at a time when public awareness was shifting, though the stories of many artists of the era still remain untold, including Alguire's own until this publication.

Section Endnotes:

1. Michael Barrier, *The Animated Man: A Life of Walt Disney* (Berkeley, CA: University of California Press, 2007), 276.
2. Richard Holliss, *Starburst*, 1982, pp. 16-19, https://www.dix-project.net/item/3353/starburst-magazine-issue-4-6-wolfgang-reitherman-interview, 17.
3. Christian Renaut, "Interview with Richard Rich from August 1987," in *Walt's People: Talking Disney With the Artists Who Knew Him*, ed. Didier Ghez, vol. 2 (Xlibris, 2005).
4. Michael Barrier, "Interview with Frank Thomas and Ollie Johnston on July 13, 1987," in *Walt's People: Talking Disney With the Artists Who Knew Him*, ed. Didier Ghez, vol. 17 (Theme Park Press, 2015).
5. Edward Sumner, "Interview with Wolfgang Reitherman," in *Walt's People: Talking Disney With the Artists Who Knew Him*, ed. Didier Ghez, vol. 23 (Theme Park Press, 2019).

Interview with Danny Alguire by Hal Smith and Chris Tyle

Alguire home, Beaverton, Oregon—July, 1977

When he realized that Chris Tyle and I were both interested in finding out more about Benny Strickler, Danny invited us to his home in Beaverton, Oregon in the summer of 1977 to tape an interview concerning Strickler's background, and Danny's own relationship with him. Fortunately, the brittle cassette held together for over 30 years, and jazz historian Dave Radlauer was able to transcribe almost all of the dialogue.

At times, small adjustments have been made to improve the readability of the conversation. Alguire's charming Oklahoma flair for speech has been maintained as much as possible. The interview recording begins with Danny helping the interviewers determine who might be amongst Benny Strickler's surviving family members. —Hal Smith

Danny Alguire: The best information would come from [Benny's] wife, Frances. She'd know it all.

Hal Smith: Would she be willing to talk about it, though?

Alguire: I think so. She's proud of him. That's what was wonderful about her. I guess she and Benny went to high school together. They used to come out to Los Angeles in 1935 or '36 when there was nothing going on with their two little kids, just to make a living. Benny loved jazz but his first thing was his family, boy.
    He and Bob Logan were playing with some guy named Lee, not a nice guy. It was a hotel-style band. Benny stuck it out as long as

he could. But once he had a little money saved, he came home one night and just said, "I'm sorry, Francis. I can't play with a guy like that." So she said ok. They didn't know where the next day's food would come from, but she stuck with him.

He kept playing with different bands. I didn't know too much. I'd see Benny off and on. I heard once—though I can't vouch for whether it's actually true, but I think it's a great story—that Benny had a chance to play with [Artie] Shaw. He might have even tried out. That was when Shaw wanted the trumpets to bend notes. Benny said, "I can't play that. I don't bend notes for anybody. I don't care who it is." He just didn't think that was honest [laughter]. Benny would play anything but he'd have to do it righteous or his own way.

Benny came to play. You'd often see loafers, guys who didn't want to play or guys that would complain all the time. "Oh you're not going to play that tune are you?" I had a tenor man one time who was like that. I'd name a tune and he'd go, "Can you get something better than that?" So I'd ask, "Well what do you want to play?" He'd just say, "Well you know, some of the good ones." You couldn't call a tune he liked, but he'd never name something. Hell, there were a lot of tunes up on the stand you may not like but you [still] play them. But Benny always came to play.

One night on the bandstand, Benny had a fever blister with a split lip. I asked Benny if I should take his parts and try to help, and he'd say "Oh no, I can make it alright." He'd play just keen and then take his horn down saying, "How's it look?" It was bleeding. So he'd say, "You know it only hurts when I take the horn away. As long as I keep the pressure on, it's O.K.." [Laughter]. I almost threw up. He looked like someone had cut him with a knife. But he played all night.

Chris Tyle: That'd fire you up.

Alguire: Benny was the most unselfish person I ever knew in my life. We had a recording session where we played a theme. Benny had always taken the chorus on. But at the session he told Alex Brashear to take the trumpet section. Alex says, "No, Benny! You should do it." He'd say, "No I got too much ensemble." This was a lie, but he just wanted Alex to have it. He'd do it to me all the time. "Dan, you play on this."

The thing he used to say that was absolutely true was, "Make the tune sound good. Everyone play together and make the tune sound good." What he meant was for everyone to think and listen to each other. I remember one time he said, "If you think you can make the tune sound good by laying out, [then] lay out!" [Laughter]. That was his big thing: make the tune sound good.

Alguire then briefly reviews some recordings.

Alguire: You know we made a lot of big band stuff [with Bob Wills and His Texas Playboys] that was never released. Did you know about that?

Tyle: No.

Alguire: Well there was a guy that called me up one day and said, "I understand you used to work with Bob Wills." I can't remember his name right now. I think he was involved with the John Edwards Memorial Foundation. But he was doing work on Bob Wills. There had been one recording session that we'd done as a band. We made maybe 18 tunes, and there were three or four big band tunes that were never released. He had these tunes on tape. But there weren't any where Benny played the chorus. Benny was so damn unselfish. He was just that kind of a guy.

Smith: Did he play a lead that you'd recognize and know that was him?

Alguire: Only on "Ten Years." Benny was always thin. He never ate right. He was so busy playing that he didn't think about eating [...] He didn't watch his health or his eating habits. He just lived to play. That might have led to his tuberculosis. You couldn't get any meat on him. He was a beanpole, about six feet tall, and probably didn't weigh 135 pounds.

Tyle: Did he have tuberculosis when the Wills band broke up?

Alguire: He didn't know it. He never missed a day. There was maybe one time it happened. Benny was sick. So Alex Brashear played the first part and I took second part [in the trumpet section].

The war came along and everyone went to war. About August of '42 is when I left the band and came back to Los Angeles. Shortly after that Benny came through. There was this place on Slauson and Vermont called "The Wheel." This was a long time ago, the fall of '42. It was a big hangout for jazz guys sitting in and everything. I walked in there one day, and by God, Benny was sitting there playing. He was on his way to San Francisco to take Lu Watters' place.

There is a break in the conversation and the recording. It resumes with Alguire discussing his essay on Benny Strickler.

Alguire: There was a critic from Los Angeles who wrote an article for an English magazine about Benny. I read it. It was good but it didn't say what I wanted to say about Benny. So I wrote this article and sent it to Paul Affeldt and he printed it. It's about four or five pages long. [...] I wanted to get it down before I forgot it [even] then. I wrote keen and warm stuff, the things I remembered about Benny. For instance, Bob Wills had a way that really kept you alert. Nothing was ever real set in the band. You really watched him because he loved to catch you talking or something, and he'd say, "Take it, Dan."

[Laughter]. It wasn't in the arrangement. He'd love to catch guys. When Benny took one he always stood up. So sometimes Wills would go, "Take it, Benny!" and boy he'd get up. He used to have this way of wrapping his legs around the chair, you know? So one time Benny got up and he was hung up in the chair. He was wrestling with his foot and just playing his ass off! [Laughter].

Tyle: What kind of horn did he play?

Alguire: Trumpet. Never played a cornet. He liked the trumpet. I hadn't been in the band two weeks, and one day I had a sticky valve on my trumpet and I was fiddling with it with oil. Bob Wills walked and asked what was the matter. I said, "Oh just a sticky valve." He says, "That's a pretty old horn, isn't it?" I said it was. So he bought Alex and I two cornets. But Benny stayed with his trumpet. I think the reason is, playing in big bands like he did, and playing lead, he probably got around better with the trumpet.

The conversation moves to the Bob Wills band repertoire, and the diversity of tunes.

Alguire: Boy, some of these things we played, you'd never know it was the Bob Wills band. We used to play "South Rampart Street Parade" or "Begin the Beguine." This would be in the big towns with more sophisticated people. In the smaller towns he'd turn on the country. Bob had a sixth sense of knowing what to do right. I remember one time we even played "Softly as in a Morning Sunrise," the Artie Shaw arrangement. We had the musicians.

Tyle: But you wouldn't record those types of songs?

Alguire: No. COLUMBIA or OKEH didn't want to get too far out, which was right, I guess. It's a shame that in those days they didn't have tape recorders. Someone could've picked that stuff up on the stand.

Smith: Do you suppose anyone's gotten air shots of the band?

Alguire: Well that's possible because we used to broadcast every day at noon. Five days a week from Tulsa.

Tyle: And you'd play these big band tunes?

Alguire: Yes. A little bit of everything. I remember one time there was a big strike, so we couldn't play our own tunes. We had to play jazz tunes like "Jazz Me Blues," which they'd call the "Tulsa Stomp." [Laughter].

After listening to a record, Alguire tells the story of Benny Strickler's joining the Lu Watters Yerba Buena Jazz Band in San Francisco in the early years of World War Two. Alguire begins by describing their brief reunion in Los Angeles.

Alguire: I asked Benny what was happening. He said, "Well the Wills band is breaking up. I got this call." I'm not sure who called him, probably Burt Bales or one of those guys down there. Benny said, "I'm on my way up to Frisco to take Lu Watters' place in the band." Benny used to go through there with a hotel-style band and he'd run down and sit in, so he knew them all.

Smith: No kidding?

Alguire: So when Lu left they thought oh God the only man they knew who they thought could take his place was Benny! So they got a hold of him in some way. Bales was later telling me about this.

Benny was on his way out there. He left his family back in Fayetteville, Arkansas. He was going to get them out there later. That was his plan. I guess Benny was 4-F. If he was sick then or knew it then he didn't say anything. I don't think he knew he had tuberculosis. Have you ever heard how long he was up in San Francisco before he got sick? I heard it wasn't very long.

Smith: Just a few months, I think.

Alguire: No more than that. He was on the bandstand one night and started hemorrhaging. They got him to a hospital and it was TB. And so he went back to Fayetteville and went into a sanitorium. Nowadays they can do so much more with TB than they could then. They could've cured him, maybe.

When the war was over—I got out of the Navy in November '45—first chance I had I went back to Oklahoma City to see my folks. I hadn't seen them since I'd been in the war. While I was there—it must have been December or the early part of '46—I called Benny on the phone in Fayetteville and talked to him. We exchanged good greetings and I asked him how he was feeling. He said, "Fine, I'm out of the sanitorium. I'm starting to blow a little. In fact the Wills band was over here on some jobs and I went down to sit in with them. I'm blowing to get my lips back. Everything's fine. I'm going to blow again!" I said, "Oh that's marvelous, Benny. Glad to hear it." He continued saying, "I feel fine and I'll come on back to California." I don't how much later it was but he had a relapse and just suddenly died. I'm sure glad I got to talk to him.

Man, as far as Benny was concerned, he was going to go right on! I know he was miserable trying to get well so he could play. He lived to play. I never saw such a dedicated guy, such a nice guy. I remember in this article I wrote, I said I was so glad I got to know Benny and to play with him, or words to this effect. I'll always remember Benny. He was a fine musician, a gentlemen, and a great friend. He was a very small town, honest, polite guy. His feet never left the ground. I think if he had been famous it wouldn't have bothered him. He'd say "yes ma'am" or "no ma'am" to older people, you know? Very courteous and soft-spoken. Very humble.

Boy, he came to play. He just lived for music. "Let's just make the tune sound good," he'd say. I used to pick up on these things he used to say. One time he said, "If you don't have a meeting of minds you don't have a meeting of music." That was another thing he harped on all the time. He'd give us lectures, you know? It wasn't "listen to me" but "here's what I think." He'd just turn to you and say, "You know what? Boy, if you don't think alike you can't play alike. You have to think alike. You have to have a meeting of minds before you can have a meeting of music. You know what I mean?" And then he might think, "I'm not getting through to him," so he'd go over it again! [Laughter]. I'd say, "What do you mean by think alike?" And he'd go, "You got to listen to each other all the time. Always listen to everybody so that you're with everybody and you're playing together. You got to make the tune sound good." He would harp all the time. Make the tune sound good. One time he said, "If it would sound better without playing, don't play!" [Laughter]. That's something, isn't it? So it wasn't just musicianship. Benny as a person was just marvelous to be around. If he wasn't playing he was talking about interesting things.

Smith: Did he really get a boot out of playing that San Francisco style with Bales, Bob Helm, and all those guys?

Alguire: That was his first love. That's what he really wanted to do.

Smith: The old stuff? The King Oliver and Lu Watters type of stuff?

Alguire: If he had been in the Watters band as Bob Scobey had been as second trumpet, that would've been exactly what he was looking for. In fact if he hadn't gotten sick, I think he would've just stayed in San Francisco. That was his first love. His love was King Oliver and Louis Armstrong and all the old guys. He thought that was the greatest music in the world.

Smith: We wondered if he liked Harry James and Yank Lawson and other later guys? Or just the pioneer stuff?

Alguire: Yes I remember he liked Yank because I did too. Yank played a pretty simple style. So did Watters. I know Benny admired Watters. It was because it was honest. Yank Lawson played a lot of notes, but I liked his style. I'm pretty sure I talked about it with Benny. But boy he liked Oliver, and he liked Bix Beiderbecke too.

Smith: When he played with Bales and Helm and those guys do you think he knew those tunes from records of "Kansas City Stomp" or "Dippermouth Blues" or do you think he picked them up when he was there?

Alguire: He knew them all! I'm pretty sure he must have gotten them off records because he knew all those tunes.

Smith: Watters didn't say, here's a neat tune, listen to this. Benny knew them before he started playing?

Alguire: Sure he did. If not, he could hear it once or twice and have it! He had a bitch of an ear. He didn't make many mistakes. I don't remember him making any! I used to think, gee the guy ain't human! He never split a note.

Tyle: He sounds so sure of himself.

Alguire: You're exactly right. Courage. I know you'll agree with me on this. To be a good trumpet player you have to be really courageous. You have to really believe you can do it. The top note? I'll get it. You know you can get it and you do get it. If you don't think you can get it you won't. That's the quality that Benny had that I didn't have enough of. I was a little on the temperate side. Benny didn't back away from anything. He knew he could do it, and did.

So he was not only a marvelous musician but just a wonderful guy personally. Just fun to be around. He was a great talker. He always talked to you like he only had about five minutes to tell you. He had a good sense of humor, but he was all business on the stand. Bob never caught him napping. He was the most alert guy. He was the kind of a take charge guy, but I don't mean to say he was bossy in any way. He just cleverly got you to do things! [Laughter]. But he was always honest about it, you know? He'd say something like, "Don't play so loud on this part coming in." It was just the way he thought it ought to go. "Just don't come in so strong, O.K.?"

I just learned so much from Benny. Of course, Alex Brashear was a great player too. Hell, I was playing third, remember. Alex was playing second. Benny would compliment me. He'd say, "One good thing is that we all think alike on our phrasing." He'd always be like that.

"That's good, Dan. That's good phrasing." I'd say, "Hell, I'm listening to you!" I always thought the trumpets sounded great together. Of course, they made it easy.

I wasn't a terrific reader when I first went into the Wills band. But after a few months, gee I was reading pretty good. Not as good as Benny. We'd get some new stuff, and we'd go two or three times rehearsing. Of course, Benny would have it down the first time. He'd help me.

"Lost Love" Lyrics

Written by Danny Alguire—October 28, 1976

Lost love, the only love I've known

I just can't believe it's lost forever

You never said goodbye, dear

Or even told me why, dear

I'm sad and so blue

And feeling oh so lonely

Please dear, say you're just pretending

Love like ours must have a happy ending

We'll never let it die, dear

And if you'll only try, dear

Our love will never be lost again

Alguire's Chili Recipe— September 16, 1977

Well known by friends, colleagues, and acquaintances alike was Danny Alguire's chili recipe, which he often made for parties over the decades. Musician and editor Hal Smith was able to procure a copy of it from Alguire before his passing. It is included here along with Alguire's original note to Hal and his wife, June.

Dear Hal and June,

Enclosed is the recipe. I used a few more hot peppers than usual. Suggest about 4 or 5 if you found it too hot (I used 9).

Thanks so much for coming and bringing your "tapes." It was fun. Will drop by your joint some Friday or Saturday and see your cats. Appreciate the Benny copy. I'll save this for sure.

Let me know when and if you and Chris [Tyle] want to get together and talk about Benny.

Best to you,
Danny

Texas Chili

Texas chili differs from other chilis in that suet is used in its preparation. This suet must be fresh, white kidney suet. Another requirement of Texas chili is perfectly lean meat. If the meat has too much fat in it, it renders out a different taste. Lean round steak trimmed and double-ground is best.

With handwritten note from Danny included below this text: To Hal & June with all my "HOT." Happy eating! Your friend, Danny Alguire

Preparing the Spice Mix

Into a bowl that holds about one quart, place the following ingredients:

- 1 ½ ounces chili powder
- ½ teaspoon fresh comino (cumin), crushed
- ½ teaspoon oregano
- 1 teaspoon paprika
- 2 or 3 cloves garlic, minced
- 4 to 8 (*if you can take it*) small, dry, red chilies, crushed
- 1 to 3 dashes Tabasco sauce (hot, but sharpens the taste)
- 1 small can green chilies, diced (if desired)

Pour 1 pint boiling water over the condiments and stir until blended.

Cooking the Meat

Slice ¾ pound kidney suet into ¼ inch slabs, place in 12 inch cast iron skillet and render over a hot flame. There should be about ½ inch of melted suet in bottom of skillet. Remove unrendered pieces of suet.

Dice 1 onion (big or little) and sauté in the suet until it starts to brown.

Add 3 pounds ground beef and brown *only* until the red color is gone. Constantly separate the meat so that it becomes individual grains, like bee-bees. Add 1 teaspoon salt and ½ teaspoon pepper.

Note: From the time you start cooking the meat until you add the spice mix, someone has to be stirring—so the meat stays separated.

Making the Chili

Pour combination of spices and water over the meat and stir thoroughly. Add a small can of tomato sauce, if desired. Turn the fire very low and simmer for about an hour until *all* the water is cooked out. Keep skillet uncovered and stir the chili occasionally.

Chili can be served with *separately* cooked beans (small reds or pintos, *never kidney beans*) or it goes great with spaghetti. Sounds so good I think I'll go make a batch myself.

Recommended Listening

Compiled by Hal Smith

Danny Alguire

- Jim Beatty Jazz Band: The Battle Hymn of the Republic; A Salute to the Bi-Centennial. Tri-AD 501 (LP) 1976. *Out of print.*
- Jim Beatty Jazz Band: The Joys Of Jazz. Tri-AD 906 (LP) 1977. *Out of print.*
- Jim Beatty Jazz Band: Strictly Dixie And Blues. JBD—5 (CD). Includes eight tracks from Tri-AD 501 and six tracks from Tri-AD 906.
- Jim Beatty Jazz Band: The West Coast Years. JBD—1 (CD). Includes three tracks from Tri-Ad 906.
- Firehouse Five Plus Two: Dixieland Jazz Vol. 2; The Snader Telescriptions, Storyville Films Video DVD 16009. Includes all six "telescriptions" of the Firehouse Five Plus Two, filmed in 1951. (Remainder of DVD is telescriptions by Pete Daily (1950) and Red Nichols (1951).
- Firehouse Five Plus Two: Around The World. Good Time Jazz GTJCD—10044—2.
- Firehouse Five Plus Two: At Disneyland. Good Time Jazz GTJCD—10049—2.
- Firehouse Five Plus Two: Crashes A Party. Good Time Jazz GTJCD—10038—2.
- Firehouse Five Plus Two: Dixieland Favorites. Good Time Jazz FCD—60—008.
- Firehouse Five Plus Two: The Firehouse Five Plus Two Story. Good Time Jazz 220552 (2-CD set). Includes GTJ recordings

from 1949—1954 originally issued on 78 rpm, 45 rpm, EP and 10" and 12" LPs.
- Firehouse Five Plus Two: Goes South. Good Time Jazz GTCD—12018—2.
- Firehouse Five Plus Two: Goes To A Fire. Good Time Jazz GTJCD—10052—2.
- Firehouse Five Plus Two: Goes To Sea. Good Time Jazz GTJCD—10028—2.
- Firehouse Five Plus Two: Havin' A Blast. Jasmine JASCD 807. Includes nine tracks from the "Goes To Sea" album plus all tracks from "Dixieland Favorites," "Around The World" and seven tracks from "At Disneyland."
- Firehouse Five Plus Two: Live At Earthquake McGoon's. GHB BCD 450.
- Firehouse Five Plus Two: Plays For Lovers. Good Time Jazz GTCD—12014—2.
- Firehouse Five Plus Two: Settin' The World On Fire—The Whole Story, Vol. 1. Jasmine JASCD 426 (2-CD set). Includes Good Time Jazz recording sessions 1949—1952 with alternate takes; a 1950 78/45 release which was never issued on LP plus material from the "Goes South" and "Plays For Lovers" albums.
- Firehouse Five Plus Two: Stoking The Fire—The Whole Story, Vol. 2. Jasmine JASCD 460 (2-CD set). Includes the remaining tracks from the "Goes South," "Plays for Lovers," and "Goes to Sea" albums plus appearances on Bing Crosby's radio program; the soundtracks of the Snader Telescriptions; and the soundtracks from the band's three appearances on the "Stars Of Jazz" television programs.
- Firehouse Five Plus Two: Twenty Years Later. Good Time Jazz GTJCD—10054—2.
- Merle Travis: Guitar Rags and a Too Fast Past Bear Family BCD 15637 (5-CD set). Includes "Won'tcha Be My Baby?"

and "Dry Bread" recorded in 1950 with Danny Alguire on cornet, plus Southwestern-style playing by studio trumpeters Jack McTaggart and Virginia Cushman.
- Merle Travis: Rare Performances 1946—1981 Vestapol DVD 13012. Includes the 1951 Snader Telescriptions by Merle Travis and his Westerners with Danny Alguire on cornet.
- T. Texas Tyler: The Man With a Million Friends. Bronco Buster CD 9012. Includes 1946 commercial recordings.
- T. Texas Tyler: Live 1948—1950, vol. 2. British Academy of Country Music BACM CD D 419. Includes live broadcasts from the Riverside Rancho in Los Angeles, 1950. There are two versions of "Goodnight Waltz," which was co-composed by Danny Alguire and T. Texas Tyler.
- Bob Wills and His Texas Playboys: San Antonio Rose Bear Family 000001953 (11-CD, 1 DVD set) Includes all recordings by Danny Alguire, Benny Strickler and Tubby Lewis with Bob Wills and His Texas Playboys, plus several tracks with Alex Brashear.
- Bob Wills and His Texas Playboys: A Tribute to Bob Wills: 50th Anniversary Texas Playboys Reunion Delta DLP-1161 (2 LPs) 1984. *Out of print.*

Alex Brashear

- Merle Haggard: A Tribute to the Best Damn Fiddle Player in the World (or, My Salute to Bob Wills) Koch CD KOC 3—7900—2.
- Merle Travis: The Legend of Merle Travis Country Stars CTS5411 (recorded 1979).
- Merle Travis: The Merle Travis Story - 24 Greatest Hits CMH Records CD-9018. (Note: This CD contains the same material as Country Stars CTS5411. Both are listed in case one of the CDs goes out of print).

- Bob Wills and His Texas Playboys: Faded Love Bear Family BCD 16550 (13-CD, 1 DVD set). Includes all remaining commercial recordings made by Alex Brashear with Bob Wills and His Texas Playboys, plus a 1971 reunion session organized by Merle Haggard.
- Bob Wills and His Texas Playboys: The Tiffany Transcriptions Collectors Choice Music CCM 991 (10-CD Box Set). Transcription recordings by Bob Wills and His Texas Playboys with Alex Brashear on numerous tracks.
- Johnny Lee Wills: Reunion. Flying Fish FF069 (LP) 1978. *Out of print.*

Miscellaneous

- Bing Crosby and Some Jazz Friends. Decca CD AAGRD 603. Includes Bing Crosby with Bob Crosby "When My Dreamboat Comes Home" with a full trumpet chorus by John "Yank" Lawson plus a Southwestern-style chorus by studio trumpeter Carroll "Cappy" Lewis on "Deep In The Heart of Texas."
- Bob Crosby and his Bob Cats: March of the Bob Cats. Living Era CD AJA 571. Includes small-band sides with Southwestern-style playing by hornmen Yank Lawson on several tracks plus Sterling Bose ("Loopin' The Loop") and Billy Butterfield ("Mournin' Blues").
- Bob Crosby and his Orchestra: Big Band Dixieland. Jasmine JASMCD 2564. This collection of big band sides by the Crosby Orchestra includes excellent Southwestern-style trumpet by Yank Lawson—particularly on "The Old Spinning Wheel" and "Vieni, Vieni."
- Jimmie Davis: Don't Take My Sunshine Away; Vintage Hillbilly Blues and Ballads, 1932—1949. Jasmine CD

JASMCD 3701. Includes tracks with studio trumpeter Bill Graham playing a realistic Southwestern Style.
- Tex Williams & His Western Caravan: Vintage Collections. Capitol CD 7243—8—36184—2. Includes the million-seller "Smoke, Smoke, Smoke (That Cigarette)" with a Southwestern-style solo by studio trumpeter Mannie Klein.

Benny Strickler

- Seger Ellis and his Choirs of Brass. Alamac QSR—2408 (LP). *Out of print.*
- Lu Watters: The Complete Good Time Jazz Recordings. Good Time Jazz 4GTJCD 4409—2 (4-CD set). Includes six transcription recordings of Benny Strickler with the Wartime version of the Yerba Buena Jazz Band.

Ed Lewis

- Bennie Moten's Kansas City Orchestra: Kansas City Breakdown: The Victor Recordings, volume 2. Frog CD DGF 30. Includes the top-selling version of "South" recorded in 1928 with the seminal Southwestern style trumpeter Ed Lewis.

Bibliography

"Alchiba (AK-23)." Naval History and Heritage Command, September 14, 2018. https://www.history.navy.mil/browse-by-topic/ships/modern-ships/alchiba--ak-23-.html.

Alguire, G. B. "24,000,000 Brooms a Year: A Review of the Broom and Broomcorn Situation." *Brooms, Brushes & Handles*, November 1920. https://books.google.com/books?id=JiAK57WWzWEC&printsec=frontcover#v=onepage&q&f=false.

Angeleno, Cholly. "Cocktail Parties Keep Smart Set 'Jumping.'" *Los Angeles Examiner*, August 31, 1950. Kimball Family Collection, Box 12.

Archerd, Armand. "Cupid KO'd as Reunion Between Shelley-Farley Blocked by Film." *Los Angeles Evening Herald & Express*, July 26, 1950. Kimball Family Collection, Clipping Files.

"Around the Circuit." *Los Angeles Evening Herald & Express*, March 22, 1950. Kimball Family Collection, Box 12.

Asman, James. "Listen for the Firehouse Five Plus Two." *The Daily Mirror* (United Kingdom), August 9, 1950. Kimball Family Collection, Clipping Files.

Avakian, George. "The Record Changer." *The Record Changer*, September 1949.

Barrier, Michael. "Interview with Frank Thomas and Ollie Johnston on July 13, 1987." In *Walt's People: Talking Disney With the Artists Who Knew Him*, edited by Didier Ghez, Vol. 17. Theme Park Press, 2015.

Barrier, Michael. *The Animated Man: A Life of Walt Disney*. Berkeley, CA: University of California Press, 2007.

"Bill Anderson, Dead at 86." Variety, January 14, 1998. https://variety.com/1998/film/news/bill-anderson-dead-at-86-1117436357/.

"Bill Anderson; Film, TV Producer for Disney." Los Angeles Times, January 13, 1998. http://articles.latimes.com/1998/jan/13/news/mn-7858.

"Bill Peet." D23, n.d. https://d23.com/walt-disney-legend/bill-peet/.

Brent, Brandy. "Carousel." *The Los Angeles Times*, January 27, 1950. Kimball Family Collection, Box 12.

"Broomcorn." Alternative Fieldcrops Manual. Purdue University, n.d. https://hort.purdue.edu/newcrop/afcm/broomcorn.html.

Brubeck, Dave. "'Jazz' Evolvement As Art Form." *Downbeat*, January 27, 1950. Kimball Family Collection, Box 12.

Carlin, George. "Firehouse Five's Wives Monday Night Widows." *The Mirror* (Los Angeles, CA), October 19, 1949. Kimball Family Collection, Box 12.

Coates, Paul V. "Well, Medium, and Rare." *The Mirror* (Los Angeles, CA), April 19, 1950. Kimball Family Collection, Clipping Files.

Crocker, Harry. "Behind the Makeup: Round the Town." *Los Angeles Evening Herald & Express*, January 26, 1950. Kimball Family Collection, Box 12.

Crocker, Harry. "Behind the Makeup: Round the Town." *Los Angeles Examiner*, February 24, 1950. Kimball Family Collection, Box 12.

Crocker, Harry. *Western Union Telegram*. April 23, 1950. Harry Crocker to The Firehouse Five Plus Two, Mocambo, Sunset Strip, Hollywood, CA. Kimball Family Collection, Box 11.

"Demand for Brush Heavier." *Journal Gazette*. July 26, 1929. Newspapers.com.

Disney Family Album: Frank Thomas. Directed by Michael Bonifer. Disney Channel, 1985. Youtube.

Gary, Priolo P. "USS Alchiba (AKA-6)." NavSource Online: Amphibious Photo Archive, n.d. https://www.navsource.org/archives/10/02/02006.htm.

Fallstrom, Bob. "Joyful Return: Jazz Drummer Monte Mountjoy Home After Longest Road Trip." *Herald and Review* (Decatur, IL), October 6, 1992. Newspapers.com.

"Fire House 5 Plus 2 Record Disney TV Show." *The Hollywood Reporter*, November 22, 1950, 11. Kimball Family Collection, Box 12.

"Government Broomcorn Inspection." *Journal Gazette*. June 24, 1926. Newspapers.com.

Greene, Robert S. "The Firehouse Five Plus Two." *The Record Changer*, September 1949.

Gwynn, Edith. "Edith Gwynn's Hollywood." *The Mirror* (Los Angeles, CA), April 10, 1950. Kimball Family Collection, Box 12.

Heffernan, Harold. "Shades of the 1920s: Now It's the Banjo Returning to Favor." *St. Louis Post-Dispatch*, August 13, 1950. Newspapers.com.

Helen Lang to Lester Koenig. April 27, 1950. Evergreen Record Sales Company, Seattle, Washington. Kimball Family Collection, Box 11.

Holly, Hal. "Firehouse Chief Kimball Scorns Pollack Hassle." *Downbeat*, June 2, 1950, 9. Kimball Family Collection, Box 12.

Holly, Hal. "The Hollywood Beat: Coast Shaken By Dixie Versus N.O. Jazz Scrap." *Downbeat*, March 10, 1950, 9. Kimball Family Collection, Box 12.

Holly, Hal. "The Hollywood Beat: Says L.A. Deejays Unfair To 'Love Drunk' Warbler." *Downbeat*, March 24, 1950, 8. Kimball Family Collection, Box 12.

Holly, Hal. "The Hollywood Beat: Sunset Strip Club Sets Lamare For Steady Stint." *Downbeat*, April 7, 1950, 9. Kimball Family Collection, Box 12.

Holly, Hal. "Pollack Says Firehouse 5 Is 'Just a Cornball Crew.'" *Downbeat*, May 5, 1950, 12. Kimball Family Collection, Box 12

"Hollywood Teletopics." *Downbeat*, April 7, 1950, 9. Kimball Family Collection, Box 12.

"Interview with Frank Thomas and Ollie Johnston." Interview by Michael Barrier. MichaelBarrier.com. November 2, 2014. http://www.michaelbarrier.com/Interviews/ThomasJohnston1987/ThomasJohnston1987.html.

"Interview with Frank Thomas by Don Peri." In *Working with Disney: Interviews with Animators, Producers, and Artists*, edited by Don Peri, 3-16. University Press of Mississippi, 2011.

"Interview with Hal Smith." E-mail interview by Lucas O. Seastrom. August 31, 2017.

"Interview with Ted Thomas." E-mail interview by Lucas O. Seastrom. August 31, 2017.

"Interview with Ted Thomas." Interview by Lucas O. Seastrom. January 11, 2016.

"Interview with Ward Kimball by Jim Korkis." In *Walt's People: Talking Disney with the Artists Who Knew Him*, edited by Didier Ghez, 74-104. Vol. 2. Xlibris, 2006.

"Interview with Ward Kimball from June 6, 1969." Interview by Michael Barrier. MichaelBarrier.com. August 2003. http://www.michaelbarrier.com/Interviews/Kimball/interview_ward_kimball.htm.

"Jazz Band and Cleffers Set for Repub. Musical." *The Hollywood Reporter*, May 5, 1950, 10. Kimball Family Collection, Box 12.

Kaler, Jim. "Alchiba (Alpha Corvi)." STARS, University of Illinois, n.d. http://stars.astro.illinois.edu/sow/alchiba.html.

Kimball, Ward. *Payroll Spreadsheets - 2nd Quarter 1950*. Kimball Family Collection, Box 11.

Kimball, Ward. *Payroll Spreadsheets - 4th Quarter 1950*. Kimball Family Collection, Box 11.

Kimball, Ward. *The Ward Kimball Journals*. March 1, 1948. Ledger Volume 3 - 1948 Kimball Family Collection.

Lambe, Joe. "Fab Ballroom a Part of Midtown's Rich Past." Midtown KC Post, November 20, 2013. http://midtownkcpost.com/fab-ballroom-a-part-of-midtowns-rich-past/.

Lewis, J. Sam. "South Plains Territory Is Being Boomed as Broomcorn Growing Center." *Lubbock Avalanche-Journal*, April 21, 1935. Newspapers.com.

"Lindsay District Brush Situation." *Journal Gazette*. November 8, 1928. Newspapers.com.

Markel, Dr. Howard. "The 'Strange' Death of Warren G. Harding." PBS, August 2, 2015. https://www.pbs.org/newshour/health/strange-death-warren-harding.

Miller, Diane Disney. *The Story of Walt Disney*. Compiled by Pete Martin. New York: Disney Editions, 2005.

Muir, Florabel. "Reporting." *The Mirror* (Los Angeles, CA), August 29, 1950. Kimball Family Collection, Box 12.

Muir, Florabel. "Reporting." *The Mirror* (Los Angeles, CA), February 21, 1950. Kimball Family Collection, Box 12.

Muir, Florabel. "Reporting." *The Mirror* (Los Angeles, CA), January 24, 1950. Kimball Family Collection, Box 12.

Muir, Florabel. "Reporting: That Old, Free Spirit." *The Mirror* (Los Angeles, CA), January 31, 1950. Kimball Family Collection, Box 12.

"Music: Dixieland Revival." *Fortnight*, April 14, 1950, 18. Kimball Family Collection, Clipping Files.

"Next Week: 'East Lynne.'" *Daily Variety*, October 25, 1950, 2. Kimball Family Collection, Clipping Files.

"Night of the Long Lances: Guadalcanal: Forgotten Valor—USS Alchiba (AK-23)." Naval History and Heritage Command, December 7, 2017. https://www.history.navy.mil/about-us/leadership/director/directors-corner/h-grams/h-gram-013.html#1.

"Our Brands: King." Conn Selmer, n.d. https://www.conn-selmer.com/en-us/our-brands/king.

Parsons, Louella. "Clark Gable Awaits Permission of MGM to Make Independent Film, Lone Star.'" *Los Angeles Examiner*, April 6, 1950. Kimball Family Collection, Box 12.

Perk, Hans. "Prod. 2069 (Alice) - Seq. 03.0 - Doorknob." A. Film L.A. November 24, 2007. http://afilmla.blogspot.com/2007/11/prod-2069-alice-seq-030-doorknob_24.html.

Perk, Hans. "Prod. 2069 (Alice) - Seq. 05.0 - Walrus..." A. Film L.A. November 27, 2007. http://afilmla.blogspot.com/2007/11/prod-2069-alice-seq-050-walrus_27.html.

Perk, Hans. "Prod. 2069 (Alice) - Seq. 07.5 - Cheshire Cat." A. Film L.A. December 9, 2007. http://afilmla.blogspot.com/2007/12/prod-2069-alice-seq-075-cheshire-cat_09.html.

Perk, Hans. "Prod. 2069 (Alice) - Seq. 08.0 - Mad Tea Party (I)." A. Film L.A. December 18, 2007. http://afilmla.blogspot.com/2007/12/prod-2069-alice-seq-080-mad-tea-party-i_18.html.

Pignatelli, Sepulveda. "The Smart Set: Adios." *Los Angeles Examiner*, April 21, 1950. Kimball Family Collection, Clipping Files.

"Pla-Mor Ballroom Photograph Collection." Pla-Mor Ballroom Photograph Collection | Digital Special Collections. University of Missouri - Kansas City, n.d. https://dl.mospace.umsystem.edu//umkc/islandora/object/umkc:plamor.

"The Pla-Mor." kcjazzlark, May 27, 2013. http://www.kcjazzlark.com/2013/05/the-pla-mor.html.

Remo. "USS Alchiba (AK-23, AKA-6)." Naval Warfare, November 22, 2011. http://navalwarfare.blogspot.com/2011/11/uss-alchiba-ak-23-aka-6.html.

Renaut, Christian. "Interview with Richard Rich from August 1987." Essay. In *Walt's People: Talking Disney With the Artists Who Knew Him*, edited by Didier Ghez, Vol. 2. Xlibris, 2005.

"Robert Stevenson, 81, Dies; Directed Walt Disney." The New York Times , May 2, 1986. https://www.nytimes.com/1986/05/02/obituaries/robert-stevenson-81-dies-directed-walt-disney-films.html.

Roddy, Joseph. "Dixieland Jazz Is "Hot" Again." *Look*, June 6, 1950. Kimball Family Collection, Clipping Files.

Smith, Hal. "For Whom the Brass Bell Tolls: A Personal Appreciation of the Firehouse Five Plus Two on Their Fiftieth Anniversary." *Frisco Cricket - San Francisco Traditional Jazz Foundation*, Spring 1999.

Starr, Jimmy. "Ex-Office Boy Wins MGM Second Lead." *Los Angeles Evening Herald & Express*, April 26, 1950. Kimball Family Collection, Box 12.

Stein, Herb. "Rambling Reporter." *The Hollywood Reporter*, April 4, 1950, 2. Kimball Family Collection, Box 12.

Sumner, Edward. "Interview with Wolfgang Reitherman." In *Walt's People: Talking Disney With the Artists Who Knew Him*, edited by Didier Ghez, Vol. 23. Theme Park Press, 2019.

"Ted Lewis Biography." The Ted Lewis Museum, n.d. https://www.tedlewismuseum.org/ted-lewis-biography.

"That Good-Time Sound." *Time*, March 6, 1950, 48-49. Kimball Family Collection, Box 12.

Thoburn, Joseph Bradfield. *A Standard History of Oklahoma: An Authentic Narrative of Its Development from the Date of the First European Exploration Down to the Present Time, Including Accounts of the Indian Tribes, Both Civilized and Wild, of the Cattle Range, of the Land Openings and the Achievements of the Most Recent Period*. Vol. 4. American Historical Society, 1916. Google Books.

Thomas, Bob. "Walt Disney Is Making Movie for Television." *Mt. Vernon Register* (Mt. Vernon, IL), November 17, 1950. Newspapers.com.

Townsend, Charles R. *'San Antonio Rose': The Life and Music of Bob Wills*. University of Illinois Press, 1986.

"U.S.S. Alchiba 'Notes Taken on Friday, August 7, 1942.'" Florida State University , 1942.

Institute on World War II and the Human Experience, Roy Gerald King Papers.

About the Editors and Contributors

Lucas O. Seastrom is a writer, historian, and filmmaker living in northern California. Born and raised in the rural Sacramento Valley, he has received degrees in cinema from both California State University Monterey Bay and San Francisco State University. He has published articles and essays on the Walt Disney Studios and general animation history for the Walt Disney Family Museum and the Hyperion Historical Alliance among others. His work in non-fiction filmmaking has been screened at the Philip Glass Days and Nights Film Festival and the National Gallery of Art. Seastrom works for Lucasfilm in San Francisco as a writer and historian.

Hal Smith is a drummer, bandleader, historian, writer, and educator in central Arkansas. He has lived in various cities across the United States for over six decades, listening to and working with some of the greatest musicians of the Traditional Jazz Revival—including musicians who played with the Firehouse Five Plus Two. He has played drums on over 200 recording sessions plus radio broadcasts and television programs. Smith leads his own New Orleans-style jazz bands and also freelances with other groups. He is a contributing writer for the *Jazz Rambler* and the *Syncopated Times* and has taught at Adult Jazz Camps in New Orleans and San Diego. He has been a "Superfan" of the Firehouse Five Plus Two since hearing them live at Disneyland in 1962.

Didier Ghez is the author of the books *Disneyland Paris—From Sketch to Reality, Disney's Grand Tour, They Drew as They Pleased—The Hidden Art of Disney's Golden Age, They Drew as They Pleased—The Hidden Art of Disney's Musical Years, They Drew as*

They Pleased—The Hidden Art of Disney's Late Golden Age, *They Drew as They Pleased—The Hidden Art of Disney's Mid-Century Era*, and *They Drew as They Pleased—The Hidden Art of Disney's Early Renaissance*, and serves as managing editor of the *Walt's People* book series (26 volumes released to date). In 2018, he was honored with ASIFAHollywood's June Foray Award for significant and benevolent impact on the art and industry of animation.

Theodore Thomas

Filmmaker and musician Theodore Thomas has enjoyed active careers in both fields. Fittingly, his first film was about a South Indian master musician. His second was about a young boy growing up in the countryside of Japan. These two efforts landed a staff position at the Walt Disney Studios developing films for what would become Epcot, followed by work on National Geographic Society Specials and PBS flagship programs. Thomas's projects for television garnered a National Emmy, a Writers Guild of America Award, and two WGA Award nominations.

His films, in a range of genres, are characterized by their insight, pathos, and humor. He co-directed the Japan-US feature documentary *Return from Space*, essaying the personal experiences of moonwalking astronauts. His children's fantasy *Where the Toys Come From* won the San Francisco International Film Festival's Golden Gate Award. *Frank and Ollie*, the story of Thomas's animator father and his best friend, debuted at the Sundance Film Festival, won the People's Choice Award at Worldfest Houston, and was an audience favorite at festivals around the world. *Walt & El Grupo* provided an unprecedented look at Walt Disney's little known 1941 trip to Latin American countries, and *Growing Up With Nine Old Men* shared insights with fellow children of Walt Disney's renowned artists.

Alongside his classical musical training as a child, Thomas was also surrounded by traditional jazz and the music of the Firehouse Five Plus Two—his first public jazz performance was at age 10 in elementary school playing "Fidgety Feet." As an adult he has played with a long line of west coast-based bands in a range of traditional styles including Lu Watters, the Firehouse Five Plus Two, jug band, jump, and New Orleans revival. With the New Orleans style band Gremoli, he has recorded for GHB, DARGASON, JAZZ CRUSADE, and on the soundtrack of the feature documentary *Frank and Ollie*. Internationally, he has appeared numerous times in Japan, both with touring groups and with Japan's foremost New Orleans style group, The New Orleans Rascals.

Chris Tyle
Born in 1955 in Vancouver, Washington, Chris Tyle is a second-generation jazz musician, playing cornet, clarinet, saxophone, and drums. Tyle's knowledge of early jazz music and its styles translates into a unique ability to eerily capture the sounds of the pioneers of jazz.

Tyle's father, Axel, hailed from Copenhagen, Denmark, moving to Portland, Oregon as a child. As a student he studied cornet and drums and played with early jazz groups on the West Coast. He was a founding member of the Castle Jazz Band, and in 1943, while stationed in Boston, played with jazz greats Sidney Bechet, Bunk Johnson, and Pops Foster.

As a teenager, Chris Tyle became interested in early jazz music, and by age twenty-one he was playing cornet professionally with his father in a group led by trumpeter and bassist Don Kinch.

In 1979, Tyle performed and recorded with the Turk Murphy Jazz Band of San Francisco. He then returned to Portland and formed a highly-successful swing group, Wholly Cats, which featured vocalist Rebecca Kilgore and drummer Hal Smith. When Wholly Cats broke up in 1985, Tyle left full-time music performance to work a "day gig," but continued performing part-time.

In 1989, Tyle moved to New Orleans, where he performed and recorded with a number of groups, including the Silver Leaf Jazz

Band, which he formed in 1992, and who appeared six nights-a-week at the Can-Can Jazz Cafe in the Royal Sonesta Hotel on Bourbon Street until October, 2002. During that stint the band recorded seven compact discs for GOOD TIME JAZZ, STOMP-OFF and JAZZOLOGY.

Tyle has many recordings to his credit. His first was with the Turk Murphy Jazz Band, and since that time he has recorded over 50 CDs on the STOMP OFF, JAZZOLOGY, G.H.B., and GOOD TIME JAZZ labels as a member of over a dozen bands. Tyle has also performed as a guest artist with bands in England, Denmark, Japan, Brazil, Switzerland, France, Norway, and Germany.

In December, 2002, Tyle returned to his home in Portland, Oregon, where he continued to work with bands both nationally and internationally. In 2015 he retired to live a quiet life in southwest France. He occasionally plays music at home.

Alguire's "Epilogue #2"

Discovered in the Cormack family collection, this additional epilogue is a single-page, handwritten epitaph written by Alguire himself. The precise date is unknown, but likely during the early 1990s not long before his passing.

As I reflect on the closing years of my life, I am very happy with the way it has unfolded. For all my earlier years of failure and frustration, the last part of my life more than made up for the early struggle. It's like climbing up a very steep hill—it's so rewarding to reach the top.

There are only three of us still around from the great 1941-42 big band, Bob Wills and His Texas Playboys!

Four of the Firehouse Five Plus Two have passed on. All great musicians. I miss them all!

> And if I should live to be
> The last leaf on the tree,
> In the spring,
> Let them laugh, as I do now,
> At the old forsaken bough
> Where I cling.
> —from "The Last Leaf" by Oliver Wendell Holmes

Index

Numbers in **bold** indicate photographs

101 Dalmatians 118, 143, 156, 163, 229
20,000 Leagues Under the Sea 114
"31st Street Blues" 86

Adventures of Ichabod and Mr. Toad, The 99, 120, 213
Affeldt, Paul xvi, 182, 236
Agnew, Red **50**
Alguire, Bernice 3, 20, 24-25, 36, 38, 55, 74
Alguire, Betty viii, 45-46, 49, 50, 55, 57, 58, 63, 64, 66, 67, 75, 77-78, 88, 129, 130-131, 170
Alguire, Bud 3, 20, 24, 34-35, 38, 39, 42, 43, 45
Alguire, D. E. 16, 17
Alguire, G. B. 1-3, 5, 6, 7-8, 9, 16, 17-18, 19-20, 22-23, 24, 25, 27, 28, 30, 34, 35, 36, 38, 39, 45, 55, 74
Alguire, George 3, 5, 8, 9, 17-18, 20, 24-25, 28, 34-35, 36, 38-39, 41
Alice in Wonderland 101, 118, 215, 221
Anderson, Bill 132, 133-134,
Anderson, Ken 230
Andrews Sisters 99, 213
"Anvil Stomp" 193, 203, 205
Aristocats, The 161, 162, **162**, 163, 169, 230

Armstrong, Louis xi, 24, 94, 98, 111, 175, **176**, 185, 189, 205, 219, 241
Around the World 247, 248
Ash, Marvin 122
"Asleep in the Deep" 120
At Disneyland 247, 248
"At The Jazz Band Ball" 177, 201
"Auntie Skinners' Chicken Dinner" 205
Autry, Gene 116

Babes in Toyland 152
"Baby Snatcher Blues, The" 123
Bacon, Jim 100
Bahn, Betty *see* Alguire, Betty
Balay, George 59, 184
Bales, Burt 86, 187, 190, 238, 240, 241
Ball, Lucille 200, 212
Ball, Ralph "Zulu" 120, **176**
"Ballad of Davy Crockett, The" 120, 127
"Ballin' the Jack" 196
Bambi 118, 160, 164, 169
Banjo Kings, The 115, **119**
Bardin, Bill 195
"Bare Necessities" 159, 164
Barrier, Michael 210, 214, 223, 224, 229, 232
Bates, G.B. 63, 65, 66, 67
Battle Hymn of the Republic: A Salute to the Bi-Centennial, The **171**, 247

Bay City Jazz Band 204
"Beale Street Mama" 205
Beatty, Jim 170-171, **171**, 179, 191, 247
"Beaumont Rag" 191
Bechet, Sidney 219, 262
Bednar, Bill 33
Bednar, Gerald 33
"Bee's Knees" 186
"Begin the Beguine" 237
Beiderbecke, Bix xi, 98, 185, 189, 205, 241
Berle, Milton 101, 125, 200, 220
"Bibbidi-Bobbidi-Boo" 213
Big Band Dixieland 250
"Big Beaver" 48, 61, 183, 194
"Bill Bailey" 203
Bing Crosby and Some Jazz Friends 250
"Birmingham Papa (Your Memphis Mama's Comin' to Town)" 202
"Blues My Naughty Sweetie Gave to Me" 203
Bob Wills and His Texas Playboys viii, xiii, xv, **47**, 49, **50**, **53**, **54**, 86, 111, 182, 189, 194-195, 224, 235, 249-250, 264
"Boot Heel Drag" 194
Boran, Arthur 220
Bose, Sterling 194, 250
Botkin, Perry 99, **119**
Brashear, Alex 48, **50**, **54**, 56, 59, 75, 180, 184, 185, 187, 190, 194, 195, 235, 236, 237, 242, 249-250
Brent, Brandy 211
Brooks, Harvey **xii**
Brubeck, Dave 207
Bruns, George 120-121, 122, 127, 152, **162**, 164, 167, **168**, 170, 179, 200, 204, 205
Bryant, Ben **60**, **170**

Bryant, Irene vii, **162**, **168**, 170, 172
Bryant, Joshua **60**, **170**
"Buffalo Gals" 17-18
Butterfield, Billy 194, 250
"Bye Bye Blues" 203

Cabot, Sebastian 160
"Cake Walkin' Babies" 187, 188
"Canal Street Blues" 86
Carlson, Bob 229
Carmichael, Hoagy 219
Carrere, Bernard **xii**
Carroll, John 218
Castle Jazz Band 120, 191, 262
"Charleston, The" 218
"Chattanooga Choo-Choo" 54
Chesnut, Ed 38, 39, 70-71
Chips Ahoy 133
Cinderella 108, 118, 120, 213-214
Clark, Les 117
Clemmons, Larry 158, 163-164
Cline, Patsy 90
"Come Back, Sweet Papa" 203
Condon, Eddie 219
Conrad, Bob 33
Coon-Sanders Nighthawks 189
"Copenhagen" 194, 203
Costa, Mary 140
Crashes a Party 247
Crocker, Harry 210, 212
Crosby, Bing 98-99, 125, 163, 194, 200, 212-213, 219, 224, 248, 250
Crosby, Bob 58-59, 194, 250
Cushman, Virginia 249

Daily, Pete 216, 247
Daley, Dan 100
Darby, Ken 213
"Dardanella" 7

Darensbourg, Joe **xii**, 111, 199, 200, 206
Dart, Bill 86, 190
Davis, Jimmie 250
Davis, Marc 117
Davis, Shakey 33
"Deck of Cards, A" 90, 93
Decker, Don 89
Deems, Barrett **176**
"Deep in the Heart of Texas" 250
Delay, Mike **xii**
"Dippermouth Blues" 86, 187, 241
Disney Family Album 222
Disney, Lillian 153, 209, 210
Disney, Walt vii, viii-ix, xii, xiv-xv, 10, 11, 27, 32, 42, 93, 94, 95-96, 98-99, 101, 103, 104, 108, 110, 111, 112, 114-115, 116-118, 119-120, 121, 122, 125, 126, 127, 128, 129, 130, 131, 132-134, 135-136, 137-139, 142, 143-144, 145, 146, 147, 148-152, 153-154, 156-157, 158, 159, 160, 161, 163-164, 165, 167, 169, 170, 171, 172, 173, 175, 178, 191, 199, 200, 208, 209-211, 213-214, 215, 218, 219, 221, 222, 229-231
Dixieland Favorites 247, 248
Dixieland Jazz Vol. 2: The Snader Telescriptions 247
"Doctor Jazz" 203
Dodds, Baby 94
Dodds, Johnny 94, 205
Domreis, Norman 170
Don't Take My Sunshine Away 250
Dorsey, Jimmy 11
Dorsey, Tommy 25, 59
"Dry Bread" 249
Duer, Neal 59, 184

Dumbo 108, 216
Duncan, Tommy **50**, 55, 184

Eckland, K. O. **xii**, **xiii**, 122, 192, 200, 203-204, 205
Ed Wynn Show, The 215
Ellis, Seger 185-186, 194, 251

Faded Love 249
Fantasia 120, 141
Farrell, Charlie 101
Faye, Alice 158-159
Ferguson, Joe Frank **60**
"Fidgety Feet" 86, 179-180, 187, 195, 262
Fink Street Five (Plus Two) 205
"Fire Chief Rag" 191, 196
Firehouse Five Plus Two Story, The 206, 247-248
Firehouse Five Plus Two, The viii-ix, xii, **xii**, **xiii**, xiii, xv, 1, 10, 26, 27, 32, 44, 51, 83, 85-86, 94, 95, **95**, 96-128, **98**, **109**, **119**, **122**, **123**, **124**, **125**, 129-130, 132, 155, 162, **165**, 165-168, **166**, **168**, 169, 170, 172-173, 174-179, **176**, 180-181, 189, 191-192, 193, 195-197, 198-206, 207-226, 247-248
Firehouse Five Story Vol. 1, The 10
Fitzgerald, Bob 184
Fitzgerald, Ella 99
"Five Foot Two" 212
Fleming, "Slim" 65-66
Forrest, Billie **168**
Forrest, Eddie **xii**, **xiii**, 116, **116**, **124**, **125**, **168**, 173, **176**, 178, 201, 203, 205
Freeman, John 93
Funicello, Annette 152

Gabor, Eva 137, 161
Garland, Judy 100, 200
Gentry, Dave 171
Geronimi, Clyde 12
Gerry, Vance 173
Gerson, Betty Lou 156
Goes South 248
Goes to a Fire 248
Goes to Sea 248
Goff, Flossie **168**
Goff, Harper **95**, 97, **98**, 99, 102, 104, 112, 114, 115, **119**, 126, 167, **168**, 199, 208
Goodman, Benny 7, 11, 48, 100, 219
"Goodnight Waltz" 249
Grable, Betty 100
Graham, Bill 194, 250
Great Locomotive Chase, The 115
Grounds for Marriage 116, 200
Grove, Olan 50, 64-65
Groves, Earl **54**
Guild, Delane 171
Guitar Rags and a Too Fast Past 248-249

Hafer, Harold 33
Haggard, Merle 190, 249
Hall, Edmond **176**
Hall, Minor "Ram" 111, 200
Hansen, Ed 230
Harlan, Don **47**, **50**, **54**, 59, 184
Harrah, Bill 96, 130
Harris, Phil 137, 158-160, 161, **162**
Havin' a Blast 248
Helm, Bob 85, 190, 193, 240, 241
Hendricks, Bob 77, 82
Herbert, Victor 6, 11
Hines, Earl 189

Hit Parade of 1951 116, 200, 218
Hogg, Ima 8
Holley, Joe 184
Holly, Hal 215-216, 217-218
"Home in San Antone" viii, 58, **60**, 81-82, 85, 189, 190
"Honeysuckle Rose" 41
Hopper, Hedda 100
Horne, Ellis 86, 192
Hurter, Albert 12

"I Ain't Gonna Give Nobody None O' This Jelly Roll" 204
"I Can't Believe That You're in Love with Me" 203
"Ida, Sweet As Apple Cider" 189
Illusion of Life: Disney Animation, The xv, 122, 128
"In the Blue Ridge Mountains of Virginia" 6
"Indian Summer" 6
"Italian Street Song" 6

James, Harry 100, 194, 241
"Jazz Me Blues" 238
"Jazzin' Babies Blues" 188
Jim Beatty Jazz Band **171**, 191, 247
Jimmie Thornton and his Orchestra 39
"Jingle Bells" 101, 220, 221
Johnson, Bunk 198, 218, 262
Johnson, Van 212, 218
Johnson, Wayne **50**, **54**
Johnston, Ollie xv, 117, 122, 136-137, 142, 143, 147, 158, 159-160, 164, 169, 230
Jones, Dale **176**
Jones, Darrell **50**, **54**, 59
"Joys of Jazz, The" 171

Jungle Book, The 120, 157-160, 161, 163, 164, 230
"Just Because" 203

Kahl, Milt 117, 230
Kansas City Breakdown: The Victor Recordings, Volume 2 251
"Kansas City Stomp" 187, 195, 241
Karger, Freddie 220
Kazebier, Nate 194
Kelly, Walt 108
Kernberger, Bill 131
Kimball, Betty 42, **168**
Kimball, Chloe **119**
Kimball, John **168**
Kimball, Ward viii, **xii**, xiii, 32, 42, 85, 86, 93, 94-97, **95**, **98**, 100, 101-104, 105, 106-110, **109**, 110, 111, 112, 113, 114, 116, 117, 119, **119**, 120, 121, 122, 123, **123**, **124**, 125, **125**, 128, 129, 130, 131-132, 151-152, 153, **166**, 167, **168**, 169, 172, 175, **176**, 177, 178, 181, 193, 199, 200-201, 202, 203, 204, 205, 206, 207, 208-209, 210, 213, 214, 216, 217, 221, 222, 223
Kinch, Don 120, 121, 122, **122**, **123**, **124**, 128, **168**, 170, 178, 179, 180, 196, 200, 201, 204, 205, 262
Kinney, Jack 134
"Kiss Me Again" 6
Klein, Mannie 194, 250
Koenig, Les 96, 97, 123, 129-130, 199, 206, 214
Kubrick, Stanley 219
Kyle, Billy **176**
Lady and the Tramp 118, 120, 155

Lamare, Nappy 200, 216-217
Lang, Eddie 205
Lang, Helen 214-215
Larson, Eric 117
Lawson, John "Yank" 194, 241, 250
Lawyer, Betty *see* Kimball, Betty
Legend of Merle Travis, The 249
"Let's Ride with Bob (blues)" 186-187
Levin, Floyd 182
Lewerke, Jack 129, 131
Lewis, Carroll "Cappy" 164, 250
Lewis, Ed 33, 193-194, 195, 197, 251
Lewis, George **119**, 198, 219
Lewis, Ted 7, 11
Lewis, Tubby 194, 249
Light Crust Doughboys, The 52
Linton, Fred R. 10
Little Mermaid, The xv
"Little Orphan Annie" 191
Live 1948—1950, Vol. 2 249
Live at Earthquake McGoon's 248
Logan, Bob 185-186, 233-234
Lombardo, Guy 201
"Loopin' the Loop" 250
Lord, Nathan **168**
"Lost Love" 243
Lounsbery, John 117, 230, 231
Lu Watters Yerba Buena Jazz Band 85, 94, 180, 195, 238, 251
Lu Watters: The Complete Good Time Jazz Recordings 251
Lucas, Johnny 94, 96-97, 199
Lund, Sharon Disney 148, 153
MacDonald, James 97, 115, 116, 126, 132, 134, 135, 167, 199
Mallery, Clarke 93, **95**, 97, **98**, 120-121, 199, 208, 210
Man and the Moon 108

Man in Space 108
Man With a Million Friends, The 249
Manone, Wingy 186, 194
Many Adventures of Winnie-the-Pooh, The 230
March of the Bob Cats 250
Marrero, Lawrence **119**
Mars and Beyond 108
Martin, Dean 161
Martin, Pete 153, 210
Mary Poppins 149, 153
Mayo, O.W. **50**
McAuliffe, Leon **50**, **54**, 55, **60**, 184
McCarthy, Senator Joe 96
McCormack, Charlotte Bryant vii-ix, **60**
McDonald, Lt. William vii, 74, 77, 86
McDonald, Marie 218
McTaggart, Jack 249
"Me and My Shadow" 11
Melody 108, 151, 154
"Memphis Blues" 99, 203
Mercer, Johnny 100, 219
Middleton, Velma **176**
"Milenburg Joys" 203
Miller, Ann 100
Miller, Diane Disney 148, 153, 210
Miller, Glenn 59
Miller, Ron 148-149
"Mississippi Rag" 203
Mordecai, Harry 190
Morrison, Charlie 99-100, 102, 103, 209, 211, 216, 217
Morton, Jelly Roll xi, 94, 198, 201, 205, 216
Moten, Bennie 31, 33, 189, 193, 194, 251
Mountjoy, Monte **95**, 97, 104, 111, 112-114, 115-116, **119**, 199, 208

"Mournin' Blues" 250
Muir, Florabel 210-212, 219
Murphy, Turk 83, 85-86, 94, 111, 120, 121, 190, 198, 200, 204, 205, 216, 262, 263
Music Land 11-12
"Muskrat Ramble" 203, 216
Musso, Vido 194
"My Confession" 186

Nelson, David 78
Nelson, Harriet 78
Nelson, Ozzie 78
Nelson, Ricky 78
Newman, Bill 115, 122, **123**, 200, 204, 205
Nicholas, Albert 111, 200
Nichols, Charles "Nick" 151-152, 153-154
Nichols, Red 98, 185, 189, 219, 247
Norris, Bill 33, 38-39, 41, 45
Norris, George 39, 41

O'Daniel, W. Lee 52
"Old-Spinning Wheel, The" 250
Oliver, King xi, 94, 198, 202, 240, 241
One Hour in Wonderland 111, 221
Ory, Kid xi, 94, 111, 198, 199, 200, 205, 216, 218

"Pagan Love Song" 10
"Panama" 203
Parsons, Louella 100
Pavageau, Slow Drag **119**
Peet, Bill 156-157, 163
Penner, Ed 93, **95**, 97, 101, **119**, 119-120, 127, 155, 199, 208, 210, 213
Pepke, Pete 171
Peter Pan 118

Pinocchio 108, 120, 141, 153
Plays for Lovers 248
Pollack, Ben 194, 216, 217
Probert, George 104, 105, 106, 121, **123, 124, 125**, 128, **168**, 175, **176**, 178, 193, 196, 202, 203, 204, 205
Purnell, Alton **119**

Rare Performances 1946—1981 249
Redd, Alton **xii**
Reitherman, Wolfgang "Woolie" 117, 135, 140, 141-142, 144-147, 150, 156, 157, 169, 173, 229-232
"Remember Me" 90
Rescuers, The 115, 164, 231
Reunion 250
Rich, Richard 231
"Riverside Blues" 203
Roberts, Dick 115, **119, 124, 125, 176**, 178, 201, 204, 205
Robin Hood 118, 161-162, 163, 230, 231
Robinson, Jim **119**
Rogers, Ginger 100, 200
Roosevelt, Franklin D. 35, 39
Rose, Wally 128, 200
Rotary Club Boys Band 8, 9, 24, 189
Roundtree, Red 115, **119**
Russell, Pee Wee 219
Ryman, Herb 218
Ryman, Lucille 218

"Saints" 203
"Salute to the Bicentennial" 171
"San" 203
"San Antonio Rose" 85, 191, 196, 203
Sanders, George 160

Sands, Tommy 152
Sauers, Charley 78
Scobey, Bob xi, 121, 128, 196, 204, 240
Scott, Bud 199
Seastrom, Lucas O. 207-226, 227-228, 229-232
Sebring, Leonard 12
Seger Ellis and his Choirs of Brass 251
Settin' the World on Fire—The Whole Story, Vol. 1 248
"Shake That Thing" 86
Shamblin, Eldon **47, 50, 54**, 184
Sharpsteen, Tom **119**
Shaw, Artie 48, 120, 234, 237
Shirley, Bill 140
Short, Bob 200
"Silver Bells" 99
Sinatra, Frank 152
Sinatra, Nancy 152
Singleton, Zutty 111, 200
Sleeping Beauty 117, 120, 127, 135-136, 138, 141, 155-156, 229
Smith, Hal 61, 177-179, 180, 192, 193-197, 198-206, 233-242, 244, 247-251
Smith, John 204
"Smoke, Smoke, Smoke (That Cigarette)" 250
Snow White and the Seven Dwarfs 115, 117, 118, 142, 144, 160, 211, 230
"Softly as in a Morning Sunrise" 237
Souchon, Doc **xii**, 202
"South" 193, 194, 203, 251
South Frisco Jazz Band 204
"South Rampart Street Parade" 237

Spanier, Muggsy 11, 219
"St. Louis Blues" 203
Stanwyck, Barbara 100, 212
Stars of Jazz 248
Stevenson, Robert 149-150, 153
Stoking the Fire—The Whole Story, Vol. 2 248
"Storyville Blues" 203
Strickler, Benny xi, xv-xvi, 33, 46, **47**, 48, **50**, **53**, **54**, 59, 61, 175, 178-179, 180, 182-188, **183**, 189, 190, 193, 194-195, 196, 197, 203, 233-242, 249, 251
Stricklin, Al **50**, **54**, **60**, 184
Strictly Dixie and Blues 247
"Sweet Georgia Brown" 203
"Sweet Temptation" 195
Sword in the Stone, The 118, 143, 157, 163, 229

Takach, Frank 73
"Take Me Back to Tulsa!" 86
Teagarden, Jack 11, 48, 219
"Temptation" 105, 106, 123
"Ten Years" 186, 194-195, 236
Tex Williams & His Western Caravan 250
"Thine Alone" 6
Thing, The 114
Thomas, Bob 221
Thomas, Frank xv, xvi, 93, **95**, **97**, 98-99, 101, 104, 105, 106, 110, 116, 117, 118, 119, **119**, 122, **124**, **125**, 126-127, 128, 142, 147, 158, 159, 160, 167, **168**, 169, 172, 174, 175, 176, **176**, 176, 178, 199, 201, 203-204-205, 208, 210, 213-214, 220, 221-222, 230, 231

Thomas, Theodore xvi, **168**, 174-177
Three Caballeros, The 108
Tierney, Louie **47**, **50**, **54**, 59, 184
Tiffany Transcriptions, The 250
"Tiger Rag" 11, 97, 168, 193, 203, 205, 212
"Tishomingo Blues" 203
Tomlins, Gene **50**, **54**, 184
Tomorrowland 108
Toot, Whistle, Plunk and Boom 108, 151, 152, 154
Townsend, Dr. Charles 51
Travis, Merle 195, 248-249
Tribute to Bob Wills: 50th Anniversary Texas Playboys Reunion, A 249
Tribute to the Best Damn Fiddle Player in the World (or, My Salute to Bob Wills), A 249
"Tulsa Stomp" *see* "Jazz Me Blues"
Twenty Years Later 248
Tye, M.D., Reuben P. 1-2, 5, 13-16
Tyle, Chris xvi, 178-181, 189-192, 233-242, 244
Tyler, T. Texas 89, 90-91, **91**, **92**, 93, 95, 126, 191, 195-196, 249

U.S.S. Alchiba 74, 76-79, 82-84, **84**, 171, 227-228
"Under the Double Eagle" 198

Van Wie, Bill 33
Vaughan, B. J. 30-32, 33, 44
Venuti, Joe 48, 186, 194
"Vieni, Vieni" 250
Vintage Collections 250

Walt Disney's Bambi: The Story and the Film 164
Walters, Albert "Fernandez" **119**

Wantland, Jack 36
Watkins, Joe **119**
Watters, Lu xi, 83, 85, 94, 111, 121, 187, 190, 195, 196, 198, 201, 204, 236, 238, 240, 241, 251, 262
"We Might As Well Forget It" 195
Weirbach, Dave 171
West Coast Years, The 247
"When My Baby Smiles At Me" 11
"When My Dreamboat Comes Home" 194
"When You and I Were Young, Maggie" 18
"White Cliffs of Dover" 54
Whiteman, Paul 7, 11-12
"Whose Heart Are You Breaking Now?" 186
Wills, Betty **60**
Wills, Bob viii, xiii, xv, xvi, 46, 47-52, **47**, **49**, **50**, **53**, **54**, 54, 55-59, 61, 62, 63, 75, 81, 85, 86, 91, 104, 111, 115, 126, 128, 169, 171, 175, 180, 182, 183-184, 186, 187, 189-190, 191, 194, 195, 199, 224, 235, 236-237, 238, 239, 242, 249-250, 264

Wills, Johnny Lee 250
Winnie the Pooh and the Blustery Day 163
Winnie the Pooh and the Honey Tree 163
Winnie the Pooh and Tigger, Too 163
Wolfe, Rube 186
"Won'tcha Be My Baby?" 248
Wood, Woody 48, **50**, **54**, 59, 184, 190
"Working Man Blues" 203
"World Is Waiting for the Sunrise, The" 97
Wright, Lammar 33
Wrightsman, Stan 122
Wyler, William 96
Wynn, Ed 101, 125, 200, 215, 221

"Yellow Dog Blues" 203
"Yes Sir! That's My Baby" 10, 99, 100, 105, 213
"You've Got to See Mama Ev'ry Night" 203, 205
Young, Trummy **176**

www.ingramcontent.com/pod-product-compliance
Lightning Source LLC
Chambersburg PA
CBHW052057230426
43662CB00036B/1228